The Prayer Book

All the prayers, songs,
hymns, canticles, psalms,
and blessings in the Bible

compiled and edited by
Eugene S. Geissler

Ave Maria Press • Notre Dame, Indiana

Contents

Editor's Preface

I have often looked for exactly this kind of prayer book.

The reason was that the Bible seemed the way to go if I wanted to pray seriously. It is true that sickness, tragedies, loneliness, and other kinds of troubles tend to make us spontaneously turn to the Lord for help: "Help me, God!" "May the good Lord help me!" "O God, come to my help!" "Lord, where are you? Why did you let this happen to me?" "Rescue me, Lord. You are the only one who can!" Even a curse in time of trouble is a kind of turning to God as though God is to blame because he is the boss, the governor, the president. He is, indeed, and then some.

God is a good place to begin if we want to pray. So we go to his revelation to get beyond the help-me, give-me response to life's needs and vicissitudes. The apostles asked Jesus to teach them how to pray, when they saw him praying. Paul told us that the Spirit would teach us to pray. The Old Testament offers a rich harvest of prayers that the Lord God taught to his people through certain ones chosen for the purpose of teaching others. The Lord will teach us, too, especially if we begin with the prayers he has already given to his people.

Through the prayers he has given us we learn quickly the fundamental attitudes asked of us before God's great mystery: awe and reverence which lead to praise and thanksgiving, and our own helplessness which leads to surrender, confidence and trust in God's goodness. The psalms, for instance, reflect well these two fundamental attitudes of praise and petition. Over one-third of the psalms are prayers of lament and trust, cries for help to him who can help us; and almost another third are prayers of praise and thanksgiving to him without whom we have and are nothing.

Naturally, we have suspected (and people have also been trying to tell us) that the psalms are the way to pray. But not everyone suspects that there are another two or three times as many other prayers in the Bible very much like them. In some of them, like prophetic prayers, God does most of the talking to us instead of the other way around. Imagine not only what you can learn from that, but how you can be lifted up by his talking to you: "Did our hearts not burn within us as he talked to us along the way?" Ah yes, it is scriptural prayers—over 500 of them—that make prayer a "conversation with him who loves us" long before we have reached the heights of mystical prayer, if ever. The Lord, so good once more, has left none of us deprived. He is available. He has provided.

There are all kinds of ways to use this Bible Prayer Book: for Bible reading, a page or two a day over a year, for instance; but the best way, no doubt, is to use it as a prayer book for personal and family prayer. I look forward to using it this way. For five years I have read a psalm a day to my family gathered for prayer on weekday mornings, and that has enriched our relationship with the Lord. Each time, some word or phrase or line insinuates itself more deeply into my consciousness in a new way. Naturally, I hope it does the same for the others, too. Now I am going to do it with "all the prayers, songs, hymns, canticles, and blessings in the Bible." I look forward to what the Lord has in store for us.

It hardly needs to be pointed out, but I will do it anyway, that the Bible Prayer Book is also useful as a source book for occasional and special use, as a reference book to find a certain prayer or prayers that you know are somewhere in the Bible, and as a resource book to build up an enlarged and available storehouse of prayer for school, parish and community libraries. A detailed contents-index in the back of the book will help locate, suggest, inspire prayers for various needs and uses.

When Paul DeCelles, cofounder and coordinator of the People of Praise charismatic community in South Bend, asked me if I was writing anything these days, I told him I was thinking of collecting all the prayers of the Bible into a prayer book. "That sounds like a wonderful idea!" he answered. Sometimes that's all a person needs—a word of encouragement.

The best recommendation for using this Bible Prayer Book is that the compiler and editor has only 20 or 30 pages in the book and the Lord has the other 500.

The Lord's peace on all who read herein!

EUGENE S. GEISSLER
July 25, 1980

General Introduction

After only a few years of entering into daily prayer before the Lord, most persons would have become aware of the exhaustibility of man-made prayers, on the one hand, and the durability of scriptural prayers, on the other. That fact is the primary motivation for this book.

That fact also suggests the genius and wisdom of the church in building its official prayer life on the Scriptures. It is true that the private devotions of the people of God have produced in the past, and continue to produce in the present, a constant stream of man-made prayers, many of them gathered into books. These prayer books are a beautiful expression of the ongoing vitality of the human heart toward God, but the prayers have on the whole a temporary and transient quality about them, a kind of fatal flaw, by which they come and go. In my own lifetime I have witnessed the passing of the prayers of the last generation, as did the generation before me, as will those coming after.

Not so with the prayers of the Bible, not so. They last, they remain, because they are durable. For the person at prayer before the Lord daily, they are the only prayers, with perhaps a few exceptions, that are inexhaustible. One reason may be that they are the prototypes of all prayer, but the main reason, no doubt, is that they are the living word of God who tempers his living word to the person before him as he does the wind to the newly shorn lamb. God is good that way.

It seemed that it would be an easy task to "collect" all the prayers of the Bible into one prayer book. The big thing was to have had such a wonderful idea! But as always, everything costs more than you think it does, and everything takes longer than you think it will. Still, if ever a work turned out to be a labor of love, this was it. I present it humbly, having discovered in the process of doing it that it was the Lord who had already done the work by multiplying the bread, so to speak, and that I was hopefully his servant rather than an imposter in distributing it to the multitude.

One of the problems was deciding what prayer was, and after that determination, deciding in 500 different cases whether this and that qualified. It should have been easy, but it wasn't. Another person, more learned in the Scriptures, might have found it a simpler task. But I doubt it. All the Bible is prayer, it is said, and today we hear a lot about "praying the Scriptures." It is a bit presumptuous, therefore, a bit difficult to say this is a prayer and that isn't. God forgive me my mistakes, and he probably will forgive me sooner than the learned men and scholars. (This is a good place to mention that I owe a considerable debt to *The Jerome Biblical Commentary*.)

Prayer has many definitions. Prayer, for instance, is the lifting up of the mind and heart to God. That was a catechism definition 50 years ago. In a more recent definition, prayer is an opening to God. But the definition used for the purposes of this collection is that prayer is a conversation with God, a definition close to St. Teresa's: Prayer is a conversation with him who loves us. According to this definition, much of prophecy in the Bible qualifies as prayer, insofar as it is God speaking to man.

So, prayer is man's word to God and God's response, and God's word to man and man's response. Part of the richness and inexhaustibility of the bible prayers is this exchange between God and man and man and God. But it is also the very thing that complicated the matter of selection—especially since I wanted to be able to say that "this prayer book contains all the prayers in the Bible." In the end it has to be a relative statement.

I have refrained from adding anything of my own to the prayers, even such logical things as short introductory statements to situate prayers in their contexts. The point was to keep it purely and simply a "bible prayer book," and to make no pretense to historical, scientific, or scholarly explanation. Sometimes the title given to a prayer does say something extra, as for instance, "Second Song of the Suffering Servant," but that extra will, let us hope, not be a distraction but a help. The biblical reference is always given at the end of a prayer if anyone is interested in going beyond what is offered by the prayer itself.

There is, however, a brief introduction to each main section of the prayer book: The Old Testament, The Psalms, The New Testament.

In general, this prayer book is a collection of all the prayers, songs, hymns, canticles, psalms and blessings in the Bible. Obviously, it is not always possible to distinguish these from one another and to identify the proper category for each entry, so the impossible has not been done. Prayer, song, hymn, canticle, psalm and blessing are often part of the title, and that identification is at least sometimes useful.

The order of the prayers as a whole follows the sequence in the Catholic Bible even though the imprimatured version of the Good News Bible used for this prayer book does not. There are exceptions, however. The Psalms are a section by themselves between the Old and the New Testaments. This seemed the proper placing of these most loved and most revered of all prayers. They are a "collection of collections" from Israel's long prayer history and, looking forward, they are the prime source of prayer for Christ, the first Christians, and the church following after.

Now about something else. Besides prayers, songs, hymns, canticles, psalms and blessings, there are occasional entries that might be called "encounters with God." They seem to have a special prayer character of their own—a kind of confrontation between man and God—for example, Jesus and the two disciples on the way to Emmaus. Though not exactly "prayers," they often include a conversation between God and man.

Finally, there are selected passages here and there in this prayer book whose richness might give a person at prayer something to think about and meditate on, for example, the Beatitudes. Strictly speaking, they are not prayers, but certainly landmark statements from the Lord to mankind.

Except when otherwise noted, the Good News Bible in "Today's English" is used because its popular language is easily understood by modern men and women.

Prayers, Songs, Hymns, Canticles, and Blessings

In the Old Testament

Introduction

1) In the prehistory account of man in the first 11 chapters of Genesis, prayer as we know it does not play a great part. Before the fall, there is the hint that God was wont to walk in the garden "in the cool of the evening" and talk with man. Then, after the birth of a son in place of Abel, and the birth of a grandson, Enosh, there is the phrase: "At that time men began to call upon the name of the Lord." For this prayer book that is a significant beginning. The prayers in Genesis, with a few exceptions, are blessings.

After Abraham, Moses marks a significant advance in man's conversation with God. He might well be called "a man of prayer," just as he is called the Lord's first "prophet." Moses prayed, he celebrated in prayerful praise and powerful song, he pleaded with God for the people, and he exhorted the people to prayer. And God spoke to Moses! With him the "conversation with God" reaches a new level, ending with the Song of Moses and his blessing of the Israelites.

2) In the so-called historical books, from Joshua to Maccabees, a great variety of prayers expresses a great variety of emotions in a variety of situations; for example, the Canticle of Deborah expresses elation after military victory, and the Canticle of Hannah, joy in the Lord after the birth of Samuel. Here also is David, the warrior-king, the harp-playing poet, author of the Lord's praises and of many of the psalms. He will always be in a class by himself: a man of war and of prayer, full of praise and full of song, whose relationship with the Lord is probably best ex-

plained by this line from Scripture following his anointing: "Immediately the spirit of the Lord took control of David and was with him from that day on."

Among the historical books, the deutero-canonical Tobit, Judith and Esther offer prayers of a special type: from Tobit out of a domestic context, and in Judith and Esther from two women saviors of God's people.

3) In the wisdom literature, there is the memorable exchange between Job and God. The Song of Songs is a love poem, a celebration of love's ardor and faithfulness: on the literal level between a man and a woman, on a covenant level between God and his people, and on a mystical level between God and the individual human spirit.

There are quite a number of entries from the deuterocanonical books of Wisdom and Sirach. Most of these cannot strictly be called prayers, though they certainly lift up the heart and mind to God; and the subject of wisdom, so prominent in each, is more than human wisdom. It helps to think of these books as syntheses of human and divine wisdom. A line like, "I am the word spoken by the Most High," immediately suggests a wisdom more than human.

4) In the Old Testament, prayer as a conversation with God reaches a climax in the prophets, and among these, Isaiah is the most prayerful of prophets. As God's spokesman he mediates God's word to the people, much of it about a coming

Messiah and the blessings he will bring. Many of these prayers are aptly called songs. Deutero-Isaiah is outstanding for the intensity and concentration of "prophetic prayer." For instance, the four songs of the Suffering Servant are a developed and mysterious prayer that in the end looks forward to Jesus himself.

5) Jeremiah suffered from being called by the Lord to pronounce judgment on the people he loved. His life was made miserable because he was a prophet. But the fire in his heart and the sensitivity of his soul have enriched the biblical conversation with God. "I will be their God and they shall be my people," becomes a familiar refrain in both Jeremiah and in Ezekiel. Ezekiel, a man of visions and of imagination, called for renewal of heart. His prayers are full of hope. Daniel, too, is a man of visions. His prayers are full of the praise of God.

6) The "Twelve Prophets" or so-called "Minor Prophets" yield a rich variety of prayer full of God's love for his people, full of calls to repentance, songs of peace, praise and forgiveness. Each looks forward to the Lord's coming and adds new details to the big picture emerging, for example, Micah's song of universal peace, and Joel's song about a universal spirit on everyone.

The last entry is from Malachi, ending this section of the prayer book on a note of God's mercy: "They will be my people," says the Lord Almighty. "On the day when I act, they will be my very own. I will be merciful to them as a father is merciful to the son who serves him."

Pentateuch

At That Time Men Began to Call Upon the Name of the Lord

And Adam knew his wife again, and she bore
a son and called his name Seth, for she said,

"God has appointed for me another child
instead of Abel, for Cain slew him."

To Seth also a son was born, and he called
his name Enosh.

At that time men began to call upon the
name of the Lord.

Gn 4:25-26 (RSV)

God's Call to Abraham

The Lord said to Abram,

"Leave your country, your relatives,
    and your father's home,
    and go to a land I am going to show you.
I will give you many descendants,
    and they will become a great nation.
I will bless you and make your name famous,
    so that you will be a blessing.

I will bless those who bless you,
But I will curse those who curse you.
And through you I will bless all the
    nations."

Gn 12:1-3

Melchizedek Blesses Abraham

When Abram came back from his victory. . .
    the king of Sodom went out to meet
        him. . . .

And Melchizedek, who was king of Salem
   and also a priest of the Most High God,
   brought bread and wine to Abram, blessed
      him, and said,

   "May the Most High God,
   who made heaven and earth,
   bless Abram!
   May the Most High God,
   who gave you victory over your enemies,
   be praised!"

And Abram gave Melchizedek a tenth of all. . .
   he had recovered.

Gn 14:17-20

God Calls to Abraham a Second Time

Abraham looked around and saw a ram
   caught in a bush by its horns.
He went and got it and offered it
   as a burnt offering
   instead of his son.
Abraham named that place "The Lord
      Provides."
And even today people say,
"On the Lord's mountain he provides."

The angel of the Lord called to Abraham
   from heaven a second time:

"I make a vow by my own name —
   the Lord is speaking —
   that I will richly bless you.
Because you did this and did not keep back
   your only son from me,

I promise to give you as many descendants
   as there are stars in the sky
   or grains of sand along the seashore.
Your descendants will conquer their enemies.
All the nations will ask me to bless them
   as I have blessed your descendants—
   all because you obeyed my command."

Gn 22:13-18

Abraham's Servant Prays for Success in Finding a Wife for Isaac

"Lord, God of my master Abraham, give me success today and keep your promise to my master. Here I am at the well where the young women of the city will be coming to get water. I will say to one of them, 'Please, lower your jar and let me have a drink.' If she says, 'Drink, and I will also bring water for your camels,' may she be the one that you have chosen for your servant Isaac. If this happens, I will know that you have kept your promise to my master."

Before he had finished praying, Rebecca arrived with a water jar on her shoulder. She was the daughter of Bethuel, who was the son of Abraham's brother Nahor and his wife Milcah. She was a very beautiful young girl and still a virgin. She went down to the well, filled her jar, and came back. The servant ran to meet her and said, "Please give me a drink of water from your jar."

She said, "Drink, sir," and quickly lowered her jar from her shoulder and held it while he drank.

When he had finished, she said, "I will also bring water for your camels and let them have all they want."

Then the man knelt down and worshiped the Lord. He said "Praise the Lord, the God of my master Abraham, who has faithfully kept his promise to my master. The Lord has led me straight to my master's relatives."

Gn 24:12-19, 26-27

A Blessing on Rebecca

So they let Rebecca and her old family
     servant go with Abraham's servant
     and his men.
And they gave Rebecca their blessing in
     these words:
  "May you, sister, become the
     mother of millions!
  May your descendants conquer
     the cities of their enemies!"

Gn 24:59-60

Isaac Blesses Jacob

"The pleasant smell of my son is like the
     smell of a field which the Lord has blessed.
May God give you dew from heaven and make
     your fields fertile!
May he give you plenty of grain and wine!
May nations be your servants,
     and may peoples bow down before you.

May you rule over all your relatives,
and may your mother's descendants
bow down before you.
May those who curse you be cursed,
and may those who bless you be blessed."
Gn 27:27-29

God Confirms the Blessing on Jacob

Jacob lay down to sleep, resting his head
on a stone.
He dreamed that he saw a stairway reaching
from earth to heaven,
with angels going up and coming down on
it.
And there was the Lord standing beside him.

"I am the Lord, the God of Abraham and
Isaac,"
he said.
"I will give to you and your descendants
this land on which you are lying.
They will be as numerous as the specks of
dust on the earth.
They will extend their territory in all
directions, and through you and your
descendants I will bless all the nations.
Remember, I will be with you and protect you
wherever you go, and I will bring you
back to this land.
I will not leave you until I have done
all that I have promised you."

Jacob woke up and said,
"The Lord is here! He is in this place,
and I didn't know it!"

He was afraid and said,
> "What a terrifying place this is!
> It must be the house of God;
> it must be the gate that opens into heaven."

Jacob got up early next morning,
> took the stone that was under his head,
> and set it up as a memorial.
Then he poured olive oil on it
> to dedicate it to God.

Then Jacob made a vow to the Lord:
"If you will be with me and protect me
> on this journey I am making and give me
> food and clothing, and if I return safely to
> my father's home, then you will be my God.
This memorial stone which I have set up
> will be the place where you are worshiped,
> and I will give you a tenth of everything
> you give me."

Gn 28:11-18, 20-22

Jacob's Prayer Before Meeting Esau

> "God of my grandfather Abraham and God of
> my father Isaac, hear me!
> You told me, Lord, to go back to my land
> and to my relatives;
> and you would make everything go well
> for me.
> I am not worth all the kindness and
> faithfulness that you have shown me, your
> servant.

I crossed the Jordan with nothing but a
walking stick, and now I have come back
with these two groups.
Save me, I pray, from my brother Esau.
I am afraid—afraid that he is coming to attack
us and destroy us all, even the women
and children.
Remember that you promised to make
everything go well for me and to give me
more descendants than anyone could count,
as many as the grains of sand along the
seashore."

Gn 32:9-12

Jacob Reassured by God

Jacob packed up all he had and went to
Beersheba, where he offered sacrifices
to the God of his father Isaac.

God spoke to him in a vision at night and
called,
"Jacob, Jacob!"

"Yes, here I am," he answered.

"I am God, the God of your father," he said.
"Do not be afraid to go to Egypt;
I will make your descendants a great nation
there.
I will go with you to Egypt, and I will bring
your descendants back to this land.
Joseph will be with you when you die."

Gn 46:1-4

Jacob Blesses the Sons of Joseph

"May God, whom my fathers
    Abraham and Isaac served,
    bless these boys!
May God, who had led me to
    this very day, bless them!
May the angel, who has rescued me
    from all harm, bless them!
May my name and the name of
    my fathers Abraham and Isaac
    live on through these boys!
May they have many children,
    many descendants!"

Gn 48:15-16

Jacob Blesses Joseph

"It is your father's God who helps you,
The Almighty God who blesses you
With blessings of rain from above
And of deep waters from beneath the ground,
Blessings of many cattle and children,
Blessings of grain and flowers,
Blessings of ancient mountains,
Delightful things from everlasting hills.
May these blessings rest on the head of Joseph,
On the brow of the one set apart from his
    brothers."

Gn 49:25-26

The Canticle of Moses

"I will sing to the Lord because he has won a
      glorious victory;
   he has thrown the horses and their riders
      into the sea.
The Lord is my strong defender;
   he is the one who has saved me.
He is my God, and I will praise him,
   my father's God, and I will sing about his
      greatness.
The Lord is a warrior;
   the Lord is his name.

"He threw Egypt's army and its chariots into
      the sea;
   the best of its officers were drowned in the
      Red Sea.
The deep sea covered them;
   they sank to the bottom like a stone.

"Your right hand, Lord, is awesome in power;
   it breaks the enemy in pieces.
In majestic triumph you overthrow your foes;
   your anger blazes out and burns them up
      like straw.
You blew on the sea and the water piled up
      high;
   it stood up straight like a wall;
   the deepest part of the sea became solid.
The enemy said, 'I will pursue them and catch
      them;
   I will divide their wealth and take all I
      want;
   I will draw my sword and take all they
      have.'

But one breath from you, Lord, and the
      Egyptians were drowned;
  they sank like lead in the terrible water.

"Lord, who among the gods is like you?
Who is like you, wonderful in holiness?
Who can work miracles and mighty acts like
      yours?
You stretched out your right hand,
  and the earth swallowed our enemies.
Faithful to your promise, you led the people
      you had rescued;
  by your strength you guided them to your
      sacred land.

"You bring them in and plant them on your
      mountain,
  the place that you, Lord, have chosen for
      your home,
  the Temple that you yourself have built.
You, Lord, will be king forever and ever."

Ex 15:1-13, 17-18

The Song of Miriam

The prophet Miriam, Aaron's sister, took her
    tambourine, and all the women followed
    her, playing tambourines and dancing.

Miriam sang for them:

"Sing to the Lord, because he has won a
    glorious victory;
he has thrown the horses and their riders
    into the sea."

Ex 15:20-21

Jethro's Prayer

Moses told Jethro everything that the Lord had
　　done to the king and people of Egypt
　　in order to rescue the Israelites.
He also told him about the hardships the
　　people had faced on the way and how the
　　Lord had saved them.

When Jethro heard all this, he was happy and
　　said:

"Praise the Lord, who saved you from
　　the king and the people of Egypt!
Praise the Lord, who saved his people
　　from slavery!
Now I know that the Lord is greater
　　than all the gods,
because he did this when the Egyptians
　　treated the Israelites with such
　　contempt."

Ex 18:8-11

The Ten Commandments

God spoke, and these were his words:
"I am the Lord your God who brought you out of
Egypt, where you were slaves.

"Worship no god but me.

"Do not make for yourselves images of anything in heaven or on earth or in the water under
the earth. Do not bow down to any idol or worship it, because I am the Lord your God and I
tolerate no rivals. I bring punishment on those
who hate me and on their descendants down to
the third and fourth generation. But I show my

love to thousands of generations of those who love me and obey my laws.

"Do not use my name for evil purposes, because I, the Lord your God, will punish anyone who misuses my name.

"Observe the Sabbath and keep it holy. You have six days in which to do your work, but the seventh day is a day of rest dedicated to me. On that day no one is to work—neither you, your children, your slaves, your animals, nor the foreigners who live in your country. In six days I, the Lord, made the earth, the sky, the seas, and everything in them, but on the seventh day I rested. That is why I, the Lord, blessed the Sabbath and made it holy.

"Respect your father and your mother, so that you may live a long time in the land that I am giving you.

"Do not commit murder.

"Do not commit adultery.

"Do not steal.

"Do not accuse anyone falsely.

"Do not desire another man's house; do not desire his wife, his slaves, his cattle, his donkeys, or anything else that he owns."

Ex 20:1-17

We Will Obey the Lord

"We will obey the Lord and do everything that he has commanded."

Ex 24:7

Moses Pleads with God

"Lord, why should you be so angry with your
people, whom you rescued from Egypt with
great and mighty power?
Why should the Egyptians be able to say that
you led your people out of Egypt, planning
to kill them in the mountains and destroy
them completely?

Stop being so angry; change your mind and do
not bring this disaster on your people.
Remember your servants Abraham, Isaac, and
Jacob.
Remember the solemn promise you made
to them to give them as many descendants as
there are stars in the sky and to give your
descendants all that land you promised
would be in their possession forever."

So the Lord changed his mind and did not
bring on his people the disaster he had
threatened.

Ex 32:11-14

A Prayer of Moses

Moses heard all the people complaining as they
stood around in groups at the entrances of their
tents. He was distressed because the Lord had
become angry with them, and he said to the
Lord,

"Why have you treated me so badly? Why are
you displeased with me? Why have you given me
the responsibility for all these people? I didn't

create them or bring them to birth! Why should you ask me to act like a nurse and carry them in my arms like babies all the way to the land you promised to their ancestors? Where could I get enough meat for all these people? They keep whining and asking for meat. I can't be responsible for all these people by myself; it's too much for me! If you are going to treat me like this, have pity on me and kill me."

Nm 11:10-15

Moses Prays for the People

The Lord said to Moses, "How much longer will these people reject me? How much longer will they refuse to trust in me, even though I have performed so many miracles among them? I will send an epidemic and destroy them, but I will make you the father of a nation that is larger and more powerful than they are!"

But Moses said to the Lord, "You brought these people out of Egypt by your power. When the Egyptians hear what you have done to your people, they will tell it to the people who live in this land. These people have already heard that you, Lord, are with us, that you appear in plain sight when your cloud stops over us, and that you go before us in a pillar of cloud by day and a pillar of fire by night. Now if you kill all your people, the nations who have heard of your fame will say that you killed your people in the wilderness because you were not able to bring them into the land you promised to give them. So now, Lord, I pray, show us your power and do what you promised when you said, 'I, the Lord, am not easily angered, and I show great love and faithfulness and forgive sin and rebellion.' And now, Lord, according to the greatness of your unchanging love, forgive, I pray, the sin of these people, just as you have forgiven them ever since they left Egypt."

Nm 14:11-19

Just As a Father . . .

"Don't be afraid. . . .
The Lord your God will lead you,
    and he will fight for you,
    just as you saw him do in Egypt
    and in the desert.
You saw how he brought you safely
    all the way to this place,
    just as a father would carry his son."

Dt 1:29-31

Moses Prays to Cross the Jordan

"Sovereign Lord, I know that you have
        shown me
    only the beginning of the great and
        wonderful things you are going to do.

There is no God in heaven or on earth who
        can do the mighty things you have
        done!

Let me cross the Jordan River, Lord,
   and see the fertile land on the other
   side, the beautiful hill country and
   the Lebanon Mountains."

But because of the people the Lord was
   angry with me and would not listen.

   Dt 3:24-26

The Great Commandment

"Israel, remember this!
The Lord—and the Lord alone—is our God.
Love the Lord your God with all your heart,
   with all your soul,
      and with all your strength."

   Dt 6:4-5

You Belong to the Lord

You belong to the Lord your God.
From all the peoples on earth he chose you
   to be his own special people.

"The Lord did not love you and choose you
   because you outnumbered other peoples;
   you were the smallest nation on earth.
But the Lord loved you and wanted to keep the
   promise that he made to your ancestors.
That is why he saved you by his great might
   and set you free from slavery to the king
   of Egypt.
Remember that the Lord your God is the
   only God and that he is faithful.

He will keep his covenant and show his
constant love to a thousand generations of
those who love him and obey his
commands."

Dt 7:6-9

Moses Prays for the People

"Sovereign Lord, don't destroy your own
people, the people you rescued and
brought out of Egypt by your great
strength and power.
Remember your servants, Abraham, Isaac,
and Jacob, and do not pay attention to
the stubbornness, wickedness, and sin of
this people.
Otherwise, the Egyptians will say that you
were unable to take your people into the
land that you had promised them.
They will say that you took your people out
into the desert to kill them, because you
hated them.
After all, these are the people whom you chose
to be your own and whom you brought
out of Egypt by your great power
and might."

Dt 9:26-29

Moses Exhorts the People to Remember

"Remember these commands and cherish them.
Tie them on your arms and wear them on your
foreheads as a reminder. Teach them to your

children. Talk about them when you are at home and when you are away, when you are resting and when you are working. Write them on the doorposts of your houses and on your gates. Then you and your children will live a long time in the land that the Lord your God promised to give to your ancestors. You will live there as long as there is a sky above the earth.

"Obey faithfully everything that I have commanded you: Love the Lord your God, do everything he commands, and be faithful to him."

Dt 11:18-22

Choose Life

"Today I am giving you a choice between good and evil, between life and death. If you obey the commands of the Lord your God, which I give you today, if you love him, obey him, and keep all his laws, then you will prosper and become a nation of many people. The Lord your God will bless you in the land that you are about to occupy.

I am now giving you the choice between life and death, between God's blessing and God's curse, and I call heaven and earth to witness the choice you make. Choose life. Love the Lord your God, obey him and be faithful to him, and then you and your descendants will live long in the land that he promised to give your ancestors, Abraham, Isaac, and Jacob."

Dt 30:15-16, 19-20

The Canticle of Moses and Joshua

"Earth and sky, hear my words,
    listen closely to what I say.
My teaching will fall like drops of rain
    and form on the earth like dew.
My words will fall like showers on young
        plants,
    like gentle rain on tender grass.
I will praise the name of the Lord,
    and his people will tell of his greatness.

"The Lord is your mighty defender,
    perfect and just in all his ways;
Your God is faithful and true;
    he does what is right and fair.
But you are unfaithful, unworthy to be his
        people,
    a sinful and deceitful nation.
Is this the way you should treat the Lord,
    you foolish, senseless people?
He is your father, your Creator,
    he made you into a nation.

"Think of the past, of the time long ago;
    ask your fathers to tell you what happened,
    ask the old men to tell of the past.
The Most High assigned nations their lands;
    he determined where peoples should live.
He assigned to each nation a heavenly being,
    but Jacob's descendants he chose for
        himself.

"He found them wandering through the
      desert,
    a desolate, wind-swept wilderness.
He protected them and cared for them,
    as he would protect himself.
Like an eagle teaching its young to fly,
    catching them safely on its spreading wings,
    the Lord kept Israel from falling.
The Lord alone led his people without
    the help of a foreign god.

"He let them rule the highlands,
    and they ate what grew in the fields.
They found wild honey among the rocks;
    their olive trees flourished in stony ground.
Their cows and goats gave plenty of milk;
    they had the best sheep, goats, and cattle,
        the finest wheat, and the choicest wine.

"The Lord's people grew rich, but rebellious.
They abandoned God their Creator
    and rejected their mighty savior.
Their idolatry made the Lord jealous;
    the evil they did made him angry.
They sacrificed to gods that are not real,
    new gods their ancestors had never known,
    gods that Israel had never obeyed.
They forgot their God, their mighty savior,
    the one who had given them life.

"When the Lord saw this, he was angry
    and rejected his sons and daughters.
'I will no longer help them,' he said;
    'then I will see what happens to them,
    these stubborn, unfaithful people.'

"The Lord will rescue his people
  when he sees that their strength is gone.
He will have mercy on those who serve him,
  when he sees how helpless they are. . .

" 'I, and I alone, am God;
  no other god is real.
I kill and I give life, I wound and I heal,
  and no one can oppose what I do.' "

Moses and Joshua son of Nun recited this song,
so that the people of Israel could hear it.

Dt 32:1-20, 36, 39, 44

The Blessings of Moses on the People

These are the blessings that Moses, the man of
  God, pronounced on the people of Israel
  before he died.

The Lord came from Mount Sinai;
  he rose like the sun over Edom
  and shone on his people from Mount Paran.
Ten thousand angels were with him,
  a flaming fire at his right hand.
The Lord loves his people and protects those
  who belong to him.
So we bow at his feet
  and obey his commands.
We obey the Law that Moses gave us,
  our nation's most treasured possession.
The Lord became king of his people Israel
  when their tribes and leaders were
  gathered together.

People of Israel, no god is like your God,
    riding in splendor across the sky,
    riding through the clouds to come to your
      aid.
God has always been your defense;
    his eternal arms are your support.
He drove out your enemies as you advanced,
    and told you to destroy them all.
So Jacob's descendants live in peace,
    secure in a land full of grain and wine,
    where dew from the sky waters the ground.
Israel, how happy you are!
    There is no one like you,
    a nation saved by the Lord.
The Lord himself is your shield and your
      sword,
    to defend you and give you victory.

Dt 33:1-5, 26-29

Historical
Books

As for My Family and Me, We Will Serve the Lord

"Now then," Joshua continued,
  "honor the Lord and serve him sincerely
    and faithfully.
Get rid of the gods which your ancestors
  used to worship in Mesopotamia and Egypt,
  and worship only the Lord.

If you are not willing to serve him,
  decide today whom you will serve,
    the gods your ancestors worshiped in
      Mesopotamia or the gods of the Amorites,
    in whose land you are now living.
As for my family and me,
  we will serve the Lord."

The people replied,
"We would never leave the Lord to serve other
      gods!
The Lord our God brought our fathers and us
      out of slavery in Egypt, and
  we saw the miracles that he performed.
He kept us safe wherever we went among the
      nations through which we passed.
As we advanced into this land,
  the Lord drove out all the Amorites who
      lived here.
So we also will serve the Lord;
  he is our God."

Jos 24:14-18

The Song of Deborah

Praise the Lord!
  The Israelites were determined to fight;
  the people gladly volunteered.
Listen, you kings!
  Pay attention, you rulers!
I will sing and play music
  to Israel's God, the Lord.
Lord, when you left the mountains of Seir,
  when you came out of the region of Edom,
  the earth shook, and rain fell from the sky.
  Yes, water poured down from the clouds.
The mountains quaked before the Lord of
      Sinai,
  before the Lord, God of Israel.

In the days of Shamgar son of Anath,
  in the days of Jael,
caravans no longer went through the land,
  and travelers used the back roads.
The towns of Israel stood abandoned,
      Deborah;
  they stood empty until you came,
  came like a mother for Israel.

My heart is with the commanders of Israel,
  with the people who gladly volunteered.
  Praise the Lord!
Tell of it, you that ride on white donkeys,
  sitting on saddles,
      and you that must walk wherever you go.
Listen! The noisy crowds around the wells
  are telling of the Lord's victories,
  the victories of Israel's people!

Then the Lord's people marched down from
    their cities.
Lead on, Deborah, lead on!
    Lead on! Sing a song! Lead on!
Forward, Barak son of Abinoam,
    lead your captives away!

Jgs 5:2-7, 9-12

Ruth's Prayer to Naomi

"Don't ask me to leave you!
Let me go with you.
Wherever you go, I will go;
wherever you live, I will live.
Your people will be my people,
    and your God will be my God.
Wherever you die, I will die,
    and that is where I will be buried.
May the Lord's worst punishment
    come upon me if I let anything but death
    separate me from you!"

Ru 1:16-17

The Canticle of Hannah

"The Lord has filled my heart with joy;
    how happy I am because of what he has
        done!
I laugh at my enemies;
    how joyful I am because God has
        helped me!

"No one is holy like the Lord;
    there is none like him,
    no protector like our God.

Stop your loud boasting;
   silence your proud words.
For the Lord is a God who knows,
   and he judges all that people do.
The bows of strong soldiers are broken,
   but the weak grow strong.
The people who once were well fed
   now hire themselves out to get food,
   but the hungry are hungry no more.
The childless wife has borne seven children,
   but the mother of many is left with none.
The Lord kills and restores to life;
   he sends people to the world of the dead
   and brings them back again.
He makes some men poor and others rich;
   he humbles some and makes others great.
He lifts the poor from the dust
   and raises the needy from their misery.
He makes them companions of princes
   and puts them in places of honor.
The foundations of the earth belong to
   the Lord;
   on them he has built the world.

"He protects the lives of his faithful people,
   but the wicked disappear in darkness;
   a man does not triumph by his own
     strength.
The Lord's enemies will be destroyed;
   he will thunder against them from heaven.
The Lord will judge the whole world;
   he will give power to his king,
   he will make his chosen king victorious."

1 Sm 2:1-10

Obey the Lord

"Obey the Lord and serve him faithfully with all
your heart. Remember the great things he has
done for you."

1 Sm 12:24

* * *

In the Name of the Lord Almighty

David answered,
"You are coming against me with a sword,
    spear, and javelin,
        but I come against you in the name of
        the Lord Almighty,
        the God of the Israelite armies, which you
        have defied.
This very day the Lord will put you in my
    power;
I will defeat you and cut off your head.
And I will give the bodies of the Philistine
    soldiers to the birds and animals to
    eat.
Then the whole world will know that
    Israel has a God,
        and everyone here will see that the Lord
        does not have need of swords or
        spears to save his people.
He is victorious in battle, and he will put
    all of you in our power."

1 Sm 17:45-47

David's Song of Praise

Give thanks to the Lord, proclaim his
    greatness;
  tell the nations what he has done.
Sing praise to the Lord;
  tell the wonderful things he has done.
Be glad that we belong to him;
  let all who worship him rejoice!
Go to the Lord for help,
  and worship him continually.

You descendants of Jacob, God's servant,
  descendants of Israel, whom God chose,
  remember the miracles that God performed
  and the judgments that he gave.
The Lord is our God;
  his commands are for all the world.
Never forget God's covenant,
  which he made to last forever,
  the covenant he made with Abraham,
  the promise he made to Isaac.
The Lord made a covenant with Jacob,
  one that will last forever.
"I will give you the land of Canaan," he said.
  "It will be your own possession."

Sing to the Lord

Sing to the Lord, all the world!
  Proclaim every day the good news that he
    has saved us.
Proclaim his glory to the nations,
  his mighty acts to all peoples.

The Lord is great and is to be highly praised;
    he is to be honored more than all the gods.
The gods of all other nations are only idols,
    but the Lord created the heavens.
Glory and majesty surround him,
    power and joy fill his Temple.
Praise the Lord, all people on earth,
    praise his glory and might.
Praise the Lord's glorious name;
    bring an offering and come into his Temple.
Bow down before the Lord when he appears in
    his holiness;
    tremble before him, all the earth!
The earth is set firmly in place and cannot be
    moved.
Be glad, earth and sky!
    Tell the nations that the Lord is king.
Roar, sea, and every creature in you;
    be glad, fields, and everything in you!
The trees in the woods will shout for joy
    before the Lord,
    when he comes to rule the earth.

Give Thanks to the Lord

Give thanks to the Lord, because he is good;
    his love is eternal.
Say to him, "Save us, O God our Savior;
    gather us together; rescue us from the
    nations,
    so that we may be thankful
    and praise your holy name."
Praise the Lord, the God of Israel!
Praise him now and forever!

Then all the people said, "Amen," and
praised the Lord.

1 Ch 16:8-18, 23-36

David's Prayer of Thanksgiving

Then King David went into the Tent of the
Lord's presence, sat down, and prayed, "I am not
worthy of what you have already done for me,
Lord God, nor is my family. Yet now you are doing even more; you have made promises about
my descendants in the years to come, and you,
Lord God, are already treating me like a great
man. What more can I say to you! You know me
well, and yet you honor me, your servant. It was
your will and purpose to do this for me and to
show me my future greatness. Lord, there is none
like you; we have always known that you alone
are God. There is no other nation on earth like
Israel, whom you rescued from slavery to make
them your own people. The great and wonderful
things you did for them spread your fame
throughout the world. You rescued your people
from Egypt and drove out other nations as your
people advanced. You have made Israel your
own people forever, and you, Lord, have become
their God.

"And now, Lord God, fulfill for all time the
promise you made about me and my descendants, and do what you said you would. Your
fame will be great, and people will forever say,
'The Lord Almighty is God over Israel.' And you
will preserve my dynasty for all time. I have the
courage to pray this prayer to you, my God,

because you have revealed all this to me, your servant, and have told me that you will make my descendants kings. You, Lord, are God, and you have made this wonderful promise to me. I ask you to bless my descendants so that they will continue to enjoy your favor. You, Lord, have blessed them, and your blessing will rest on them forever."

1 Chr 17:16-27
(2 Sm 7:18-29)

David's Song of Victory

When the Lord saved David from Saul and his other enemies, David sang this song to the Lord:

The Lord is my protector;
    he is my strong fortress.
My God is my protection,
    and with him I am safe.
He protects me like a shield;
    he defends me and keeps me safe.
He is my savior;
    he protects me and saves me from violence.
I call to the Lord,
    and he saves me from my enemies.
Praise the Lord!

The waves of death were all around me;
    the waves of destruction rolled over me.

The danger of death was around me,
    and the grave set its trap for me.
In my trouble I called to the Lord;
    I called to my God for help.
In his temple he heard my voice;
    he listened to my cry for help.

The Lord reached down from above and took
    hold of me;
    he pulled me out of the deep waters.
He rescued me from my powerful enemies
    and from all those who hate me—
    they were too strong for me.
When I was in trouble, they attacked me,
    but the Lord protected me.
He helped me out of danger;
    he saved me because he was pleased with
    me.

The Lord Rewards

The Lord rewards me because I do what is
    right;
    he blesses me because I am innocent.
I have obeyed the law of the Lord;
    I have not turned away from my God.
I have observed all his laws;
    I have not disobeyed his commands.
He knows that I am faultless,
    that I have kept myself from doing wrong.
And so he rewards me because I do what is
    right,
    because he knows that I am innocent.

O Lord, you are faithful to those who are
    faithful to you,
    and completely good to those who are
    perfect.
You are pure to those who are pure,
    but hostile to those who are wicked.
You save those who are humble,
    but you humble those who are proud.

You, Lord, are my light;
   you dispel my darkness.
You give me strength to attack my enemies
   and power to overcome their defenses.

This God—how perfect are his deeds,
   how dependable his words!
He is like a shield
   for all who seek his protection.
The Lord alone is God;
   God alone is our defense.
This God is my strong refuge;
   he makes my pathway safe.
He makes me sure-footed as a deer;
   he keeps me safe on the mountains.
He trains me for battle,
   so that I can use the strongest bow.

O Lord, you protect me and save me;
   your help has made me great.
You have kept me from being captured,
   and I have never fallen.

The Lord Lives

The Lord lives! Praise my defender!
   Proclaim the greatness of the strong God
      who saves me!
He gives me victory over my enemies;
   he subdues the nations under me
   and saves me from my foes.

O Lord, you give me victory over my enemies;
   and protect me from violent men.
And so I praise you among the nations;
   I sing praises to you.
God gives great victories to his king;

he shows constant love to the one he has
   chosen,
to David and his descendants forever.

2 Sm 22:1-7, 17-37, 47-51

David's Canticle of Praise

There in front of the whole assembly King David
praised the Lord.

"Lord God of our ancestor Jacob, may you be
praised forever and ever! You are great and
powerful, glorious, splendid, and majestic.
Everything in heaven and earth is yours, and you
are king, supreme ruler over all. All riches and
wealth come from you; you rule everything by
your strength and power; and you are able to
make anyone great and strong. Now, our God,
we give you thanks, and we praise your glorious
name.

   "Yet my people and I cannot really give you
anything, because everything is a gift from you,
and we have only given back what is yours
already. You know, O Lord, that we pass
through life like exiles and strangers, as our
ancestors did. Our days are like a passing
shadow, and we cannot escape death. O Lord,
our God, we have brought together all this
wealth to build a temple to honor your holy
name, but it all came from you and all belongs to
you. I know that you test everyone's heart and
are pleased with people of integrity. In honesty
and sincerity I have willingly given all this to

you, and I have seen how your people who are gathered here have been happy to bring offerings to you. Lord God of our ancestors Abraham, Isaac, and Jacob, keep such devotion forever strong in your people's hearts and keep them always faithful to you. Give my son Solomon a wholehearted desire to obey everything that you command and to build the Temple for which I have made these preparations."

Then David commanded the people, "Praise the Lord your God!"

1 Chr 29:10-20

*   *   *

Solomon Prays for Wisdom

That night the Lord appeared to Solomon in a dream and asked him, "What would you like me to give you?"

Solomon answered, "You always showed great love for my father David, your servant, and he was good, loyal, and honest in his relation with you. And you have continued to show him your great and constant love by giving him a son who today rules in his place. O Lord God, you have let me succeed my father as king, even though I am very young and don't know how to rule. Here I am among the people you have chosen to be your own, a people who are so many that they cannot be counted. So give me the wisdom I need to rule your people with justice and to know the difference between good and evil. Otherwise, how would I ever be able to rule this great people of yours?"

1 Kgs 3:5-9

Solomon's Prayer When the Covenant Box Is Brought to the Temple

When all the leaders had gathered, the priests lifted the Covenant Box and carried it to the Temple. . . . There was nothing inside the Covenant Box except the two stone tablets which Moses had placed there at Mount Sinai, when the Lord made a covenant with the people of Israel as they were coming from Egypt.

As the priests were leaving the Temple, it was suddenly filled with a cloud shining with the dazzling light of the Lord's presence, and they could not go back in to perform their duties. Then Solomon prayed:

"You, Lord, have placed the sun in the sky,
　yet you have chosen to live in clouds and darkness.
Now I have built a majestic temple for you,
　a place for you to live in forever."

1 Kgs 8:3-4, 9-13

Solomon's Prayer to the Lord God at the Dedication of the Temple

Then in the presence of the people Solomon went and stood in front of the altar, where he raised his arms and prayed:

"Lord God of Israel, there is no god like you in heaven above or on earth below! You keep your covenant with your people and show them your love when they live in wholehearted obedience to you. You have kept the promise you made to my

father David; today every word has been fulfilled. And now, Lord God of Israel, I pray that
you will also keep the other promise you made to
my father when you told him that there would
always be one of his descendants ruling as king of
Israel, provided they obeyed you as carefully as
he did. So now, O God of Israel, let everything
come true that you promised to my father David,
your servant.

"But can you, O God, really live on earth? Not
even all of heaven is large enough to hold you, so
how can this Temple that I have built be large
enough? Lord my God, I am your servant. Listen
to my prayer, and grant the requests I make to
you today. Watch over this Temple day and
night, this place where you have chosen to be
worshiped. Hear me when I face this Temple and
pray. Hear my prayers and the prayers of your
people when they face this place and pray. In
your home in heaven hear us and forgive us.

Lord, Listen to Your People

"When your people Israel are defeated by their
enemies because they have sinned against you,
and then when they turn to you and come to this
Temple, humbly praying to you for forgiveness,
listen to them in heaven. Forgive the sins of your
people and bring them back to the land which
you gave to their ancestors.

"When you hold back the rain because your
people have sinned against you, and then when
they repent and face this Temple, humbly praying to you, listen to them in heaven. Forgive the
sins of the king and of the people of Israel, and

teach them to do what is right. Then, O Lord, send rain on this land of yours, which you gave to your people as a permanent possession.

"When there is famine in the land or an epidemic or the crops are destroyed by scorching winds or swarms of locusts, or when your people are attacked by their enemies, or when there is disease or sickness among them, listen to their prayers. If any of your people Israel, out of heartfelt sorrow, stretch out their hands in prayer toward this Temple, hear their prayer. Listen to them in your home in heaven, forgive them, and help them. You alone know the thoughts of the human heart. Deal with each person as he deserves, so that your people may obey you all the time they live in the land which you gave to our ancestors.

Listen to the Foreigner

"When a foreigner who lives in a distant land hears of your fame and of the great things you have done for your people and comes to worship you and to pray at this Temple, listen to his prayer. In heaven, where you live, hear him and do what he asks you to do, so that all the peoples of the world may know you and obey you, as your people Israel do. Then they will know that this Temple I have built is the place where you are to be worshiped.

"When you command your people to go into battle against their enemies and they pray to you, wherever they are, facing this city which you have chosen and this Temple which I have built for you, listen to their prayers. Hear them in heaven and give them victory.

If They Repent, Forgive Them, Lord

"When your people sin against you—and there is no one who does not sin—and in your anger you let their enemies defeat them and take them as prisoners to some other land, even if that land is far away, listen to your people's prayers. If there in that land they repent and pray to you, confessing how sinful and wicked they have been, hear their prayers, O Lord. If in that land they truly and sincerely repent and pray to you as they face toward this land which you gave to our ancestors, this city which you have chosen, and this Temple which I have built for you, then listen to their prayers. In your home in heaven hear them and be merciful to them. Forgive all their sins and their rebellion against you, and make their enemies treat them with kindness. They are your own people, whom you brought out of Egypt, that blazing furnace.

"Lord God, may you always look with favor on your people Israel and their king, and hear their prayer whenever they call to you for help. You chose them from all the peoples to be your own people, as you told them through your servant Moses when you brought our ancestors out of Egypt.

The Final Prayer

"Praise the Lord who has given his people peace, as he promised he would. He has kept all the generous promises he made through his servant Moses. May the Lord our God be with us as he was with our ancestors; may he never leave us or abandon us; may he make us obedient to him, so that we will always live as he wants us to live, keeping all the laws and commands he gave our ancestors. May the Lord our God remember at all times this prayer and these petitions I have made to him. May he always be merciful to the people of Israel and to their king, according to their daily needs. And so all the nations of the world will know that the Lord alone is God—there is no other. May you, his people, always be faithful to the Lord our God, obeying all his laws and commands as you do today."

1 Kgs 8:22-30, 33-53, 56-61

*   *   *

Elijah's Prayer for the Widow's Dead Son

"Give the boy to me," Elijah said. He took the boy from her arms, carried him upstairs to the room where he was staying, and laid him on the bed. Then he prayed aloud:

"O Lord my God, why have you done such a terrible thing to this widow? She has been kind enough to take care of me, and now you kill her son!" Then Elijah stretched himself out on the boy three times and prayed, "O Lord my God, restore this child to life!" The Lord answered Elijah's prayer; the child started breathing again and revived.

Elijah took the boy back downstairs to his mother and said to her, "Look, your son is alive!"

1 Kgs 17:19-23

Elijah's Prayer Over the Sacrifice

At the hour of the afternoon sacrifice the prophet
Elijah approached the altar and prayed:

"O Lord, the God of Abraham, Isaac, and
Jacob, prove now that you are the God of Israel
and that I am your servant and have done all this
at your command. Answer me, Lord, answer
me, so that this people will know that you, the
Lord, are God and that you are bringing them
back to yourself."

The Lord sent fire down, and it burned up the
sacrifice, the wood, and the stones, scorched the
earth and dried up the water in the trench.

When the people saw this, they threw
themselves on the ground and exclaimed, "The
Lord is God: the Lord alone is God!"

1 Kgs 18:36-39

The Glory of the Lord

The singers were accompanied in perfect harmony by trumpets, cymbals, and other instruments, as they praised the Lord singing:

"Praise the Lord, because he is good,
And his love is eternal."

As the priests were leaving the Temple, it was
suddenly filled with a cloud shining with the
dazzling light of the Lord's presence, and they
could not continue the service of worship.

2 Chr 5:11-14

May God Be With All of You Who Are His People

"This is the command of Cyrus, Emperor of Persia. The Lord, the God of Heaven, has made me ruler over the whole world and has given me the responsibility of building a temple for him in Jerusalem in Judah. May God be with all of you who are his people. You are to go to Jerusalem and rebuild the Temple of the Lord, the God of Israel, the God who is worshiped in Jerusalem. If any of his people in exile need help to return, their neighbors are to give them this help. They are to provide them with silver and gold, supplies and pack animals, as well as offerings to present in the Temple of God in Jerusalem."

Ezra 1:2-4

They Sang the Lord's Praises

When the men started to lay the foundation of the Temple, the priests in their robes took their places with trumpets in their hands, and the Levites of the clan of Asaph stood there with cymbals. They praised the Lord according to the instructions handed down from the time of King David. They sang the Lord's praises, repeating the refrain:

"The Lord is good, and his
    love for Israel is eternal."

Everyone shouted with all his might, praising the Lord, because the work on the foundation of the Temple had been started. *Ezra 3:10-11*

Nehemiah's Prayer for the People

"Lord God of Heaven! You are great, and we stand in fear of you. You faithfully keep your covenant with those who love you and do what you command. Look at me, Lord, and hear my prayer, as I pray day and night for your servants, the people of Israel. I confess that we, the people of Israel, have sinned. My ancestors and I have sinned. We have acted wickedly against you and have not done what you commanded. We have not kept the laws which you gave us through Moses, your servant. Remember now what you told Moses: 'If you people of Israel are unfaithful to me, I will scatter you among the other nations. But then if you turn back to me and do what I have commanded you, I will bring you back to the place where I have chosen to be worshiped, even though you are scattered to the ends of the earth.'

"Lord, these are your servants, your own people. You rescued them by your great power and strength. Listen now to my prayer and to the prayers of all your other servants who want to honor you. Give me success today and make the emperor merciful to me."

Ne 1:5-11

The People Confess Their Sins

On the twenty-fourth day of the same month the people of Israel gathered to fast in order to show sorrow for their sins. They had already separated themselves from all foreigners. They wore sackcloth and put dust on their heads as signs of grief.

Then they stood and began to confess the sins
that they and their ancestors had committed. For
about three hours the Law of the Lord their God
was read to them, and for the next three hours
they confessed their sins and worshiped the Lord
their God.

There was a platform for the Levites. . . . They
prayed aloud to the Lord their God:

"Stand up and praise the Lord your God;
    praise him forever and ever!
Let everyone praise his glorious name,
    although no human praise is great enough."
Ne 9:1-5

The Prayer of Confession

And then the people of Israel prayed this
prayer:

"You, Lord, you alone are Lord;
    You made the heavens and the stars of the
        sky.
You made land and sea and everything in
        them;
    you gave life to all.
The heavenly powers bow down and worship
        you.
You, Lord God, chose Abram
    and led him out of Ur in Babylonia;
    you changed his name to Abraham.
You found that he was faithful to you
    and you made a covenant with him.
You promised to give him the land of the
        Canaanites,

the land of Hittites and Amorites,
the land of Perizzites, Jebusites, Girgashites,
to be a land where his descendants would
live.
You kept your promise, because you are
faithful.

The Lord Saves

"You saw how our ancestors suffered in Egypt;
you heard their call for help at the Sea of
Reeds.
You worked amazing miracles against the
king,
against his officials and the people of his
land,
because you knew how they oppressed your
people.
You won then the fame you still have today.
Through the sea you made a path for your
people
and led them through on dry ground.
Those who pursued them drowned in deep
water,
as a stone sinks in the raging sea.
With a cloud you led them in daytime,
and at night you lighted their way with fire.
At Mount Sinai you came down from heaven;
you spoke to your people
and gave them good laws and sound
teachings.
You taught them to keep your Sabbaths holy,
and through your servant Moses you gave
them your laws.

The Lord Provides

"When they were hungry, you gave them
bread from heaven,
and water from a rock when they were
thirsty.
You told them to take control of the land
which you had promised to give them.
But our ancestors grew proud and stubborn
and refused to obey your commands.
They refused to obey; they forgot all you did;
they forgot the miracles you had performed.
In their pride they chose a leader
to take them back to slavery in Egypt.
But you are a God who forgives;
you are gracious and loving, slow to be
angry.
Your mercy is great; you did not forsake them.
They made an idol in the shape of a bull-calf
and said it was the god who led them from
Egypt!
How much they insulted you, Lord!
But you did not abandon them there in the
desert,
for your mercy is great.
You did not take away the cloud or the fire
that showed them the path by day and
night.
In your goodness you told them what they
should do;
you fed them manna and gave them water
to drink.
Through forty years in the desert
you provided all that they needed;
their clothing never wore out,
and their feet were not swollen with pain.

The Lord Forgives

"But your people rebelled and disobeyed you;
   they turned their backs on your Law.
They killed the prophets who warned them,
      who told them to turn back to you.
They insulted you time after time,
   so you let their enemies conquer and rule
      them.
In their trouble they called to you for help,
   and you answered them from heaven.
In your great mercy you sent them leaders
   who rescued them from their foes.
When peace returned, they sinned again,
   and again you let their enemies conquer
      them.
Yet when they repented and asked you to save
      them,
   in heaven you heard, and time after time
   you rescued them in your great mercy.
Because your mercy is great,
   you did not forsake or destroy them.
You are a gracious and merciful God!

The Lord Is Faithful

"O God, our God, how great you are!
   How terrifying, how powerful!
You faithfully keep your covenant promises.
From the time when Assyrian kings oppressed
      us,
   even till now, how much we have suffered!
Our kings, our leaders, our priests and
      prophets,
   our ancestors, and all our people have
      suffered.

Remember how much we have
  suffered!
You have done right to punish us;
  you have been faithful, even though we
  have sinned."

Ne 9:6-21, 26-28, 31-33

*   *   *

Tobit's Prayer

"You are righteous, O Lord!
You are merciful in all you do,
  faithful in all your ways.
You are the judge of this world.
I beg you, treat me with kindness.
Do not punish me for my sins,
  not even for sins of which I am
    unaware. . . .
You have often judged my ancestors for
    their sins
  and punished me for mine.
We were disloyal and rejected your
    commands,
  so your punishment has always been just.

"Now treat me as you please.
Take my life away and free me from this
    world;
  let my body return to the earth.
  I would be better off dead.
I am tormented by insults I don't deserve,
  and weighed down with despair.

Lord, give the command—
    bring all my troubles to an end,
    take me to my eternal rest.
Don't reject my prayer.
I would rather die than live in misery
    and face such cruel insults."

Tb 3:2-3, 5-6

Sarah's Prayer

"God of mercy, worthy of our praise,
    may your name always be honored,
    may all your creation praise you
        forever.

"Lord, I look to you for help.
Speak the word and set me free from this
    life;
    then I will no longer have to hear these
        insults.
You know, O Lord, that I'm still a virgin;
    I have never been defiled by a man.
Never have I disgraced myself or my
    father's name,
    as long as we have lived in this land of
        exile.
My father has no other child to be his heir,
    and there is no relative whom I can
        marry.
I have already lost seven husbands,
    so why should I live any longer?
But if it is not your will to take my life,
    at least show mercy to me.
Don't let me hear those insults again!"

Tb 3:11-15

The Prayer of Tobias

"God of our ancestors, you are worthy of
praise.

May your name be honored forever and ever
by all your creatures in heaven and on
earth.

You created Adam and gave him his wife Eve
to be his helper and support.

They became the parents of all mankind.

You said, 'It is not good for man to live alone.
I will make a suitable helper for him.'

Lord, I have chosen Sarah because it is right,
not because I lusted for her.

Please be merciful to us
and grant that we may grow old together."

Tb 8:4-7

Raguel's Prayer

"You are worthy of our praise, O God.

May your people praise you forever,
may they praise you with pure hearts.

I praise you because you have made me glad;
you have been merciful to us,

and my worst fears did not come true.

You deserve our praise, O Lord;
you were merciful to this young couple,
the only children of their parents.

Now, grant them your mercy and protection.

Let them live out their lives in happiness and
love."

Tb 8:15-17

Tobit's Prayer of Praise

"Praise God. Praise him for his greatness.
  Praise all his holy angels.
May he continue to bless us.
  Praise all his angels forever.
He brought this illness upon me,
  but now I can see my son Tobias!"

Tb 11:14-15

Raphael's Exhortation

Then Raphael called the two men aside and said to them, "Praise God and tell everyone about the good things he has done for you, so that they too will honor him and sing his praises. Let everyone know what God has done. Never stop praising him.

"It's a good idea to keep a king's secret, but what God does should be told everywhere, so that he may be praised and honored.

"If you do good, no harm will come to you.

"It is better to pray sincerely and to please God by helping the poor than to be rich and dishonest. It is better to give to the poor than to store up gold. Such generosity will save you from death and will wash away all your sins. Those who give to the poor will live full lives, but those who live a live of sin and wickedness are their own worst enemies.

"I have already told you that a king's secret ought to be kept, but the things God does should be told to everyone. . . .

"I am Raphael, one of the seven angels who stands in the glorious presence of the Lord, ready to serve him."

Tb 12:6-11, 15

Tobit's Song of Praise

"Praise the eternal God,
   praise the one who rules.
He punishes us; then he shows us mercy.
   He sends us down to the world of the dead,
   then he brings us up from the grave.
No one can escape his power.

"People of Israel, give thanks among the
      nations,
   where he sent you into exile;
   even there he showed his great power.
Let all who live hear your praise.
The Lord is our God and father forever.

"Though he punished you for your wickedness,
   he will be merciful and bring you home
   from among the nations where he scattered
      you.

"Turn to him with all your heart and soul,
   live in loyal obedience to him.
   Then he will turn to you to help you
   and will no longer hide himself.
Remember what God has done for you,
   and give thanks with all your heart.
Praise the righteous Lord;
   honor the eternal King.

"Although I live in exile in a foreign land,
   I will give thanks to the Lord
   and will speak of his great strength to a
      nation of sinners.
'Turn away from your sins, and do what
      pleases God!
Perhaps he will be gracious
   and show you his mercy.'

"I praise my God and rejoice in his greatness;
   my whole being honors the King of Heaven.

"Let everyone tell of his greatness
   and sing his praises in Jerusalem.

Praise the Lord, Jerusalem

"Jerusalem, Holy City of our God,
   he will punish you for the sins of your
      people,
   but he will be merciful to all who do right.
So give thanks to the Lord, for he is good.
   Praise the eternal King.
   Your Temple will be rebuilt
   and your people will be happy again.

"May the Lord make all you exiles glad,
   may he take care of your suffering people
   for as long as time shall last.

"Jerusalem, your light will shine brightly for
      all the world,
   and from far away many nations will come
      to you.
Their people will come to honor the Lord your
      God,
   they will bring gifts for the King of Heaven.

In your streets many generations will sing
      joyful praise,
   your name will endure forever as God's
      chosen city.
A curse will be on all who make threats against
      you,
   on all who destroy you and tear down your
      walls,
   on all who demolish your towers and burn
      your homes.
But all who honor you will be blessed forever.

Jerusalem Will Be Rebuilt

"Rejoice, Jerusalem, because of your righteous
      people;
   they will be gathered together from exile
   to praise the Lord of the ages.

"Happy are all those who love you
   and are pleased to see you prosper.
Those who mourn over your suffering now
   will one day be happy;
   your happiness will bring them joy forever.

"I praise the Lord, the great King;
   Jerusalem will be rebuilt
   and will be his home forever.

"Jerusalem, how happy I will be
   when my descendants can see your splendor
   and give thanks to the King of Heaven.

"Your gates will be built with sapphires and
      emeralds,
   and all your walls with precious stones.

Your towers will be made of gold
    and their fortifications of pure gold.
Your streets will be paved with rubies and
      precious jewels.
Joyful songs will ring out from your gates,
    and from all your houses people will shout,
    'Praise the Lord! Praise the God of Israel!'

"Jerusalem, God will bless your people,
    and they will praise his holy name forever."
Tb 13:1-18

*   *   *

Judith's Prayer

"O my God, listen to my prayer, the prayer of a widow. Your hand guided all that happened then, and all that happened before and after. You have planned it all—what is happening now, and what is yet to be. Your plans have always been carried out. Whatever you want to be done is as good as done. You know in advance all that you will do and what decisions you will make. Now the Assyrians are stronger than ever; they take pride in their cavalry and infantry. They rely on their weapons, but they do not know that you, O Lord, are a warrior who ends war. The Lord is your name. In your anger, use your power to shatter their mighty army. They plan to defile your Temple, where you are worshiped, and to hack off the corners of your altar with their swords. Look how proud and boastful they are! Pour out your fury on them!

"I am only a widow, but give me the strength to carry out my plan. Use my deceitful words to strike them all dead, master and slave alike. Let a woman's strength break their pride. Your power does not depend on the size and strength of an army. You are a God who cares for the humble and helps the oppressed. You give support and protection to people who are weak and helpless; you save those who have lost hope. Now hear my prayer, O God of my ancestor Simeon, the God in whom Israel trusts, ruler of heaven and earth, creator of the rivers and the seas, king of all creation. Hear my prayer and let my deceitful words wound and kill those who have planned such cruelty against your covenant and your holy Temple, against Mount Zion and the land you have given your people. Make your whole nation and every tribe recognize that you are God, almighty and all-powerful, and that you alone protect the people of Israel!"

Jdt 9:4-14

Judith Prays for Strength

"O Lord, God Almighty, help me with what
    I am about to do for the glory of Jerusalem.
Now is the time to rescue your chosen people
    and to help me carry out my plan to destroy
        the enemies who are threatening us.". . .
"O Lord, God of Israel, give me strength
    now."

Jdt 13:4-5, 7

In Praise of Judith

Everyone in the city was utterly amazed. They bowed down and worshiped God, praying together,

"Our God, you are worthy of great praise.
Today you triumphed over the enemies of
    your people."

Then Uzziah said, "Judith, my dear, the Most High God has blessed you more than any other woman on earth. How worthy of praise is the Lord God who created heaven and earth! He guided you as you cut off the head of our deadliest enemy. Your trust in God will never be forgotten by those who tell of God's power. May God give you everlasting honor for what you have done. May he reward you with blessings, because you remained faithful to him and did not hesitate to risk your own life to relieve the oppression of your people."

All the people replied, "Amen, amen!"

Jdt 13:17-20

The Canticle of Judith

"Praise my God and sing to him;
    praise the Lord with drums and cymbals;
    play a new song for him.
Praise him and call on him for help.
The Lord is a warrior who ends war.
    He rescued me from my pursuers
    and brought me back to his people's camp.
Down from the mountains of the north came
    the Assyrians,
    with their tens of thousands of soldiers.

Their troops blocked the rivers in the valleys;
    their cavalry covered the mountains.
They threatened to set fire to our country,
    slaughter our young men,
    dash our babies to the ground,
    take our children away as captives,
    and carry off all our young women.
But the Lord Almighty tricked them;
    he used a woman to stop them.
Their hero was not slain by young soldiers
    or attacked and killed by mighty giants.
It was Judith, the daughter of Merari,
    who brought him down with her beauty.
She gave victory to the oppressed people of
      Israel;
    when she took off her widow's clothes,
    and put on a linen dress to entice him.
She put on her rich perfumes
    and tied a ribbon around her hair.
Her dainty sandal caught his eye;
    her beauty captured his heart.
Then the sword slashed through his neck.
The Persians trembled at her daring;
    the Medes were amazed at her bravery.
Then our people shouted in victory.
    They had been weak and oppressed,
    but they forced the enemy to retreat in
      panic and fear.
We are the descendants of slaves,
    but our enemies turned and ran;
    we killed them like runaway slaves.
They were destroyed by the army of the Lord.

I Will Sing a New Song

"I will sing a new song to my God.
   O Lord, you are strong and glorious!
   You have never been defeated.
Let all creatures serve you.
   You gave the command
   and all of them came into being;
   you breathed on them,
   and all of them were created.
   No one can oppose your command.
The mountains and the seas tremble,
   and rocks melt like wax when you come
      near.
But there is mercy for all who obey you.
The Lord is more pleased with those who
      obey him
   than with all the choice meat on the altar,
   or with all the most fragrant sacrifices.
The nations who rise up against my people
      are doomed.
   The Lord Almighty will punish them on
      Judgment Day.
   He will send fire and worms to devour
      their bodies,
   and they will weep in pain forever."

                              Jdt 16:2-17

Mordecai's Prayer

"O Lord, you are the Lord and King of all creation, and everything obeys your commands. If
you wish to save Israel, no one can stop you. You
made heaven and earth and all the wonderful
things on earth. You are the Lord of all, and

there is no one who can stand against you. You know all things. You know, Lord, that when I refused to bow to that arrogant Haman, it was not because I was arrogant or trying to impress people. I simply did not want to honor any man more than I honor God. I refuse to bow to anyone but you, my Lord; and this is not because of pride. If it would help to save Israel, I would be willing even to kiss the soles of his feet.

"And now, O Lord, God and King, God of Abraham, spare your people; save us from our enemies. They are determined to destroy us; they are looking for a chance. Long ago you chose us to be your people and rescued us from the land of Egypt. Do not abandon us now. We are your chosen people, so listen to my prayer and be gracious to us. Turn our misfortune into joy so that we may live to sing your praises. Save us from death so that we can keep on praising you."

Est 4C:2-10

Esther's Prayer

"My Lord and King, only you are God. I am all alone, and I have no one to turn to but you. Help me! I am about to risk my life. O Lord, as long as I can remember, my family has told me how you chose Israel from all the nations and how in ancient times you singled out our ancestors to be your people forever. You have kept all your promises to them.

"But we have sinned against you. You handed us over to our enemies because we worshiped their gods. We deserve your punishment, O

Lord. But our enemies are no longer satisfied just to see us in slavery. They have made a solemn promise to their idols not only to destroy the people who praise you, but to do away with your Law and to remove forever the glory of your house and altar. They want the whole world to praise worthless idols and stand in awe of mortal kings forever.

"Lord, these gods are nothing; do not surrender your power to them or give our enemies the chance to laugh at our downfall. Instead, turn their evil plans against them, and make an example of that man who first planned our destruction.

"Remember us, O Lord. Come to us in this time of trouble. Give me courage, King of all gods and Ruler over all earthly powers. Give me the right words to say when I go in to face Xerxes, that savage lion. Change his heart so that he will turn against Haman, our enemy, and destroy him and his gang. Come to our rescue, O Lord. Help me; I am all alone, and I have no one to turn to but you.

"Since I came here, the only thing that has brought me joy is my worship of you, Lord God of Abraham.

"Almighty God, listen to the prayer of your people. Rescue us from these evil men, and take away my fear."

Est 4C:14-25, 29-30

Prayer of Judas Maccabeus

When Judas saw how strong the enemy's army was, he prayed:

"We will praise you, Savior of Israel.
You broke the attack of the giant by the hand
    of your servant David
    and you let Saul's son Jonathan and the
        young man who carried his weapons
        defeat the entire Philistine army.
Now in the same way let your people Israel
    defeat our enemy.
Put them to shame, in spite of all their con-
    fidence in their infantry and cavalry.
Make them afraid;
    let their bold strength melt away;
    let them tremble at the prospect of defeat.
We love and worship you;
    so let us kill our enemies,
    that we may then sing your praises."

1 Macc 4:30-33

A Blessing to the Jews in Egypt

"May God be good to you
    and keep the covenant he made with
        Abraham, Isaac, and Jacob, his faithful
        servants.
May he fill each of you with the desire to
    worship him
    and to do his will eagerly with all your heart
        and soul.
May he enable you to understand his Law and
    his commands.
May he give you peace,
    answer your prayers,
    forgive your sins,
    and never abandon you in times of trouble.
Here in Judah we are now praying for you."

2 Macc 1:2-6

Nehemiah's Prayer

"Lord God, Creator of all things, you are awesome and strong, yet merciful and just. You alone are king. No one but you is kind; no one but you is gracious and just. You are almighty and eternal, forever ready to rescue Israel from trouble. You chose our ancestors to be your own special people. Accept this sacrifice which we offer on behalf of all Israel; protect your chosen people and make us holy. Free those who are slaves in foreign lands and gather together our scattered people. Have mercy on our people, who are mistreated and despised, so that all other nations will know that you are our God. Punish the brutal and arrogant people who have oppressed us, and then establish your people in your holy land, as Moses said you would."

2 Macc 1:24-29

Wisdom
Literature

The Lord Gives and the Lord Takes Away

"I was born with nothing, and I will die with nothing. The Lord gave, and now he has taken away. May his name be praised!"

Job 1:21

Let God Be God

"When God sends us something good, we welcome it. How can we complain when he sends us trouble?"

Job 2:10

Job's Complaint to God

O God, put a curse on the day I was born;
    put a curse on the night I was conceived!
Turn that day into darkness, God.
Never again remember that day;
    never again let light shine on it.
Make it a day of gloom and thick darkness;
    cover it with clouds, and blot out the sun.
Blot that night out of the year,
    and never let it be counted again;
    make it a barren, joyless night.
Tell the sorcerers to curse that day,
    those who know how to control Leviathan.
Keep the morning star from shining;
    give that night no hope of dawn.
Curse that night for letting me be born,
    for exposing me to trouble and grief.
I wish I had died in my mother's womb
    or died the moment I was born.

Why did my mother hold me on her knees?
Why did she feed me at her breast?
If I had died then, I would be at rest now,
sleeping like the kings and rulers
who rebuilt ancient palaces.
Then I would be sleeping like princes
who filled their houses with gold and silver,
or sleeping like a stillborn child.

In the grave wicked men stop their evil,
and tired workmen find rest at last.
Even prisoners enjoy peace,
free from shouts and harsh commands.
Everyone is there, the famous and the
unknown,
and slaves at last are free.
Why let men go on living in misery?
Why give light to men in grief?
They wait for death, but it never comes;
they prefer a grave to any treasure.
They are not happy till they are dead and
buried;
God keeps their future hidden
and hems them in on every side.
Instead of eating, I mourn,
and I can never stop groaning.
Everything I fear and dread comes true.
I have no peace, no rest, and my troubles
never end.

Job 3:2-26

My Redeemer Lives

Oh, would that my words were written down!
Would that they were inscribed in a record:

That with an iron chisel and with lead
they were cut in the rock forever!
But as for me, I know that my Vindicator
  lives,
and that he will at last stand forth upon the
  dust;
Whom I myself shall see:
my own eyes, not another's, shall behold him,
and from my flesh I will see God.

Job 19:23-26 (NAB)

The Lord Answers Job

Who are you to question my wisdom
  with your ignorant, empty words?

Stand up now like a man
  and answer the questions I ask you.
Were you there when I made the world?
  If you know so much, tell me about it.
Who decided how large it would be?
  Who stretched the measuring line over it?
  Do you know all the answers?
What holds up the pillars that support the
    earth?
  Who laid the cornerstone of the world?
In the dawn of that day the stars sang
    together,
  and the heavenly beings shouted for joy.

Who closed the gates to hold back the sea
  when it burst from the womb of the earth?
It was I who covered the sea with clouds
  and wrapped it in darkness.
I marked a boundary for the sea
  and kept it behind bolted gates.

I told it, "So far and no farther!
  Here your powerful waves must stop."
Job, have you ever in all your life
  commanded a day to dawn?

Have you been to the springs in the depths of
    the sea?
  Have you walked on the floor of the ocean?
Has anyone ever shown you the gates
  that guard the dark world of the dead?
Have you any idea how big the world is?
  Answer me if you know.

Do you know where the light comes from
  or what the source of darkness is?
Can you show them how far to go,
  or send them back again?
I am sure you can, because you're so old
  and were there when the world was made!

Have you ever visited the storerooms,
  Where I keep the snow and the hail?
I keep them ready for times of trouble,
  for days of battle and war.
Have you been to the place where the sun
    comes up,
  or the place from which the east wind
    blows?

Who dug a channel for the pouring rain
  and cleared the way for the thunderstorm?
Who makes rain fall where no one lives?
Who waters the dry and thirsty land,
  so that grass springs up?
Does either the rain or the dew have a father?

Who is the mother of the ice and the frost,
    which turn the waters to stone
    and freeze the face of the sea?

Can you tie the Pleiades together
    or loosen the bonds that hold Orion?
Can you guide the stars season by season
    and direct the Big and the Little Dipper?
Do you know the laws that govern the skies,
    and can you make them apply to the earth?

Can you shout orders to the clouds
    and make them drench you with rain?
And if you command the lightning to flash,
    will it come to you and say, "At your
      service"?
Who tells the ibis when the Nile will flood,
    or who tells the rooster that rain will fall?
Who is wise enough to count the clouds
    and tilt them over to pour out the rain,
    rain that hardens the dust into lumps?

Do you find food for lions to eat,
    and satisfy hungry young lions
    when they hide in their caves,
    or lie in wait in their dens?
Who is it that feeds the ravens
    when they wander about hungry,
    when their young cry to me for food?

Do you know when mountain goats are born?
Have you watched wild deer give birth?

Job 38:2-12, 16-41; 39:1

I Spoke Foolishly, Lord

The Lord

Job, you challenged Almighty God;
   will you give up now, or will you answer?

Job

I spoke foolishly, Lord. What can I answer?
   I will not try to say anything else.
I have already said more than I should.

Then out of the storm the Lord spoke to Job once
again.

The Lord

Stand up now like a man,
   and answer my questions.
Are you trying to prove that I am unjust—
   to put me in the wrong and yourself in the
      right?
Are you as strong as I am?
   Can your voice thunder as loud as mine?
If so, stand up in your honor and pride;
   clothe yourself with majesty and glory.

Job 40:1-10

Job Repents

Then Job answered the Lord.

I know, Lord, that you are all-powerful;
   that you can do everything you want.
You ask how I dare question your wisdom
   when I am so very ignorant.
I talked about things I did not understand,
   about marvels too great for me to know.

You told me to listen while you spoke
    and to try to answer your questions.
Then I knew only what others had told me,
    but now I have seen you with my own eyes.
So I am ashamed of all I have said
    and repent in dust and ashes.

Job 42:1-6

In Praise of Wisdom

I Am Better Than Jewels

"I am Wisdom, I am better than jewels;
    nothing you want can compare with me.
I am Wisdom, and I have insight;
    I have knowledge and sound judgment.
To honor the Lord is to hate evil;
    I hate pride and arrogance,
    evil ways and false words.
I make plans and carry them out.
    I have understanding, and I am strong.
I help kings to govern
    and rulers to make good laws.
Every ruler on earth governs with my help,
    statesmen and noblemen alike.
I love those who love me;
    whoever looks for me can find me.
I have riches and honor to give,
    prosperity and success.
What you get from me is better than the finest
      gold,
    better than the purest silver.
I walk the way of righteousness;
    I follow the paths of justice,
giving wealth to those who love me,
    filling their houses with treasures.

I Am the First of the Lord's Works

"The Lord created me first of all,
 the first of his works, long ago.
I was made in the very beginning,
 at the first, before the world began.
I was born before the oceans,
 when there were no springs of water.
I was born before the mountains,
 before the hills were set in place,
before God made the earth and its fields
 or even the first handful of soil.
I was there when he set the sky in place,
 when he stretched the horizon across the
  ocean,
when he placed the clouds in the sky,
 when he opened the springs of the ocean
and ordered the waters of the sea
 to rise no further than he said.
I was there when he laid the earth's
  foundations.
I was beside him like an architect,
 I was his daily source of joy,
 always happy in his presence —
happy with the world
 and pleased with the human race.

The Man Who Finds Me Finds Life

"The man who listens to me will be happy —
 the man who stays at my door every day,
 waiting at the entrance to my home.
The man who finds me finds life,
 and the Lord will be pleased with him."
                                    Pr 8:11-31, 34-35

There Is a Season for Everything

For everything there is a season, and a time for
every matter under heaven:
    a time to be born, and a time to die;
    a time to plant, and a time to pluck up what is
        planted;
    a time to kill, and a time to heal;
    a time to break down, and a time to build up;
    a time to weep, and a time to laugh;
    a time to mourn, and a time to dance;
    a time to cast away stones, and a time to
        gather stones together;
    a time to embrace, and a time to refrain from
        embracing;
    a time to seek, and a time to lose;
    a time to keep, and a time to cast away;
    a time to rend, and a time to sew;
    a time to keep silence and a time to speak;
    a time to love, and a time to hate;
    a time for war, and a time for peace.

Ec 3:1-8 (RSV)

The Breath of Life

Our bodies will return to the dust of the earth,
and the breath of life will go back to God, who
gave it.

Ec 12:7

Man's Purpose

Have reverence for God and obey his commands,
because this is all that man was created for.

Ec 12:13

Song of Songs*

The First Song

The Woman

Your lips cover me with kisses;
　your love is better than wine.
There is a fragrance about you;
　the sound of your name recalls it.
　No woman could keep from loving you.
Take me with you, and we'll run away;
　be my king and take me to your room.
We will be happy together,
　drink deep, and lose ourselves in love.
No wonder all women love you!
Women of Jerusalem, I am dark but beautiful,
　dark as the desert tents of Kedar,
　　but beautiful as the draperies in Solomon's
　　　palace.
Don't look down on me because of my color,
　because the sun has tanned me.
My brothers were angry with me
and made me work in the vineyard.
I had no time to care for myself.
Tell me, my love,
　Where will you lead your flock to graze?
　Where will they rest from the noonday sun?
Why should I need to look for you
　among the flocks of the other shepherds?

---

*These songs have often been interpreted by Jews as a picture
of the relationship between God and his people, and by Christians as a picture of the relationship between Christ and the
church.

The Man

> Don't you know the place, loveliest of women?
> Go and follow the flock;
>> find pasture for your goats
>> near the tents of the shepherds.
>
> Your hair is beautiful upon your cheeks
> and falls along your neck like jewels.
> But we will make for you a chain of gold
>> with ornaments of silver.

The Woman

> My king was lying on his couch,
> and my perfume filled the air with fragrance.
> My lover has the scent of myrrh
>> as he lies upon my breasts.
> My lover is like the wild flowers
>> that bloom in the vineyards at Engedi.

The Man

> How beautiful you are, my love;
>> how your eyes shine with love!

The Woman

> How handsome you are, my dearest;
>> how you delight me!
> The green grass will be our bed;
> the cedars will be the beams of our house,
>> and the cypress trees the ceiling.
> I am only a wild flower in Sharon,
>> a lily in a mountain valley.

The Man

> Like a lily among thorns
>> is my darling among women.

The Woman

Like an apple tree among the trees of the
    forest,
    so is my dearest compared to other men.
I love to sit in its shadow,
    and its fruit is sweet to my taste.
He brought me to his banquet hall
    and raised the banner of love over me.
Restore my strength with raisins
    and refresh me with apples!
    I am weak from passion.
His left hand is under my head,
    and his right hand caresses me.
Promise me, women of Jerusalem;
    swear by the swift deer and the gazelles
    that you will not interrupt our love.

Sgs 1:2-2:7

The Second Song

The Woman

I hear my lover's voice.
He comes running over the mountains,
    racing across the hills to me.
My lover is like a gazelle,
    like a young stag.
There he stands beside the wall.
He looks in through the window
    and glances through the lattice.
My lover speaks to me.

The Man

Come then, my love;
    my darling, come with me.

The winter is over; the rains have stopped;
    in the countryside the flowers are in bloom.
This is the time for singing;
    the song of doves is heard in the fields.
Figs are beginning to ripen;
    the air is fragrant with blossoming vines.
Come then, my love;
    my darling, come with me.
You are like a dove that hides
    in the crevice of a rock.
Let me see your lovely face
    and hear your enchanting voice.

Catch the foxes, the little foxes,
    before they ruin our vineyard in bloom.

The Woman

My lover is mine, and I am his.
He feeds his flock among the lilies
    until the morning breezes blow
    and the darkness disappears.
Return, my darling, like a gazelle,
    like a stag on the mountains of Bether.
Asleep on my bed, night after night
    I dreamed of the one I love;
    I was looking for him, but couldn't find him.
I went wandering through the city,
    through its streets and alleys.
I looked for the one I love.
    I looked, but couldn't find him.
The watchmen patrolling the city saw me.
    I asked them, "Have you found my lover?"
As soon as I left them, I found him.

I held him and wouldn't let him go
until I took him to my mother's house,
to the room where I was born.

Promise me, women of Jerusalem;
swear by the swift deer and the gazelles
that you will not interrupt our love.

Sgs 2:8-3:5

The Third Song

The Woman

What is this coming from the desert like a
column of smoke,
fragrant with incense and myrrh,
the incense sold by traders?
Solomon is coming, carried on his throne;
sixty soldiers form the bodyguard,
the finest soldiers in Israel.
King Solomon is carried on a throne
made of the finest wood.
Its posts are covered with silver;
over it is cloth embroidered with gold.
Its cushions are covered with purple cloth,
lovingly woven by the women of Jerusalem.
Women of Zion, come and see King Solomon.
He is wearing the crown that his mother
placed on his head
on his wedding day,
on the day of his gladness and joy.

The Man

How beautiful you are, my love!
How your eyes shine with love behind
your veil.

Your hair dances like a flock of goats
  bounding down the hills of Gilead.
Your teeth are as white as sheep
  that have just been shorn and washed.
Your lips are like a scarlet ribbon;
  how lovely they are when you speak.
Your cheeks glow behind your veil.
Your neck is like the tower of David,
  round and smooth,
    with a necklace like a thousand warrior
      shields hung around it.
Your breasts are like gazelles,
  twin deer feeding among lilies.
I will stay on the hill of myrrh,
  the hill of incense,
    until the morning breezes blow
    and darkness disappears.
How beautiful you are, my love;
  how perfect you are!

Come with me from the Lebanon Mountains,
    my bride;
  come with me from Lebanon.
The look in your eyes, my sweetheart and
    bride,
  and the necklace you are wearing
  have stolen my heart.
Your love delights me,
  my sweetheart and bride.
Your love is better than wine;
  your perfume more fragrant than any spice.
The taste of honey is on your lips, my darling;
  your tongue is milk and honey for me.
Your clothing has all the fragrance of
    Lebanon.

My sweetheart, my bride, is a secret garden,
   a walled garden, a private spring;
     there the plants flourish.
They grow like an orchard of pomegranate
     trees
   and bear the finest fruits.
There is no lack of henna and nard,
   of saffron, calamus, and cinnamon,
   or incense of every kind.
Myrrh and aloes grow there
   with all the most fragrant perfumes.
Fountains water the garden,
   streams of flowing water,
     brooks gushing down from the Lebanon
     Mountains.

The Woman

Wake up, North Wind.
South Wind, blow on my garden;
   fill the air with fragrance.
Let my lover come to his garden
   and eat the best of its fruits.

The Man

I have entered my garden,
   my sweetheart, my bride.
I am gathering my spices and myrrh;
   I am eating my honey and honeycomb;
   I am drinking my wine and milk.

The Women

Eat, lovers, and drink
   until you are drunk with love! *Sgs 3:6-5:1*

The Fourth Song

The Woman

> While I slept, my heart was awake.
> I dreamed my lover knocked at the door.

The Man

> Let me come in, my darling,
>   my sweetheart, my dove.
> My head is wet with dew,
>   and my hair is damp from the mist.

The Woman

> I have already undressed;
>   why should I get dressed again?
> I have washed my feet;
>   why should I get them dirty again?
> My lover put his hand to the door,
>   and I was thrilled that he was near.
>   I was ready to let him come in.
> My hands were covered with myrrh,
>   my fingers with liquid myrrh,
>   as I grasped the handle of the door.
> I opened the door for my lover,
>   but he had already gone.
> How I wanted to hear his voice!
> I looked for him, but couldn't find him:
>   I called to him, but heard no answer.
>
> The watchmen patrolling the city found me;
>   they struck me and bruised me;
>   the guards at the city wall tore off my cape.
> Promise me, women of Jerusalem,
>   that if you find my lover,
>   you will tell him I am weak from passion.

The Women

Most beautiful of women,
  is your lover different from everyone else?
What is there so wonderful about him
  that we should give you our promise?

The Woman

My lover is handsome and strong;
he is one in ten thousand.
His face is bronzed and smooth;
  his hair is wavy,
  black as a raven.
His eyes are as beautiful as doves by a flowing
    brook,
  doves washed in milk and standing by the
    stream.
His cheeks are as lovely as a garden
  that is full of herbs and spices.
His lips are like lilies,
  wet with liquid myrrh.
His hands are well-formed,
  and he wears rings set with gems.
His body is like smooth ivory,
  with sapphires set in it.
His thighs are columns of alabaster
  set in sockets of gold.
He is majestic, like the Lebanon Mountains
  with their towering cedars.
His mouth is sweet to kiss;
  everything about him enchants me.
This is what my lover is like,
  women of Jerusalem.

The Women

Most beautiful of women,
    where has your lover gone?
Tell us which way your lover went,
    so that we can help you find him.

The Woman

My lover has gone to his garden,
    where the balsam trees grow.
He is feeding his flock in the garden
    and gathering lilies.
My lover is mine, and I am his;
    he feeds his flock among the lilies.

Sgs 5:2-6:3

The Fifth Song

The Man

My love, you are as beautiful as Tirzah,
    as lovely as the city of Jerusalem,
    as breathtaking as these great cities.
Turn your eyes away from me;
    they are holding me captive.
Your hair dances like a flock of goats
    bounding down the hills of Gilead.
Your teeth are as white as a flock of sheep
    that have just been washed.
Your cheeks glow behind your veil.
Let the king have sixty queens, eighty
        concubines,
    young women without number!
But I love only one,
    and she is as lovely as a dove.

She is her mother's only daughter,
    her mother's favorite child.
All women look at her and praise her;
    queens and concubines sing her praises.

Who is this whose glance is like the dawn?
She is beautiful and bright,
    as dazzling as the sun or the moon.
I have come down among the almond trees
    to see the young plants in the valley,
    to see the new leaves on the vines
    and the blossoms on the pomegranate trees.
I am trembling; you have made me as eager
        for love
    as a chariot driver is for battle.

The Women

Dance, dance, girl of Shulam.
Let us watch you as you dance.

The Woman

Why do you want to watch me as I dance
between the rows of onlookers?

The Man

What a magnificent girl you are!
    How beautiful are your feet in sandals.
The curve of your thighs
    is like the work of an artist.
A bowl is there,
    that never runs out of spiced wine.
A sheaf of wheat is there
    surrounded by lilies.

Your breasts are like twin deer,
   like two gazelles.
Your neck is like a tower of ivory.
Your eyes are like the pools in the city of
      Heshbon,
   near the gate of that great city.
Your nose is as lovely as the tower of Lebanon
   that stands guard at Damascus.
Your head is held high like Mount Carmel.
Your braided hair shines like the finest satin;
   its beauty could hold a king captive.
How pretty you are, how beautiful;
   how complete the delights of your love.
You are as graceful as a palm tree,
   and your breasts are clusters of dates.
I will climb the palm tree
   and pick its fruit.
To me your breasts are like bunches of grapes,
   your breath like the fragrance of apples,
   and your mouth like the finest wine.

The Woman

Then let the wine flow straight to my lover,
   flowing over his lips and teeth.
I belong to my lover, and he desires me.
Come, darling, let's go out to the countryside
   and spend the night in the villages.
We will get up early and look at the vines
   to see whether they've started to grow,
   whether the blossoms are opening
   and the pomegranate trees are in bloom.
There I will give you my love.

You can smell the scent of mandrakes,
   and all the pleasant fruits are near our door.
Darling, I have kept for you
   the old delights and the new.

Your left hand is under my head,
   and your right hand caresses me.

Promise me, women of Jerusalem,
   that you will not interrupt our love.

Sgs 6:4-8:4

The Sixth Song

The Women

Who is this coming from the desert,
   arm in arm with her lover?

The Woman

Under the apple tree I woke you,
   in the place where you were born.
Close your heart to every love but mine;
   hold no one in your arms but me.
Love is as powerful as death;
   passion is as strong as death itself.
It bursts into flame
   and burns like a raging fire.
Water cannot put it out;
   no flood can drown it.
But if anyone tried to buy love with his
      wealth,
   contempt is all he would get.

The Woman's Brothers

> We have a young sister,
>   and her breasts are still small.
> What will we do for her
>   when a young man comes courting?
> If she is a wall,
>   we will build her a silver tower.
> But if she is a gate,
>   we will protect her with panels of cedar.

The Woman

> I am a wall,
>   and my breasts are its towers.
> My lover knows that with him
>   I find contentment and peace.

The Man

> Solomon has a vineyard
>   in a place called Baal Hamon.
> There are farmers who rent it from him;
>   each one pays a thousand silver coins.
> Solomon is welcome to his thousand coins,
>   and the farmers to two hundred as their
>   share;
> I have a vineyard of my own!
>
> Let me hear your voice from the garden,
>   my love;
>   my companions are waiting to hear you
>   speak.

The Woman

> Come to me, my lover, like a gazelle,
>   like a young stag on the mountains where
>   spices grow.   Sgs 8:5-14

*   *   *

God Did Not Invent Death

God did not invent death,
and when living creatures die,
it gives him no pleasure.
He created everything so that
it might continue to exist,
and everything he created
is wholesome and good.

Ws 1:13-14

Solomon Prays for Wisdom

"God of my ancestors, merciful Lord, by your word you created everything. By your Wisdom you made man to rule all creation, to govern the world with holiness and righteousness, to administer justice with integrity. Give me the Wisdom that sits beside your throne; give me a place among your children. I am your slave, as was my mother before me. I am only human. I am not strong, and my life will be short. I have little understanding of the Law or of how to apply it. Even if a man is perfect, he will be thought of as nothing without the wisdom that comes from you."

Wisdom to Understand and Judge

"You chose me over everyone else to be the king of your people, to judge your sons and daughters. You told me to build a temple on your sacred mountain, an altar in Jerusalem, the city you chose as your home. It is a copy of that temple in heaven which you prepared at the beginning.

Wisdom is with you and knows your actions; she was present when you made the world. She knows what pleases you, what is right and in accordance with your commands. Send her from the holy heavens, down from your glorious throne, so that she may work at my side and I may learn what pleases you. She knows and understands everything, and will guide me intelligently in what I do. Her glory will protect me. Then I will judge your people fairly, and be worthy of my father's throne. My actions will be acceptable."

Who Can Ever Learn the Will of God?

"Who can ever learn the will of God? Human reason is not adequate for the task, and our philosophies tend to mislead us, because our mortal bodies weigh our souls down. The body is a temporary structure made of earth, a burden to the active mind. All we can do is make guesses about things on earth; we must struggle to learn about things that are close to us. Who, then, can ever hope to understand heavenly things? No one has ever learned your will, unless you first gave him Wisdom, and sent your holy spirit down to him. In this way people on earth have been set on the right path, have learned what pleases you, and have been kept safe by Wisdom."

Ws 9:1-18

God Is Powerful and Merciful

You can show your great power any time you wish, and no one can stand up against it. In your sight the whole world is a grain of sand, barely heavy enough to tip a pair of scales, a drop of dew on the ground in the morning. You are powerful enough to do anything, but you are merciful to everyone; you overlook our sins and give us time to repent. You love everything that exists; you do not despise anything that you have made. If you had not liked it, you would not have made it in the first place. How could anything last, if you did not want it to? How could it endure, if you had not created it? You have allowed it to exist, O Lord, because it is yours, and you love every living thing.

Your immortal spirit is in every one of them, and so you gently correct those who sin against you. You remind them of what they are doing, and warn them about it, so that they may abandon their evil ways and put their trust in you, Lord.

Ws 11:21-12:2

The True God Gives Immortality

But you, our God, are kind and true and patient. You rule the universe with mercy. Even if we sin, we know your power and are still yours. But because we know that we belong to you, we will not sin. Knowing you is perfect righteousness. Recognizing your power is where immortality begins.

Ws 15:1-3

In Praise of Wisdom

All wisdom comes from the Lord,
    and Wisdom is with him forever.

Who can count raindrops or sand along the
   shore?
   Who can count the days of eternity?
How high is the sky? How wide is the earth?
   How deep is the ocean? How profound is
   Wisdom?
   Can anyone find answers to these questions?
Wisdom was created before anything else;
   understanding has always existed.
Has anyone ever shown where Wisdom
   originates?
   Does anyone understand her subtle clever-
   ness?
There is one who is wise
   and we must stand in awe before his throne.
The Lord himself created Wisdom;
   he saw her and recognized her value,
   and so he filled everything he made with
   Wisdom.
He gave some measure of Wisdom to everyone,
   but poured her out on those who love him.

Fear of the Lord

If you fear the Lord, honor and pride will be
   yours;
   you will be crowned with happiness and
   joy.
To honor the Lord is a heartfelt delight;
   it will give you a long and happy life,
and at the end of your days all will go well for
   you.
   God will bless you on the day of your death.
To fear the Lord is the first step to Wisdom.

Wisdom is given to the faithful in their
    mothers' wombs.
She has lived with us from ancient times,
    and generations to come will rely on her.
To fear the Lord is Wisdom at her fullest;
    she satisfies us completely with her gifts
and fills our homes and our barns
    with all that our hearts can desire.
To fear the Lord is the flower of Wisdom
    that blossoms with peace and good health.
She sends knowledge and understanding like
    rain,
    and increases the honor of those who receive
    her.
To fear the Lord is the root of Wisdom;
    her branches are long life.

Si 1:1-20

Has the Lord Ever Disappointed Anyone?

Has the Lord ever disappointed anyone who put
his hope in him? Has the Lord ever abandoned
anyone who held him in constant reverence? Has
the Lord ever ignored anyone who prayed to
him? The Lord is merciful and kind; he forgives
sins and keeps us safe in time of trouble.

Si 2:10-11

The Greatness of God

The Lord, who lives forever, created the whole
universe, and he alone is just. He has given no
one enough power to describe what he has done,

and no one can investigate it completely. Who can measure his majestic power? Who can tell the whole story of his merciful actions? We cannot add to them; we cannot subtract from them. There is no way to comprehend the marvelous things the Lord has done. When we come to the end of that story, we have not even begun; we are simply at a loss for words.

Si 18:1-7

A Prayer for Help Against Sin

I wish that a guard could be placed at my mouth, that my lips could be wisely sealed. It would prevent me from making mistakes and prevent me from destroying myself with my own tongue.

O Lord, my Father and Master of my life, do not leave me at the mercy of my own words; don't let them cause my downfall. I wish I could be whipped for my thoughts, so that Wisdom could discipline my mind. I would not want to be spared when I am wrong; I would not want a single sin to be overlooked! Then I would not keep on sinning, making one mistake after another. I could not fall to my enemies and be humiliated by them.

O Lord, my father, God of my life, keep me from being arrogant; protect me from evil desires. Keep me from being overcome by greed or lust; do not leave me at the mercy of those shameless passions.

Si 22:27-23:6

Canticle of Wisdom

Listen to Wisdom! She proudly sings her own praises among the Israelites, her own people, in the assembly of the Most High, in the presence of his power.

"I am the word spoken by the Most High.
  I covered the earth like a mist.
I made my home in highest heaven,
  my throne on a pillar of cloud.
Alone I walked around the circle of the sky
  and walked through the ocean beneath
    the earth.
I ruled over all the earth and the ocean waves,
  over every nation, over every people.
I looked everywhere for a place to settle,
  some part of the world to make my
    home.

I Took Root in an Honorable People

Then my Creator, who created the universe,
  told me where I was to live.
"Make your home in Israel," he said.
  "The descendants of Jacob will be your
    people."
He created me in eternity, before time began,
  and I will exist for all eternity to come.
I served him in the sacred tent
  and then made my home on Mount Zion.
He settled me in the Beloved City
  and gave me authority over Jerusalem.
I put down roots among an honored people
  whom the Lord had chosen as his own.

I grew tall, like the cedars in Lebanon,
  like the cypresses on Mount Hermon,
like the palm trees of Engedi,
  like the roses of Jericho,
like beautiful olive trees in the fields,
  like plane trees growing by the water.
My breath was the spicy smell of cinnamon,
  of sweet perfume and finest myrrh,
of stacte, onycha, and galbanum,
  the fragrant incense in the sacred Tent.
Like an oak I spread out my branches,
  magnificent and graceful.
Like a grapevine I put out lovely shoots;
  my blossoms gave way to rich and glorious
  fruit.

Come to Me

Come to me, all you that want me,
  and eat your fill of my fruit.
You will remember me as sweeter than honey,
  better than honey from the comb.
Eat me, and you will hunger for more;
  drink me, and you will thirst for more.
Obey me, and you will never have cause for
  embarrassment;
  do as I say, and you will be safe from sin."

Si 24:1-22

Fear the Lord

Those who fear the Lord will live, because they
have put their trust in the one who can save
them. Fear the Lord, and you will have nothing
else to fear. If your trust is in him, you will never

act like a coward. People who fear the Lord are fortunate, because they know where they can look for help. The Lord watches over those who love him; he is their strong protection and firm support. He shelters them from the heat, shades them from the noonday sun, and keeps them from stumbling and falling. He makes them cheerful and puts a sparkle in their eyes. He blesses them with life and health.

Si 34:13-17

God's Justice

The Lord is fair and does not show partiality. He is not prejudiced against the poor; when someone prays who has been wronged, the Lord listens. When orphans and widows pour out their prayers, he does not ignore them. The tears running down a widow's cheek cry out in accusation against the one who has caused her distress.

Serve the Lord willingly, and the Lord will accept you; your prayers will reach the skies. The prayer of the humble person goes past the clouds and keeps on going until it reaches the Lord Most High, where it stays until he answers by seeing that justice is done and that the guilty are punished.

Si 35:12-17

Canticle of Sirach

O Lord God of the universe,
    look upon us and have mercy.

Make every nation stand in fear of you.
Take action against the foreign nations,
    and let them witness your power!
You have used us to show them how holy you
        are;
    now use them to show us how great you are.
Let them learn, as we have learned,
    that there is no God, O Lord, but you.
Give us new signs, perform new miracles;
    show us your glorious strength!
Bring on that appointed time when everyone
    can talk about the great things you do.
Gather the tribes of Israel together again,
    and give them back their land as you gave it
        to them long ago.
Lord, have mercy on Israel, the people who
        are known by your first name,
    whom you called your first-born son.
Take pity on Jerusalem, your holy city,
    where you chose to stay.
Fill your Temple on Mount Zion with your
        glory,
    and with hymns of praise.
Testify for your people, whom you created in
        the beginning;
    fulfill the prophecies that have been spoken
        in your name.
Reward those who have put their faith in you,
    and vindicate your prophets.
You have always been gracious to your people;
    listen to your servants as we pray.
Then everyone on earth will recognize
    that you are the Lord, the God of the ages.

Si 36:1-8, 11-17

A Hymn in Praise of God

Sing the Lord's praises, and thank him for all that he has done. Proclaim his glory in grateful praise! To the music of the harp, sing this song:

All that the Lord has done is very good;
all that he commands is sooner or later done.
No one should ask why things are as they are;
these questions will be answered at the right time.
He commanded, and the water piled up high,
great walls of water arose when he spoke.
Whatever he commands is promptly done;
there are no limits to his power to save.
He sees all that every human being does;
there is no way to hide from his sight.
He sees the whole of time, from beginning to end,
and nothing takes him by surprise.
No one should ask why things are as they are;
everything in creation has its purpose.

Everything made by the Lord is good;
he meets every need at the proper time.
No one can claim that some things are worse than others,
for everything is good in its proper place.
Now then, sing praises with all your heart,
and praise the name of the Lord!

Si 39:14-21, 33-35

The Glory of God in Nature

Now I will remind you of the works of the
    Lord
  and describe the things I have seen.
The words of the Lord brought his works into
    being,
  and the whole creation obeys his com-
    mands.
The light of the sun shines down on
    everything,
  and everything is filled with the Lord's
    glory.
Not even to his holy angels has the Lord given
    power
  to describe all his mighty deeds,
even though he has given them power
  to stand unharmed in his glorious presence.
He sees into the oceans and into the human
    heart,
  and he knows the secrets of both.
The Most High knows everything that can be
    known
  and understands the signs of the ages.
He knows all that has ever been and all that
    ever will be;
  he uncovers the deepest mysteries.
He takes notice of our every thought
  and hears our every word.
The orderly world shows the greatness of his
    wisdom;
  He is the same forever and ever.
Nothing can be added to him, and nothing
    taken away;

he needs no one to give him advice
All his works are beautiful, down to the
    smallest and faintest spark of light.
All these things go on forever,
    and all of them have their purpose.
All things are in pairs, each the opposite of the
    other,
    but nothing the Lord made is incomplete.
Everything completes the goodness of
    something else.
    Could anyone ever see enough of this
    splendor?

Si 42:15-25

The Lord Is Everything

The Lord is everything.
How can we find the power to praise him?
    He is greater than all his creation.
The Lord is awesome in his greatness;
    his power is overwhelming.
    Though you do your best to praise him,
    he is greater than you can ever express.
Though you honor him tirelessly and with all
    your strength,
    you still cannot praise him enough.
No one has seen him, no one can describe him;
    no one can praise him as he deserves.
Mysteries greater than these are still unknown;
    we know only a fraction of his works.
The Lord made the universe
    and then gave wisdom to devout men.

Si 43:27-33

A Benediction

Now then, give praise to the God of the universe,
who has done great things everywhere, who
brings us up from the time we are born, and
deals with us mercifully. May he give us happiness and allow us to have peace in Israel
forever. May he continue his mercy to us and
rescue us in our time of need.

Si 50:22-24

A Song of Thanksgiving

I give you thanks, O Lord and King;
    I praise you as my God and Savior.
I give you thanks,
    for you have helped me and protected me.
You have rescued me from death,
    from dangerous lies and slander.
You helped me when no one else would;
    in your great mercy you saved me
    from the many troubles I have known. . . .

I was once brought face-to-face with death;
    enemies surrounded me everywhere.
I looked for someone to help me,
    but there was no one there.
But then, O Lord, I remembered how merciful
        you are
    and what you had done in times past.
I remembered that you rescue those who rely
        on you,
    that you save them from their enemies.
Then from here on earth I prayed to you
    to rescue me from death.

I prayed, "O Lord, you are my father,
  do not abandon me to my troubles
  when I am helpless against arrogant
    enemies.
I will always praise you
  and sing hymns of thanksgiving."
You answered my prayer,
  and saved me from the threat of destruction.
And so I thank you and praise you.
  O Lord, I praise you!

Si 51:1-3, 6-12

Isaiah

Song of Everlasting Peace

"Let us go up the hill of the Lord,
    to the Temple of Israel's God.
He will teach us what he wants us to do;
    we will walk in the paths he has chosen.
For the Lord's teaching comes from Jerusalem;
    from Zion he speaks to his people."

He will settle disputes among great nations.
They will hammer their swords into plows
    and their spears into pruning knives.
Nations will never again go to war,
    never prepare for battle again.

Is 2:2-4

The Song of the Vineyard

Listen while I sing you this song,
    a song of my friend and his vineyard:
My friend had a vineyard
    on a fertile hill.
He dug the soil and cleared it of stones;
    he planted the finest vines.
He built a tower to guard them,
    dug a pit for treading the grapes.
He waited for the grapes to ripen,
    but every grape was sour.

So now my friend says, "You people who live in Jerusalem and Judah, judge between my vineyard and me. Is there anything I failed to do for it? Then why did it produce sour grapes and not the good grapes I expected?

"Here is what I am going to do to my vineyard: I will take away the hedge around it, break down

the wall that protects it, and let wild animals eat
it and trample it down. I will let it be overgrown
with weeds. I will not trim the vines or hoe the
ground; instead, I will let briars and thorns cover
it. I will even forbid the clouds to let rain fall on
it."

Israel is the vineyard of the Lord Almighty;
    the people of Judah are the vines he planted.
He expected them to do what was good,
    but instead they committed murder.
He expected them to do what was right,
    but their victims cried out for justice.

Is 5:1-7

God Calls Isaiah to Be a Prophet

I saw the Lord. He was sitting on his throne, high
and exalted, and his robe filled the whole Temple. Around him flaming creatures were standing, each of which had six wings. Each creature
covered its face with two wings, and its body
with two, and used the other two for flying.
They were calling out to each other:

"Holy, holy, holy!
The Lord Almighty is holy!
His glory fills the world."

The sound of their voices made the foundation
of the Temple shake, and the Temple itself became filled with smoke.

I said, "There is no hope for me! I am doomed
because every word that passes my lips is sinful,
and I live among a people whose every word is

sinful. And yet, with my own eyes I have seen the King, the Lord Almighty."

Then one of the creatures flew down to me, carrying a burning coal that he had taken from the altar with a pair of tongs. He touched my lips with the burning coal and said, "This has touched your lips, and now your guilt is gone, and your sins are forgiven."

Then I heard the Lord say, "Whom shall I send? Who will be our messenger?"

I answered, "I will go! Send me!"

Is 6:1-8

Song of the Prince of Peace

The people who walked in darkness
  have seen a great light.
They lived in a land of shadows,
  but now light is shining on them.
You have given them great joy, Lord;
  you have made them happy.
They rejoice in what you have done,
  as people rejoice when they harvest grain
  or when they divide captured wealth.
For you have broken the yoke that burdened
    them
  and the rod that beat their shoulders.
You have defeated the nation
  that oppressed and exploited your people,
  just as you defeated the army of Midian
    long ago.
The boots of the invading army
  and all their bloodstained clothing
  will be destroyed by fire.

A Child Is Born to Us

A child is born to us!
  A son is given to us!
  And he will be our ruler.
He will be called, "Wonderful Counselor,"
  "Mighty God," "Eternal Father,"
  "Prince of Peace."
His royal power will continue to grow;
  his kingdom will always be at peace.
He will rule as King David's successor,
  basing his power on right and justice,
  from now until the end of time.
The Lord Almighty is determined to do all
    this.

Is 9:2-7

The Peaceable Kingdom

The royal line of David is like a tree that has been cut down; but just as new branches sprout from a stump, so a new king will arise from among David's descendants.

The spirit of the Lord will give him wisdom
  and the knowledge and skill to rule his
    people.
He will know the Lord's will and will have
  reverence for him,
  and find pleasure in obeying him.
He will not judge by appearance or hearsay;
  he will judge the poor fairly
  and defend the rights of the helpless.
At his command the people will be punished,
  and evil persons will die.

He will rule his people with justice and
    integrity.

Wolves and sheep will live together in peace,
    and leopards will lie down with young
        goats.
Calves and lion cubs will feed together,
    and little children will take care of them.
Cows and bears will eat together,
    and their calves and cubs will lie down in
        peace.
Lions will eat straw as cattle do.
Even a baby will not be harmed
    if it plays near a poisonous snake.
On Zion, God's holy hill,
    there will be nothing harmful or evil.
The land will be as full of knowledge of
    the Lord
    as the seas are full of water.

Is 11:1-9

Hymn of Thanksgiving

A day is coming when people will sing,
"I praise you, Lord! You were angry with me,
    but now you comfort me and are angry no
        longer.
God is my savior;
    I will trust him and not be afraid.
The Lord gives me power and strength;
    he is my savior.
As fresh water brings joy to the thirsty,
    so God's people rejoice when he saves
        them."

A day is coming when people will sing,
"Give thanks to the Lord! Call for him to
    help you!
  Tell all the nations what he has done!
  Tell them how great he is!
Sing to the Lord because of the great things he
    has done.
  Let the whole world hear the news.
Let everyone who lives in Zion shout and sing!
  Israel's holy God is great,
  and he lives among his people."

Is 12:1-6

A Canticle of Praise

Lord, you are my God;
  I will honor you and praise your name.
You have done amazing things;
  you have faithfully carried out
  the plans you made long ago.
You have turned cities into ruins
  and destroyed their fortifications.
The palaces which our enemies built
  are gone forever.
The people of powerful nations will praise
    you;
  you will be feared in the cities of cruel
    nations.
The poor and the helpless have fled to you
  and have been safe in times of trouble.
You give them shelter from storms
  and shade from the burning heat.
Cruel men attack like a winter storm,
  like drought in a dry land.

But you, Lord, have silenced our enemies;
   you silence the shouts of cruel men,
   as a cloud cools a hot day.

Is 25:1-5

God Prepares a Banquet

Here on Mount Zion the Lord Almighty will
prepare a banquet for all the nations of the
world—a banquet of the richest food and the
finest wine. Here he will suddenly remove the
cloud of sorrow that has been hanging over all
the nations. The Sovereign Lord will destroy
death forever! He will wipe away the tears from
everyone's eyes and take away the disgrace his
people have suffered throughout the world. The
Lord himself has spoken.

When it happens, everyone will say,
   "He is our God!
   We put our trust in him,
   and he has rescued us.
   He is the Lord!
   We have put our trust in him,
   and now we are happy because
      he has saved us."

Is 25:6-9

The People's Victory Song

Our city is strong!
God himself defends its walls!
Open the city gates
   and let the faithful nation enter,
   the nation whose people do what is right.

You, Lord, give perfect peace
   to those who keep their purpose firm
   and put their trust in you.
Trust in the Lord forever;
   he will always protect us.
He has humbled those who were proud;
   he destroyed the strong city they lived in,
   and sent its walls crashing into the dust.
Those who were oppressed walk over it now
   and trample it under their feet.

Lord, you make the path smooth for good
      men;
   the road they travel is level.
We follow your will and put our hope in you;
   you are all that we desire.
At night I long for you with all my heart;
   when you judge the earth and its people,
   they will all learn what justice is.

You Alone Are Our Lord

You will give us prosperity, Lord;
   everything that we achieve
   is the result of what you do.
Lord our God, we have been ruled by others,
   but you alone are our Lord.
Now they are dead and will not live again;
   their ghosts will not rise,
      for you have punished them and destroyed
      them.
No one remembers them any more.
Lord, you have made our nation grow,
   enlarging its territory on every side;
   and this has brought you honor.

You punished your people, Lord,
and in anguish they prayed to you.
You, Lord, have made us cry out,
as a woman in labor cries out in pain.
We were in pain and agony,
but we gave birth to nothing.
We have won no victory for our land;
we have accomplished nothing.

Those of our people who have died will live
again!
Their bodies will come back to life.
All those sleeping in their graves
will wake up and sing for joy.
As the sparkling dew refreshes the earth,
so the Lord will revive those who have long
been dead.

Is 26:1-9, 12-19

God Will Bless His People

The Lord is wanting to be merciful to you. He is
ready to take pity on you because he always does
what is right. Happy are those who put their
trust in the Lord.

You people who live in Jerusalem will not
weep any more. The Lord is compassionate, and
when you cry to him for help, he will answer
you. The Lord will make you go through hard
times, but he himself will be there to teach you,
and you will not have to search for him any
more. If you wander off the road to the right or
to the left, you will hear his voice behind you
saying, "Here is the road. Follow it."

On the day when the forts of your enemies are captured and their people are killed, streams of water will flow from every mountain and every hill. The moon will be as bright as the sun, and the sun will be seven times brighter than usual, like the light of seven days in one. This will all happen when the Lord bandages and heals the wounds he has given his people.

Is 30:18-21, 25-26

A Prayer for Help

Lord, have mercy on us. We have put our hope in you. Protect us day by day and save us in times of trouble. When you fight for us, nations run away from the noise of battle.

How great the Lord is! He rules over everything. He will fill Jerusalem with justice and integrity and give stability to the nation. He always protects his people and gives them wisdom and knowledge. Their greatest treasure is their reverence for the Lord.

Is 33:2-3, 5-6

Song of Rejoicing

The desert will rejoice,
    and the flowers will bloom in the
        wastelands.
The desert will sing and shout for joy;
    it will be as beautiful as the Lebanon
        Mountains
    and as fertile as the fields of Carmel and
        Sharon.

Everyone will see the Lord's splendor,
   see his greatness and power.

Give strength to hands that are tired
   and knees that tremble with weakness.
Tell everyone who is discouraged,
   "Be strong and don't be afraid!
   God is coming to your rescue,
   coming to punish your enemies."

The blind will be able to see,
   and the deaf will hear.
The lame will leap and dance,
   and those who cannot speak will shout for
     joy.
Streams of water will flow through the desert;
   the burning sand will become a lake,
   and dry land will be filled with springs.
Where jackals used to live,
   marsh grass and reeds will grow.

There will be a highway there,
   called "The Road of Holiness."
No sinner will ever travel that road;
   no fools will mislead those who follow it.
No lions will be there;
   no fierce animals will pass that way.
Those whom the Lord has rescued
   will travel home by that road.
They will reach Jerusalem with gladness,
   singing and shouting for joy.

They will be happy forever,
   forever free from sorrow and grief.

Is 35:1-10

Hezekiah's Canticle of Praise
Upon Recovering from His Illness

I thought that in the prime of life
I was going to the world of the dead,
Never to live out my life.
I thought that in this world of the living
I would never again see the Lord
Or any living person.
My life was cut off and ended,
Like a tent that is taken down,
Like cloth that is cut from a loom.
I thought that God was ending my life.
All night I cried out with pain,
As if a lion were breaking my bones.
I thought that God was ending my life.
My voice was thin and weak,
And I moaned like a dove.
My eyes grew tired from looking to heaven.
Lord, rescue me from all this trouble.
What can I say? The Lord has done this.
My heart is bitter, and I cannot sleep.

Lord, I will live for you, for you alone;
Heal me and let me live.
My bitterness will turn into peace.
You save my life from all danger;
You forgive all my sins.
No one in the world of the dead can praise
    you;
The dead cannot trust in your faithfulness.
It is the living who praise you,
As I praise you now.
Fathers tell their children how faithful you
    are.

Lord, you have healed me.
We will play harps and sing your praise,
Sing praise in your Temple as long as we live.

Is 38:10-20

* * *

Words of Hope

"Comfort my people," says our God.
  "Comfort them!
Encourage the people of Jerusalem.
Tell them they have suffered long enough
  and their sins are now forgiven."

The Lord Is Coming

A voice cries out,
"Prepare in the wilderness a road for the Lord!
Clear the way in the desert for our God!
Fill every valley;
  level every mountain.
The hills will become a plain,
  and the rough country will be made smooth.
Then the glory of the Lord will be revealed,
  and all mankind will see it.
The Lord himself has promised this."

A voice cries out, "Proclaim a message!"
"What message shall I proclaim?" I ask.
"Proclaim that all mankind are like grass;
  they last no longer than wild flowers.

Grass withers and flowers fade
    when the Lord sends the wind blowing over
      them.
    People are no more enduring than grass.
Yes, grass withers and flowers fade,
    but the word of our God endures forever."

Jerusalem, go up on a high mountain
    and proclaim the good news!
Call out with a loud voice,
      Zion;
    announce the good news!
Speak out and do not be afraid.
Tell the towns of Judah
    that their God is coming!

The Sovereign Lord is coming to rule with
      power,
    bringing with him the people he has
      rescued.
He will take care of his flock like a shepherd;
    he will gather the lambs together
    and carry them in his arms;
    he will gently lead their mothers.

Is 40:1-11

Hymn to the Incomparable God

Can anyone measure the ocean by handfuls
    or measure the sky with his hands?
Can anyone hold the soil of the earth in a cup
    or weigh the mountains and hills on scales?
Can anyone tell the Lord what to do?
    Who can teach him or give him advice?

With whom does God consult
in order to know and understand
and to learn how things should be done?

To whom can God be compared?
How can you describe what he is like?
He is not like an idol that workmen make,
that metalworkers cover with gold
and set in a base of silver.
Do you not know?
Were you not told long ago?
Have you not heard how the world began?
It was made by the one who sits on his throne
above the earth and beyond the sky;
the people below look as tiny as ants.
He stretched out the sky like a curtain,
like a tent in which to live.

Who Is Like Him?

To whom can the holy God be compared?
Is there anyone else like him?
Look up at the sky!
Who created the stars you see?
The one who leads them out like an army,
he knows how many there are
and calls each one by name!
His power is so great—
not one of them is ever missing!

Israel, why then do you complain
that the Lord doesn't know your troubles
or care if you suffer injustice?
Don't you know? Haven't you heard?
The Lord is the everlasting God;
he created all the world.

He never grows tired or weary.
No one understands his thoughts.
He strengthens those who are weak and tired.

Even those who are young grow weak;
    young men can fall exhausted.
But those who trust in the Lord for help
    will find their strength renewed.
They will rise on wings like eagles;
    they will run and not get weary;
    they will walk and not grow weak.
Is 40:12-14, 18-22, 25-31

First Song of the Suffering Servant

The Lord says,
"Here is my servant, whom I strengthen—
    the one I have chosen, with whom I am
        pleased.
I have filled him with my spirit,
    and he will bring justice to every nation.
He will not shout or raise his voice
    or make loud speeches in the streets.
He will not break off a bent reed
    nor put out a flickering lamp.
He will bring lasting justice to all.
He will not lose hope or courage;
    he will establish justice on the earth.
    Distant lands eagerly wait for his teaching."

God created the heavens and stretched them
        out;
    he fashioned the earth and all that lives
        there;
    he gave life and breath to all its people.
And now the Lord God says to his servant,

"I, the Lord, have called you and given
    you power
  to see that justice is done on earth.
Through you I will make a covenant with all
    peoples;
  through you I will bring light to the nations.
You will open the eyes of the blind
  and set free those who sit in dark prisons.

"I alone am the Lord your God.
  No other god may share my glory;
  I will not let idols share my praise.
The things I predicted have now come true.
Now I will tell you of new things
  even before they begin to happen."

Is 42:1-9

A Song of Praise

Sing a new song to the Lord;
  sing his praise, all the world!
Praise him, you that sail the sea;
  praise him, all creatures of the sea!
Sing, distant lands and all who live there!
Let the desert and its towns praise God;
  let the people of Kedar praise him!
Let those who live in the city of Sela
  shout for joy from the tops of the mountains!
Let those who live in distant lands
  give praise and glory to the Lord!
The Lord goes out to fight like a warrior;
  he is ready and eager for battle.
He gives a war cry, a battle shout;
  he shows his power against his enemies.

Is 42:10-13

I Have Called You by Name

Israel, the Lord who created you says,
"Do not be afraid—I will save you.
I have called you by name—you are mine.
When you pass through deep waters, I will be
with you;
your troubles will not overwhelm you.
When you pass through fire, you will not be
burned;
the hard trials that come will not hurt you.
For I am the Lord your god,
the holy God of Israel, who saves you.
I will give up Egypt to set you free;
I will give up Sudan and Seba.
I will give up whole nations to save your life,
because you are precious to me
and because I love you and give you honor.
Do not be afraid—I am with you!"

Besides Me There Is No Other

"People of Israel, you are my witnesses;
I chose you to be my servant,
so that you would know me and believe me
and understand that I am the only God.
Besides me there is no other god;
there never was and never will be.

"I alone am the Lord,
the only one who can save you.
I predicted what would happen,
and then I came to your aid.
No foreign god has ever done this;
you are my witnesses.

I am God and always will be.
No one can escape from my power;
    no one can change what I do."

Is 43:1-5, 10-13

The Lord Is the Only God

The Lord says,
    Listen now, Israel, my servant,
    my chosen people, the descendants of Jacob.
I am the Lord who created you;
    from the time you were born, I have helped
      you;
Do not be afraid; you are my servant,
    my chosen people whom I love.

"I will give water to the thirsty land
    and make streams flow on the dry ground.
I will pour out my spirit on your children
    and my blessing on your descendants.
They will thrive like well-watered grass,
    like willows by streams of running water.

"One by one, people will say, 'I am the
      Lord's.'
    They will come to join the people of Israel.
Each one will mark the name of the Lord on
      his arm
    and call himself one of God's people."

The Lord, who rules and protects Israel,
    the Lord Almighty, has this to say:
"I am the first, the last, the only God;
    there is no other god but me.

Could anyone else have done what I did?
Who could have predicted all that would
happen
from the very beginning to the end of time?
Do not be afraid, my people!
You know that from ancient times until now
I have predicted all that would happen,
and you are my witnesses.
Is there any other god?
Is there some powerful god I never heard of?"
Is 44:1-8

The Lord, the Creator and Savior

The Lord says,
"Israel, remember this;
remember that you are my servant.
I created you to be my servant,
and I will never forget you.
I have swept your sins away like a cloud.
Come back to me; I am the one who saves
you."

Shout for joy, you heavens!
Shout, deep places of the earth!
Shout for joy, mountains, and every tree of the
forest!
The Lord has shown his greatness
by saving his people Israel.

"I am the Lord, your
Savior;
I am the one who created you.
I am the Lord, the Creator of all things.
I alone stretched out the heavens;
when I made the earth, no one helped me.

I make fools of fortunetellers
    and frustrate the predictions of astrologers.
The words of the wise I refute
    and show that their wisdom is foolishness.
But when my servant makes a prediction,
    when I send a messenger to reveal my plans,
    I make those plans and predictions come
        true.
I tell Jerusalem that people will live there
        again,
    and the cities of Judah that they will be
        rebuilt.
    Those cities will rise from the ruins.
With a word of command I dry up the ocean.
I say to Cyrus, 'You are the one who will rule
        for me;
    you will do what I want you to do:
    you will order that Jerusalem be rebuilt
    and that the foundations of the Temple be
        laid.' "

Is 44:21-28

Canticle of Isaiah

Does a clay pot dare argue with its maker,
    a pot that is like all the others?
Does the clay ask the potter what he is doing?
    Does the pot complain that its maker has no
        skill?
Does anyone dare say to his parents,
    "Why did you make me like this?"
The Lord, the holy God of Israel,
    the one who shapes the future, says:
"You have no right to question me about my
        children
    or to tell me what I ought to do!

The Lord of Creation and History

I am the one who made the earth
and created mankind to live there.
By my power I stretched out the heavens;
I control the sun, the moon, and the stars.
I myself have stirred Cyrus to action
to fulfill my purpose and put things right.
I will straighten out every road that he travels.
He will rebuild my city, Jerusalem,
and set my captive people free.
No one has hired him or bribed him to do
this."
The Lord Almighty has spoken.

The Lord says to Israel,
"The wealth of Egypt and Sudan will be yours,
and the tall men of Seba will be your slaves;
they will follow you in chains.
They will bow down to you and confess,
'God is with you—he alone is God.
The God of Israel, who saves his people,
is a God who conceals himself.
Those who make idols will all be ashamed;
all of them will be disgraced.
But Israel is saved by the Lord,
and her victory lasts forever;
her people will never be disgraced.' "

I Am the Lord

The Lord created the heavens—
he is the one who is God!
He formed and made the earth—
he made it firm and lasting.

He did not make it a desolate waste,
    but a place for people to live.
It is he who says, "I am the Lord,
    and there is no other god.
I have not spoken in secret
    or kept my purpose hidden.
I did not require the people of Israel
    to look for me in a desolate waste.
I am the Lord, and I speak the truth;
    I make known what is right."

Is 45:9-19

Second Song of the Suffering Servant

Listen to me, distant nations,
    you people who live far away!
Before I was born, the Lord chose me
    and appointed me to be his servant.
He made my words as sharp as a sword.
    With his own hand he protected me.
He made me like an arrow,
    sharp and ready for use.
He said to me, "Israel, you are my servant;
    because of you, people will praise me."

I said, "I have worked, but how hopeless it is!
    I have used up my strength, but have
        accomplished nothing."
Yet I can trust the Lord to defend my cause;
    he will reward me for what I do.

Before I was born, the Lord appointed me;
    he made me his servant to bring back his
        people,
    to bring back the scattered people of Israel.

The Lord gives me honor;
    he is the source of my strength.

The Lord said to me,
"I have a greater task for you, my servant.
    Not only will you restore to greatness
    the people of Israel who have survived,
but I will also make you a light to the
        nations—
    so that all the world may be saved."

Israel's holy God and savior says
    to the one who is deeply despised,
    who is hated by the nations
    and is the servant of the rulers:
"Kings will see you released
    and will rise to show their respect;
princes also will see it,
    and they will bow low to honor you."

This will happen because the Lord
    has chosen his servant;
the holy God of Israel keeps his promises.

Is 49:1-7

A Song of Restoration

The Lord says to his people,
When the time comes to save you, I will show
        you favor
    and answer your cries for help.
I will guard and protect you
    and through you make a covenant with all
        peoples.

I will let you settle once again
    in your land that is not laid waste.
I will say to the prisoners, 'Go free!'
    and to those who are in darkness,
    'Come out to the light!'
They will be like sheep that graze on the hills;
    they will never be hungry or thirsty.
Sun and desert heat will not hurt them,
    for they will be led by one who loves them.
    He will lead them to springs of water.

"I will make a highway across the mountains
    and prepare a road for my people to travel.
My people will come from far away,
    from the north and the west,
    and from Aswan in the south."

Sing, heavens! Shout for joy, earth!
    Let the mountains burst into song!
The Lord will comfort his people;
    he will have pity on his suffering people.

Even If a Mother Should Forget . . .

But the people of Jerusalem said,
"The Lord has abandoned us!
    He has forgotten us."
So the Lord answers,
"Can a woman forget her own baby
    and not love the child she bore?
Even if a mother should forget her child,
    I will never forget you.
Jerusalem, I can never forget you!
    I have written your name on the palms of
        my hands.

"Those who will rebuild you are coming soon,
   and those who destroyed you will leave.
Look around and see what is happening!
   Your people are assembling — they are
     coming home!
As surely as I am the living God,
   you will be proud of your people,
   As proud as a bride is of her jewels."

The Sovereign Lord says to his people:
"I will signal to the nations,
   and they will bring your children home.
Kings will be like fathers to you:
   queens will be like mothers.
They will bow low before you and honor you;
   they will humbly show their respect for you.
Then you will know that I am the Lord;
   no one who waits for my help will be
     disappointed."

Is 49:8-18, 22-23

Third Song of the Suffering Servant

The Sovereign Lord has taught me what to
     say,
   so that I can strengthen the weary.
Every morning he makes me eager
   to hear what he is going to teach me.
The Lord has given me understanding,
   and I have not rebelled
   or turned away from him.
I bared my back to those who beat me.
   I did not stop them when they insulted me,
   when they pulled out the hairs of my beard
   and spit in my face.

But their insults cannot hurt me
 because the Sovereign Lord gives me help.
I brace myself to endure them.
 I know that I will not be disgraced,
 for God is near,
 and he will prove me innocent.
Does anyone dare bring charges against me?
 Let us go to court together!
 Let him bring his accusation!
The Sovereign Lord himself defends me—
 who, then, can prove me guilty?
All my accusers will disappear;
 they will vanish like moth-eaten cloth.

All of you that have reverence for the Lord
 and obey the words of his servant,
the path you walk may be dark indeed,
 but trust in the Lord, rely on your God.
         Is 50:4-10

How Wonderful on the Mountains!

How wonderful it is to see
 a messenger coming across the mountains,
 bringing good news, the news of peace!
He announces victory and says to Zion,
 "Your God is king!"
Those who guard the city are shouting,
 shouting together for joy.
They can see with their own eyes
 the return of the Lord of Zion.

Break into shouts of joy,
 you ruins of Jerusalem!

The Lord will rescue his city
and comfort his people.
The Lord will use his holy power;
he will save his people,
and all the world will see it. . . .

The Lord your God will lead you
and protect you on every side.

Is 52:7-10, 12

Fourth Song of the Suffering Servant

The Lord says,
"My servant will succeed in his task;
he will be highly honored.
Many people were shocked when they saw
him;
he was so disfigured that he hardly looked
human.
But now many nations will marvel at him,
and kings will be speechless with
amazement.
They will see and understand
something they had never known."

The people reply,
"Who would have believed what we now
report?
Who could have seen the Lord's hand in this?
It was the will of the Lord that his servant
grow like a plant taking root in dry ground.
He had no dignity or beauty
to make us take notice of him.
There was nothing attractive about him,
nothing that would draw us to him.
We despised him and rejected him;

he endured suffering and pain.
No one would even look at him —
we ignored him as if he were nothing.

He Endured Our Suffering

"But he endured the suffering
that should have been ours,
the pain that we should have borne.
All the while we thought that his suffering
was punishment sent by God.
But because of our sins he was wounded,
beaten because of the evil we did.
We are healed by the punishment he suffered,
made whole by the blows he received.
All of us were like sheep that were lost,
each of us going his own way.
But the Lord made the punishment fall on
him,
the punishment all of us deserved.

"He was treated harshly, but endured it
humbly;
he never said a word.
Like a lamb about to be slaughtered,
like a sheep about to be sheared,
he never said a word.
He was arrested and sentenced and led off to
die.
and no one cared about his fate.
He was put to death for the sins of our people.
He was placed in a grave with evil men,
he was buried with the rich,
even though he had never committed a crime
or ever told a lie."

His Death Was a Sacrifice

The Lord says,
"It was my will that he should suffer;
  his death was a sacrifice to bring
    forgiveness.
And so he will see his descendants;
  he will live a long life,
  and through him my purpose will succeed.
After a life of suffering, he will again have joy.
  he will know that he did not suffer in vain.
My devoted servant, with whom I am pleased,
  will bear the punishment of many
  and for his sake I will forgive them.
And so I will give him a place of honor,
  a place among great and powerful men.
He willingly gave his life
  and shared the fate of evil men.
He took the place of many sinners
  and prayed that they might be forgiven."
Is 52:13-53:12

The Lord's Love for Us

Jerusalem, you have been like a childless
    woman,
  but now you can sing and shout for joy.

Now you will have more children
  than a woman whose husband never left
    her.
Make the tent you live in larger;
  lengthen its ropes and strengthen the pegs!
You will extend your boundaries on all sides;
  your people will get back the land

that the other nations now occupy.
Cities now deserted will be filled with
people.

You Are Like a Young Wife

Do not be afraid—you will not be disgraced
again:
you will not be humiliated.
You will forget your unfaithfulness as a
young wife,
and your desperate loneliness as a widow.
Your Creator will be like a husband to you—
the Lord Almighty is his name.
The holy God of Israel will save you—
he is the ruler of all the world.

Israel, you are like a young wife,
deserted by her husband and deeply
distressed.
But the Lord calls you back to him and says:
"For one brief moment I left you:
with deep love I will take you back.
I turned away angry for only a moment,
but I will show you my love forever."
So says the Lord who saves you. . . .

My Love for You Will Never End

"The mountains and hills may crumble,
but my love for you will never end;
I will keep forever my promise of peace."
So says the Lord who loves you.

Is 54:1-8, 10

A Song of God's Mercy

The Lord says,
"Come everyone who is thirsty —
  here is water!
Come, you that have no money —
  buy grain and eat!
Come! Buy wine and milk —
  it will cost you nothing!
Why spend money on what does not satisfy?
  Why spend your wages and still be hungry?
Listen to me and do what I say,
  and you will enjoy the best food of all.

"Listen now, my people, and come to me,
  come to me, and you will have life!
I will make a lasting covenant with you
  and give you the blessings I promised to
    David. . . .
I, the Lord your God, the holy God of Israel,
  will make all this happen;
  I will give you honor and glory."

Turn to the Lord and Pray

Turn to the Lord and pray to him,
  now that he is near.
Let the wicked leave their way of life
  and change their way of thinking.
Let them turn to the Lord, our God;
  he is merciful and quick to forgive.

"My thoughts," says the Lord, "are not like
    yours,
  and my ways are different from yours.

As high as the heavens are above the earth,
    so high are my ways and thoughts above
        yours.

"My word is like the snow and the rain
    that come down from the sky to water the
        earth.
They make the crops grow
    and provide seed for planting and food to
        eat.
So also will be the word that I speak—
    it will not fail to do what I plan for it;
    it will do everything I send it to do.

"You will leave Babylon with joy:
    you will be led out of the city in peace.
The mountains and hills will burst into
        singing,
    and trees will shout for joy.
Cypress trees will grow where now there are
        briers;
    myrtle trees will come up in place of thorns.
This will be a sign that will last forever,
    a reminder of what I, the Lord, have done."
                                    Is 55:1-3, 5-13

God Promises Help and Healing

The Lord says, "Let my people return to me. Remove every obstacle from their path! Build the road and make it ready!

"I am the high and holy God who lives forever. I live in a high and holy place, but I also live with people who are humble and repentant, so that I can restore their confidence and hope. . . . I will heal them. I will lead them and help them, and I will comfort those who mourn, I offer peace to all, both near and far! I will heal my people."

Is 57:14-15, 18-19

My Favor Will Shine on You

The Lord says, "The kind of fasting I want is this: remove the chains of oppression and the yoke of injustice, and let the oppressed go free. Share your food with the hungry and open your homes to the homeless poor. Give clothes to those who have nothing to wear, and do not refuse to help your own relatives.

"Then my favor will shine on you like the morning sun, and your wounds will be quickly healed. I will always be with you to save you; my presence will protect you on every side. When you pray, I will answer you. When you call to me, I will respond."

Is 58:6-9

The Lord Rescues His People

The Lord says to his people,"I will come to Jerusalem to defend you and to save all of you that turn from your sins. And I make a covenant with you: I have given you my power and my teachings to be yours forever, and from now on you are to obey me and teach your children and your descendants to obey me for all time to come."

Is 59:20-21

The Glory of the New Jerusalem

Arise, Jerusalem, and shine like the sun;
The glory of the Lord is shining on you!
Other nations will be covered by darkness,
But on you the light of the Lord will shine;
The brightness of his presence will be with
    you.
Nations will be drawn to your light,
And kings to the dawning of your new day.

Look around you and see what is happening;
Your people are gathering to come home!
Your sons will come from far away;
Your daughters will be carried like children.
You will see this and be filled with joy;
You will tremble with excitement.
The wealth of the nations will be brought to
    you;
From across the sea their riches will come.

Great caravans of camels will come, from
    Midian and Ephah.
They will come from Sheba, bringing gold
    and incense.
People will tell the good news of what the
    Lord has done!

"No longer will the sun be your light by day
Or the moon be your light by night:
I, the Lord, will be your eternal light;
The light of my glory will shine on you.
Your days of grief will come to an end.
I, the Lord, will be your eternal light,
More lasting than the sun and moon."

Is 60:1-6, 19-20

The Good News of Deliverance

The Sovereign Lord has filled me with his
    spirit.
He has chosen me and sent me
To bring good news to the poor,
To heal the broken-hearted,
To announce release to captives
And freedom to those in prison.
He has sent me to proclaim
That the time has come
When the Lord will save his people
And defeat their enemies.
He has sent me to comfort all who mourn,
To give to those who mourn in Zion
Joy and gladness instead of grief,
A song of praise instead of sorrow.
They will be like trees
That the Lord himself has planted.
They will all do what is right,
And God will be praised for what he has done,
They will rebuild cities that have long been in
    ruins.

The Lord says,
"I love justice and hate oppression and crime.
I will faithfully reward my people
And make an eternal covenant with them.
They will be famous among the nations;
Everyone who sees them will know
That they are a people whom I have blessed."

Jerusalem rejoices because of what the Lord
    has done.
She is like a bride dressed for her wedding.

God has clothed her with salvation and
     victory.
As surely as seeds sprout and grow,
The Sovereign Lord will save his people,
And all the nations will praise him.

Is 61:1-4, 8-11

Your God Will Delight in You

I will speak out to encourage Jerusalem;
I will not be silent until she is saved,
And her victory shines like a torch in the night.
Jerusalem, the nations will see you victorious!
All their kings will see your glory.
You will be called by a new name.
A name given by the Lord himself.
You will be like a beautiful crown for the
     Lord.
No longer will you be called "Forsaken,"
Or your land be called "The Deserted Wife."
Your new name will be "God Is Pleased with
     Her."
Your land will be called "Happily Married,"
Because the Lord is pleased with you
And will be like a husband to your land.
Like a young man taking a virgin as his bride,
He who formed you will marry you.
As a groom is delighted with his bride,
So your God will delight in you.

Is 62:1-5

Song of the Conquering Hero

Who is this so splendidly dressed in red, march-
ing along in power and strength?

It is the Lord, powerful to save, coming to announce his victory.

"Why is his clothing so red, like that of a man who tramples grapes to make wine?"

The Lord answers, "I have trampled the nations like grapes, and no one came to help me. I trampled them in my anger, and their blood has stained all my clothing. I decided that the time to save my people had come; it was time to punish their enemies. I was amazed when I looked and saw that there was no one to help me. But my anger made me strong, and I won the victory myself. In my anger I trampled whole nations and shattered them. I poured out their lifeblood on the ground."

The Lord's Goodness to Israel

I will tell of the Lord's unfailing love;
  I praise him for all he has done for us.
He has richly blessed the people of Israel
  because of his mercy and constant love.

Is 63:1-7

A Prayer for Mercy and Help

Lord, look upon us from heaven, where you live in your holiness and glory. Where is your great concern for us? Where is your power? Where are your love and compassion? Do not ignore us. You are our father. Our ancestors Abraham and Jacob do not acknowledge us, but you, Lord, are our father, the one who has always rescued us. Why do you let us stray from your ways? Why do you make us so stubborn that we turn away from you? Come back, for the sake of those who serve you, for the sake of the people who have always been yours.

We, your holy people, were driven out by our enemies for a little; they trampled down your sanctuary. You treat us as though you had never been our ruler, as though we had never been your people.

Tear the Sky and Come Down

Why don't you tear the sky open and come down? The mountains would see you and shake with fear. They would tremble like water boiling over a hot fire. Come and reveal your power to your enemies, and make the nations tremble at your presence! There was a time when you came and did terrifying things that we did not expect; the mountains saw you and shook with fear. No one has ever seen or heard of a God like you, who does such deeds for those who put their hope in him. You welcome those who find joy in doing what is right, those who remember how you want them to live. You were angry with us, but we went on sinning; in spite of your great anger we have continued to do wrong since ancient times. All of us have been sinful; even our best actions are filthy through and through. Because of our sins we are like leaves that wither and are blown away by the wind. No one turns to you in prayer, no one goes to you for help. You have hidden yourself from us and have abandoned us because of our sins.

You Are Our Father

But you are our father, Lord. We are like clay, and you are like the potter. You created us, so do not be too angry with us or hold our sins against us forever. We are your people; be merciful to us. Your sacred cities are like a desert; Jerusalem is a deserted ruin, and our Temple, the sacred and beautiful place where our ancestors praised you, has been destroyed by fire. All the places we loved are in ruins. Lord, are you unmoved by all this? Are you going to do nothing and make us suffer more than we can endure?   *Is 63:15-64:12*

Song of the New Creation

The Lord says, "I am making a new earth and new heavens. The events of the past will be completely forgotten. Be glad and rejoice forever in what I create. The new Jerusalem I make will be full of joy, and her people will be happy. I myself will be filled with joy because of Jerusalem and her people. There will be no weeping there, no calling for help. Babies will no longer die in infancy, and all people will live out their life span. Those who live to be a hundred will be considered young. To die before that would be a sign that I had punished them. People will build houses and get to live in them—they will not be used by someone else. They will plant vineyards and enjoy the wine—it will not be drunk by others. Like trees, my people will live long lives. They will fully enjoy the things that they have worked for. The work they do will be successful, and their children will not meet with disaster. I will bless them and their descendants for all time to come. Even before they finish praying to me, I will answer their prayers. Wolves and lambs will eat together; lions will eat straw, as cattle do, and snakes will no longer be dangerous. On Zion, my sacred hill, there will be nothing harmful or evil."   *Is 64:17-25*

Rejoice with Jerusalem

"My holy city is like a woman who suddenly gives birth to a child without ever going into labor. Has anyone ever seen or heard of such a thing? Has a nation ever been born in a day? Zion will not have to suffer long, before the nation is born. Do not think that I will bring my people to the point of birth and not let them be born." The Lord has spoken.

> Rejoice with Jerusalem; be glad for her,
>   all you that love this city!
> Rejoice with her now,
>   all you that have mourned for her!
> You will enjoy her prosperity,
>   like a child at its mother's breast.

The Lord says, "I will bring you lasting prosperity; the wealth of the nations will flow to you like a river that never goes dry. You will be like a child that is nursed by its mother, carried in her arms, and treated with love. I will comfort you in Jerusalem, as a mother comforts her child. When you see this happen, you will be glad; it will make you strong and healthy. Then you will know that I, the Lord, help those who obey me, and I show my anger against my enemies."

Is 66:7-13

Jeremiah

Ezekiel

Daniel

The Call of Jeremiah

The Lord said to me, "I chose you before I gave you life, and before you were born I selected you to be a prophet to the nations."

I answered, "Sovereign Lord, I don't know how to speak; I am too young."

But the Lord said to me, "Do not say that you are too young, but go to the people I send you to, and tell them everything I commanded you to say. Do not be afraid of them, for I will be with you to protect you. I, the Lord, have spoken!"

Then the Lord reached out, touched my lips, and said to me, "Listen, I am giving you the words you must speak. Today I give you authority over nations and kingdoms to uproot and to pull down, to destroy and to overthrow, to build and to plant." . . .

"Listen, Jeremiah! Everyone in this land — the kings of Judah, the officials, the priests, and the people — will be against you. But today I am giving you the strength to resist them; you will be like a fortified city, an iron pillar, and a bronze wall. They will not defeat you for I will be with you to protect you. I, the Lord, have spoken."

Jr 1:4-10, 18-19

God's Care for Israel

The Lord told me to proclaim this message to everyone in Jerusalem:

"I remember how faithful you were when
   you were young,
   how you loved me when we were first
   married;

you followed me through the desert,
   through a land that had not been planted.
Israel, you belonged to me alone;
   you were my sacred possession.
I sent suffering and disaster
   on everyone who hurt you.
I, the Lord, have spoken.

Israel's Unfaithfulness

"You deserted me, the Lord your God,
   while I was leading you along the way.
You will learn how bitter and wrong it is
   to abandon me, the Lord your God,
   and no longer to have reverence for me.
I, the Sovereign Lord Almighty, have spoken."
                                    Jr 2:1-3, 17, 19

I Wanted You to Call Me Father

"Israel, I wanted to accept you as my son
   and give you a delightful land,
   the most beautiful land in all the world.
I wanted you to call me father
   and never again turn away from me.
But like an unfaithful wife,
   you have not been faithful to me.
I, the Lord, have spoken."

A noise is heard on the hilltops:
   it is the people of Israel crying and pleading
   because they have lived sinful lives
   and have forgotten the Lord their God.
Return, all of you who have turned away from
      the Lord:
   he will heal you and make you faithful.
                                    Jr 3:19-22

Lord, There Is No One Like You

Lord, there is no one like you;
    you are mighty,
    and your name is great and powerful.
Who would not honor you, the king of all
       nations?
    You deserve to be honored.
There is no one like you
    among all the wise men of the nations
    or among the kings.
You, Lord, are the true God
    you are the living God
    and the eternal king.
When you are angry, the world trembles;
    the nations cannot endure your anger.

Jr 10:6-7, 10

A Hymn of Praise to God

The Lord made the earth by his power;
    by his wisdom he created the world
    and stretched out the heavens.
At his command the waters above the sky roar;
    he brings clouds from the ends of the earth.
He makes lightning flash in the rain
    and sends the wind from his storeroom. . . .

The God of Jacob is not like other gods;
    he is the one who made everything,
    and he has chosen Israel to be his very own
       people.
The Lord Almighty is his name.

Jr 10:12-13, 16

Jeremiah's Prayer for Justice

Lord, I know that no one is the master of his
   own destiny;
   no person has control over his own life.
Correct your people, Lord,
   but do not be too hard on us
   or punish us when you are angry;
   that would be the end of us.
Turn your anger on the nations that do not
   worship you.
They have killed your people;
   they have destroyed us completely
   and left our country in ruins.

Jr 10:23-25

Jeremiah Questions the Lord

Lord, if I argued my case with you,
   you would prove to be right.
Yet I must question you about matters of
   justice.
Why are wicked men so prosperous?
   Why do dishonest men succeed?
You plant them, and they take root;
   they grow and bear fruit.
They always speak well of you,
   yet they do not really care about you.
But, Lord, you know me;
   you see what I do
   and how I love you. . . .
How long will our land be dry,
   and the grass in every field be withered?

Animals and birds are dying
because of the wickedness of our people,
people who say, "God doesn't see what we
are doing."

Jr 12:1-4

A Song of Lament

The Lord said to me concerning the drought,
"Judah is in mourning;
its cities are dying,
its people lie on the ground in sorrow,
and Jerusalem cries out for help.
The rich people send their servants for water;
they go to the cisterns,
but find no water;
they come back with their jars empty.
Discouraged and confused,
they hide their faces.
Because there is no rain
and the ground is dried up,
the farmers are sick at heart;
they hide their faces.
In the field the mother deer
abandons her newborn fawn
because there is no grass.
The wild donkeys stand on the hilltops
and pant for breath like jackals;
their eyesight fails them
because they have no food.
My people cry out to me,
'Even though our sins accuse us,
help us, Lord, as you have promised.

We have turned away from you many times;
    we have sinned against you.
You are Israel's only hope;
    you are the one who saves us from disaster.
Why are you like a stranger in our land,
    like a traveler who stays for only one night?
Why are you like a man taken by surprise,
    like a soldier powerless to help?
Surely, Lord, you are with us!
    We are your people;
    do not abandon us.' "   *Jr 14:1-9*

Jeremiah Tells of His Sorrow

"May my eyes flow with tears day and night,
    may I never stop weeping,
for my people are deeply wounded
    and are deeply hurt.
When I go out in the fields,
    I see the bodies of men killed in war;
when I go into the towns,
    I see people starving to death.
Prophets and priests carry on their work,
    but they don't know what they are doing."

The People Plead with the Lord

Lord, have you completely rejected Judah?
    Do you hate the people of Zion?
Why have you hurt us so badly
      that we cannot be healed?
We looked for peace, but nothing good
      happened;
    we hoped for healing, but terror came
      instead.

We have sinned against you, Lord;
   we confess our own sins
   and the sins of our ancestors.
Remember your promises and do not
    despise us;
   do not bring disgrace on Jerusalem,
   the place of your glorious throne.
Do not break the covenant you made with us.
None of the idols of the nations can send rain;
   the sky by itself cannot make the showers
    fall.
We have put our hope in you, O Lord our
    God,
   because you are the one who does these
    things.

Jr 14:17-22

Jeremiah Complains to the Lord

What an unhappy man I am! Why did my mother bring me into the world? I have to quarrel and argue with everyone in the land. I have not lent any money or borrowed any; yet everyone curses me. Lord, may all their curses come true if I have not served you well, if I have not pleaded with you on behalf of my enemies when they were in trouble and distress. . . .

The Lord said to me,"I will send enemies to carry away the wealth and treasures of my people, in order to punish them for the sins they have committed throughout the land. I will make them serve their enemies in a land they know nothing about, because my anger is like fire, and it will burn forever."

Second Exchange with the Lord

Then I said, "Lord, you understand. Remember me and help me. Let me have revenge on those who persecute me. Do not be so patient with them that they succeed in killing me. Remember that it is for your sake that I am insulted. You spoke to me, and I listened to every word. I belong to you, Lord God Almighty, and so your words filled my heart with joy and happiness. I did not spend my time with other people, laughing and having a good time. In obedience to your orders I stayed by myself and was filled with anger. Why do I keep on suffering? Why are my wounds incurable? Why won't they heal? Do you intend to disappoint me like a stream that goes dry in the summer?"

To this the Lord replied, "If you return, I will take you back, and you will be my servant again. If instead of talking nonsense you proclaim a worthwhile message, you will be my prophet again. The people will come back to you, and you will not need to go to them. I will make you like a solid bronze wall as far as they are concerned. They will fight against you, but they will not defeat you. I will be with you to protect you and keep you safe. I will rescue you from the power of wicked and violent men. I, the Lord, have spoken."

Jr 15:10-11, 13-21

Jeremiah's Prayer of Confidence

Lord, you are the one who protects me and gives me strength; you help me in times of trouble. Na-

tions will come to you from the ends of the earth
and say, "Our ancestors had nothing but false
gods, nothing but useless idols. Can a man make
his own gods? No, if he did, they would not really be gods."

"So then," says the Lord, "once and for all I
will make the nations know my power and my
might: they will know that I am the Lord."

Jr 16:19-21

Like Names Written in the Dust

The Lord says,
"I will condemn the person
who turns away from me
and puts his trust in man,
in the strength of mortal man.
He is like a bush in the desert,
which grows in the dry wasteland,
on salty ground where nothing else grows.
Nothing good ever happens to him.
But I will bless the person
who puts his trust in me.
He is like a tree growing near a stream
and sending out roots to the water.
It is not afraid when hot weather comes,
because its leaves stay green;
it has no worries when there is no rain;
it keeps on bearing fruit."

Lord, you are Israel's hope;
all who abandon you will be put to shame.
They will disappear like names written in the
dust,
because they have abandoned you,
the Lord,
the spring of fresh water. *Jr 17:5-8, 13*

Jeremiah Asks the Lord for Help

Lord, heal me and I will be completely well; rescue me and I will be perfectly safe. You are the one I praise!

The people say to me, "Where are those threats the Lord made against us? Let him carry them out now!"

But, Lord, I never urged you to bring disaster on them; I did not wish a time of trouble for them. Lord, you know this; you know what I have said. Do not be a terror to me; you are my place of safety when trouble comes. Bring disgrace on those who persecute me, but spare me, Lord. Fill them with terror, but do not terrify me. Bring disaster on them and break them to pieces.

Jr 17:14-18

Jeremiah's Complaint

Lord, you have deceived me,
 and I was deceived.
You are stronger than I am,
 and you have overpowered me.
Everyone makes fun of me;
 they laugh at me all day long.
Whenever I speak, I have to cry out
 and shout, "Violence! Destruction!"
Lord, I am ridiculed and scorned all the time
 because I proclaim your message.
But when I say, "I will forget the Lord
 and no longer speak in his name,"
then your message is like a fire
 burning deep within me.

I try my best to hold it in,
    but can no longer keep it back.
I hear everybody whispering,
    "Terror is everywhere!
    Let's report him to the authorities!"
Even my close friends wait for my downfall.
"Perhaps he can be tricked," they say;
    "then we can catch him and get revenge."
But you, Lord, are on my side, strong and
    mighty,
    and those who persecute me will fail.
They will be disgraced forever,
    because they cannot succeed.
Their disgrace will never be forgotten.
But, Almighty Lord, you test men justly;
    you know what is in their hearts and minds.
So let me see you take revenge on my enemies,
    for I have placed my cause in your hands.
Sing to the Lord!
    Praise the Lord!
He rescues the oppressed from the power of
    evil men.

A Prayer in Despair

Curse the day I was born!
Forget the day my mother gave me birth!
Curse the man who made my father glad
    when he brought him the news.
    "It's a boy! You have a son!"
May he be like those cities
    that the Lord destroyed without mercy.
May he hear cries of pain in the morning
    and the battle alarm at noon,
    because he didn't kill me before I was born.

Then my mother's womb would have been my
grave.
Why was I born?
Was it only to have trouble and sorrow,
to end my life in disgrace?

Jr 20:7-18

God's Judgment on the Nations

"The Lord will roar from heaven
and thunder from the heights of heaven.
He will roar against his people;
he will shout like a man treading grapes.
Everyone on earth will hear him,
and the sound will echo to the ends of the
earth.
The Lord has a case against the nations.
He will bring all people to trial
and put the wicked to death.
The Lord has spoken."

Jr 25:30-31

I Will Keep My Promise
to Bring You Home

"The Lord Almighty, the God of Israel, says to
all those people whom he allowed Nebuchadnezzar to take away as prisoners from Jerusalem to
Babylonia: 'Build houses and settle down. Plant
gardens and eat what you grow in them. Marry
and have children. Then let your children get
married, so that they also may have children.
You must increase in numbers and not decrease.

Work for the good of the cities where I have made you go as prisoners. Pray to me on their behalf, because if they are prosperous, you will be prosperous too.'

"The Lord says, 'When Babylonia's seventy years are over, I will show my concern for you and keep my promise to bring you back home. I alone know the plans I have for you, plans to bring you prosperity and not disaster, plans to bring about the future you hope for. Then you will call to me. You will come and pray to me, and I will answer you. You will seek me, and you will find me because you will seek me with all your heart. Yes, I say, you will find me, and I will restore you to your land. I will gather you from every country and from every place to which I have scattered you, and I will bring you back to the land from which I had sent you away into exile. I, the Lord, have spoken.' "

Jr 29:4-7, 10-14

The Lord Will Save His People

"My people, do not be afraid,
    people of Israel, do not be terrified.
I will rescue you from that faraway land,
    from the land where you are prisoners.
You will come back home and live in peace;
    you will be secure, and no one will make
        you afraid.
I will come to you and save you.
I will destroy all the nations
    where I have scattered you,
    but I will not destroy you.

I will not let you go unpunished;
    but when I punish you, I will be fair.
I, the Lord, have spoken.

The Lord Will Restore His People

"I will restore my people to their land
    and have mercy on every family;
Jerusalem will be rebuilt
    and its palace restored.
The people who live there will sing praise;
    they will shout for joy.
By my blessing they will increase in numbers;
    my blessing will bring them honor.
I will restore the nation's ancient power
    and establish it firmly again;
    I will punish all who oppress them.
Their ruler will come from their own nation,
    their prince from their own people.
He will approach me when I invite him,
    for who would dare come uninvited?
They will be my people,
    and I will be their God.
I, the Lord, have spoken."

Jr 30:10-11, 18-22

Canticle of Jeremiah

Take Up Your Tambourines

The Lord says, "The time is coming when I will be the God of all the tribes of Israel, and they will be my people. In the desert I showed mercy to those people who had escaped death. When the people of Israel longed for rest, I appeared to them from far away. People of Israel, I have always loved you, so I continue to show you my constant love. Once again I will rebuild you. Once again you will take up your tambourines and dance joyfully. Once again you will plant vineyards on the hills of Samaria, and those who plant them will eat what the vineyards produce. Yes, the time is coming when watchmen will call out on the hills of Ephraim, 'Let's go up to Zion, to the Lord our God.' "

Sing With Joy

The Lord says,
"Sing with joy for Israel,
    the greatest of the nations.
Sing your praise,
    'The Lord has saved his people;
    he has rescued all who are left.'
I will bring them from the north
    and gather them from the ends of the earth.
The blind and the lame will come with them,
    pregnant women and those about to give
        birth.
They will come back a great nation.
My people will return weeping,
    praying as I lead them back.
I will guide them to streams of water,
    on a smooth road where they will not
        stumble.
I am like a father to Israel,
    and Ephraim is my oldest son."

Dance and Rejoice

The Lord says,
"Nations, listen to me
    and proclaim my words on the far-off
        shores.
I scattered my people, but I will gather them
    and guard them as a shepherd guards his
        flock.
I have set Israel's people free
    and have saved them from a mighty nation.
They will come and sing for joy on Mount Zion
    and be delighted with my gifts—
    gifts of grain and wine and olive oil,
    gifts of sheep and cattle.
They will be like a well-watered garden;
    they will have everything they need.
Then the girls will dance and be happy,
    and men, young and old, will rejoice.
I will comfort them and turn their mourning
        into joy,
    their sorrow into gladness.
I will fill the priests with the richest food
    and satisfy all the needs of my people.
I, the Lord, have spoken."

Wipe Away Your Tears

The Lord says,
"A sound is heard in Ramah,
    the sound of bitter weeping.
Rachel is crying for her children;
    they are gone,
    and she refuses to be comforted.
Stop your crying
    and wipe away your tears.

All that you have done for your children
    will not go unrewarded;
        they will return from the enemy's land.
There is hope for your future;
    your children will come back home.
I, the Lord, have spoken.

"I hear the people of Israel say in grief,
'Lord, we were like an untamed animal,
    but you taught us to obey.
Bring us back;
    we are ready to return to you,
        the Lord our god.
We turned away from you,
    but soon we wanted to return.
After you had punished us,
    we hung our heads in grief.
We were ashamed and disgraced
    because we sinned when we were young.'

You Are the Child I Love Best

"Israel, you are my dearest son,
    the child I love best.
Whenever I mention your name,
    I think of you with love.
My heart goes out to you;
    I will be merciful.
Set up signs and mark the road;
    find again the way by which you left.
Come back, people of Israel,
    come home to the towns you left.
How long will you hesitate, faithless people?
I have created something new and different,
    as different as a woman protecting a man."
                                    Jr 31:1-22

I Will Be Their God and They Will Be My People

The Lord says,
"The time is coming when I will make a new covenant with the people of Israel and with the people of Judah. It will not be like the old covenant that I made with their ancestors when I took them by the hand and led them out of Egypt. Although I was like a husband to them, they did not keep that covenant. The new covenant that I will make with the people of Israel will be this: I will put my law within them and write it on their hearts. I will be their God, and they will be my people. None of them will have to teach his fellow countryman to know the Lord, because all will know me, from the least to the greatest. I will forgive their sins and I will no longer remember their wrongs. I, the Lord, have spoken."

The Lord provides the sun for light by day,
    the moon and the stars to shine at night.
He stirs up the sea and makes it roar;
    his name is the Lord Almighty.
He promises that as long as the natural order
      lasts,
    so long will Israel be a nation.
If one day the sky could be measured
    and the foundations of the earth explored,
    only then would he reject the people of
      Israel
    because of all they have done.
The Lord has spoken.

Jr 31:31-37

Jeremiah's Prayer

After I had given the deed of purchase to Baruch, I prayed:

"Sovereign Lord, you made the earth and the sky by your great power and might; nothing is too difficult for you. You have shown constant love to thousands, but you also punish people for the sins of their parents. You are a great and powerful God; you are the Lord Almighty. You make wise plans and do mighty things; you see everything that people do, and you reward them according to their actions.

"Long ago you performed miracles and wonders in Egypt, and you have continued to perform them to this day, both in Israel and among all the other nations, so that you are now known everywhere. By means of miracles and wonders that terrified our enemies, you used your power and might to bring your people Israel out of Egypt. You gave them this rich and fertile land, as you had promised their ancestors. But when they came into this land and took possession of it, they did not obey your commands or live according to your teaching; they did nothing that you had ordered them to do. And so you brought all this destruction on them.

"The Babylonians have built siege mounds around the city to capture it, and they are attacking. War, starvation, and disease will make the city fall into their hands. You can see that all you have said has come true. Yet, Sovereign Lord, you are the one who ordered me to buy the field in the presence of witnesses, even though the city is about to be captured by the Babylonians."

Jr 32:16-25

The Lord's Answer

The Lord, the God of Israel, said to me, "Jeremiah, the people are saying that war, starvation, and disease will make this city fall into the hands of the king of Babylonia. Now listen to what else I have to say.

I Am Going to Gather the People

"I am going to gather the people from all the countries where I have scattered them in my anger and fury, and I am going to bring them back to this place and let them live here in safety. Then they will be my people, and I will be their God. I will give them a single purpose in life: to honor me for all time, for their own good and the good of their descendants. I will make an eternal covenant with them. I will never stop doing good things for them, and I will make them fear me with all their heart, so that they will never turn away from me. I will take pleasure in doing good things for them, and I will establish them permanently in this land.

Fields Will Once Again Be Bought

"Just as I have brought this disaster on these people, so I am going to give them all the good things that I have promised. The people are saying that this land will be like a desert where neither people nor animals live, and that it will be given over to the Babylonians. But fields will once again be bought in this land. People will buy them, and the deeds will be signed, sealed, and witnessed. This will take place in the territory of Benjamin, in the villages around Jerusalem, in the towns of Judah, and in southern Judah. I will restore the people to their land. I, the Lord, have spoken.

You Will Hear Again Shouts of Gladness

"In these places you will hear again the shouts of gladness and joy and the happy sounds of wedding feasts. You will hear people sing as they bring thank offerings to my Temple; they will say:

    'Give thanks to the Lord Almighty,
      because he is good
      and his love is eternal.' "

Jr 32:36-44; 33:11

The Lord's Unfailing Love

The Lord's unfailing love and mercy still
    continue,
    Fresh as the morning, as sure as the sunrise.
    The Lord is all I have, and so in him I put
    my hope.

The Lord is good to everyone who trusts in
    him,
    So it is best for us to wait in patience—to
    wait for him to save us—
    And it is best to learn this patience in our
    youth.

When we suffer, we should sit alone in silent
    patience;
  We should bow in submission, for there
    may still be hope.
  Though beaten and insulted, we should
    accept it all.

The Lord is merciful and will not reject us
    forever.
  He may bring us sorrow, but his love for us
    is sure and strong.
  He takes no pleasure in causing us grief or
    pain.

Lm 3:22-33

I Cried Out to the Lord

"I was trapped like a bird by
  enemies who had no cause to hate me.
  They threw me alive into a pit and closed
    the opening with a stone.
  Water began to close over me, and I thought
    death was near.

"From the bottom of the pit, O Lord, I cried
    out to you,
  And when I begged you to listen to my cry,
    you heard.
  You answered me and told me not to be
    afraid.

"You came to my rescue, Lord, and saved my
    life."

Lm 3:52-58

A Prayer for Mercy

Remember, O Lord, what has happened to us.
  Look at us, and see our disgrace.

Our property is in the hands of strangers;
  foreigners are living in our homes.

Our fathers have been killed by the enemy,
  and now our mothers are widows.

We must pay for the water we drink;
  we must buy the wood we need for fuel.

Driven hard like donkeys or camels,
  we are tired, but are allowed no rest.
To get food enough to stay alive,
  we went begging to Egypt and Assyria.

Our ancestors sinned, but now they are gone,
  and we are suffering for their sins.

People No Longer Make Music

We are ruled by men who are no better than
    slaves,
  and no one can save us from their power.

Murderers roam through the countryside;
  we risk our lives when we look for food.

Hunger has made us burn with fever
  until our skin is as hot as an oven.

Our wives have been raped on Mount Zion
    itself;
  in every Judean village our daughters have
    been forced to submit.

Our leaders have been taken and hanged;
   our old men are shown no respect.

Our young men are forced to grind grain
   like slaves;
   boys go staggering under heavy loads of
   wood.

The old people no longer sit at the city gate,
   and the young people no longer make music.

But You, O Lord, Are King Forever

Happiness has gone out of our lives;
   grief has taken the place of our dances.

Nothing is left of all we were proud of.
   We sinned, and now we are doomed.

We are sick at our very hearts
   and can hardly see through our tears,

because Mount Zion lies lonely and deserted,
   and wild jackals prowl through its ruins.

But you, O Lord, are king forever
   and will rule to the end of time.

Why have you abandoned us so long?
   Will you ever remember us again?

Bring us back to you, Lord! Bring us back!
   Restore our ancient glory.

Or have you rejected us forever?

Lm 5:1-22

The Prayer for Deliverance

"You, O Lord, are the God of Israel who brought

your people out of Egypt with great power and with signs, miracles, and wonders. You showed your mighty strength and gained a glorious reputation, which is still recognized today. O Lord, our God, we have sinned: we have been unfaithful: we have disobeyed all your commands. But do not be angry with us any longer. Here among the nations where you have scattered us, only a few of us are left. Listen to our prayers of petition, Lord, and rescue us for the sake of your own honor. Let those who have taken us into exile be pleased with us. Then the whole world will know that you are our Lord our God and that you have chosen the nation of Israel to be your own people.

"O Lord, look down from heaven and see our misery. Listen to our prayer. Open your eyes and look upon us. Those in the world of the dead with no breath left in their bodies cannot offer praises to you or proclaim how just you are. Only the living, O Lord, can offer you praise and acknowledge your justice, even though they may be suffering greatly, bent and weak, hungry and with failing eyesight.

We Pray to You for Mercy

"O Lord our God, we pray to you for mercy, but not because of any good things done by our ancestors and our kings. You turned your anger and wrath against us, just as you had threatened to do when your servants the prophets spoke your word to us and said, 'Bend your backs and serve the king of Babylonia, and you can remain in the land that I gave to your ancestors. But if you refuse to obey my command to serve him, I will bring to an end every sound of joy and celebration in the towns of Judah and in Jerusalem. Even the happy sounds of wedding feasts will no longer be heard. The whole land will be desolate and uninhabited.'

"But we did not obey your command to serve the king of Babylonia, so you carried out the threat that you had made when you spoke through your servants the prophets, when you said that the bones of our kings and of our ancestors would be taken from their tombs and scattered. And now here they lie exposed to the heat of the day and to the frost of the night. They died in torment from famine, war, and disease. And because of the sin of the people of Israel and Judah, you have reduced your own Temple to ruins, even as it is today.

In Exile You Will Remember Me

"But, Lord, you have been patient with us and have shown us great mercy, as you promised through your servant Moses on the day you commanded him to write your Law in the presence of the Israelites. 'If you do not obey me,' you said, 'you will be reduced to a handful among nations where I will scatter you. I know that you will not obey me, because you are a stubborn people. But when you are taken into exile in another land, you will come to your senses. Then you will realize that I am the Lord your God and I will give you a desire to know and a mind with which to understand. There in the land of exile you will praise me and remember me. You will stop being so stubborn and wicked, for you will remember what happened to your ancestors when they sinned against the Lord. Then I will bring you back to the land that I solemnly promised to give to your ancestors, to Abraham, Isaac, and Jacob, and it will be yours again. I will increase your population, and you will never again be reduced to a small number. I will make an everlasting covenant with you; I will be your God and you will be my people. I will never again remove you, the people of Israel, from the land that I gave you.'

Hear Us, O Lord, and Have Mercy

"O Lord Almighty, God of Israel, from the depth of our troubled, weary souls we cry out to you. Hear us, O Lord, and have mercy on us, because we have sinned against you. You reign as king forever. O Lord Almighty, God of Israel, hear our prayer. We are no better off than dead men. Our ancestors sinned against you, the Lord their God. They refused to obey you, and we are suffering the consequences of their sin. Forget the sinful things that our ancestors did in the past; at a time like this, think only of your power and reputation, for you are the Lord our God, and we will praise you. You have made us fear you, so that we might pray to you. Here in exile we will praise you because we have turned away from the sins of our ancestors. You have scattered us among the nations, and you have made them despise and curse us. You are punishing us for the sins of our ancestors when they rebelled against you, the Lord our God."   *Ba 2:11-3:8*

How Great Is the Universe!

O Israel, how great is the universe in which God dwells! How vast is all that he possesses! There is no end to it; there is no way to measure how wide or how high it is.

Ba 3:24-25

*   *   *

They Shall Be My People

"So tell them what I, the Sovereign Lord, am saying. I will gather them out of the countries where I scattered them, and will give the land of Israel back to them. When they return, they are to get rid of all the filthy, disgusting idols they find. I will give them a new heart and a new mind. I will take away their stubborn heart of stone and will give them an obedient heart. Then they will keep my laws and faithfully obey all my commands. They will be my people, and I will be their God."

Ez 11:17-20

God's Promise of Hope

This is what the Sovereign Lord says:

"I will take the top of a tall cedar
    and break off a tender sprout;
I will plant it on a high mountain,
    on Israel's highest mountain.
It will grow branches and bear seed
    and become a magnificent cedar.

Birds of every kind will live there
and find shelter in its shade.
All the trees in the land will know
that I am the Lord.
I cut down the tall trees
and make low trees grow tall.
I wither up the green trees
and make the dry trees become green.

I, the Lord, have spoken. I will do what I have
said I will do."

Ez 17:22-24

The Good Shepherd

"I, the Sovereign Lord, tell you that I myself will
look for my sheep and take care of them in the
same way as a shepherd takes care of his sheep
that were scattered and are brought together
again. I will bring them back from all the places
where they were scattered on that dark,
disastrous day. I will take them out of foreign
countries, gather them together, and bring them
back to their own land.

"I will lead them back to the mountains and
the streams of Israel and will feed them in pleasant pastures. I will let them graze in safety in the
mountain meadows and the valleys and in all the
green pastures of the land of Israel. I myself will
be the shepherd of my sheep, and I will find
them a place to rest. I, the Sovereign Lord, have
spoken.

"I will look for those that are lost, bring back
those that wander off, bandage those that are

hurt, and heal those that are sick. . . . I will give
them a king like my servant David to be their one
shepherd, and he will take care of them. I, the
Lord, will be their God, and a king, like my servant David will be their ruler. I have spoken. I
will make a covenant with them that guarantees
their security. . . .

I Will Bless Them

"I will bless them and let them live around my
sacred hill. There I will bless them with showers
of rain when they need it. The trees will bear
fruit, the fields will produce crops, and everyone
will live in safety on his own land. When I break
my people's chains and set them free from those
who made them slaves, then they will know that
I am the Lord. The heathen nations will not
plunder them any more, and the wild animals
will not kill and eat them. They will live in safety, and no one will terrify them. I will give them
fertile fields and put an end to hunger in the
land. The other nations will not sneer at them
any more. Everyone will know that I protect
Israel and that they are my people. I, the
Sovereign Lord, have spoken.

"You, my sheep, the flock that I feed, are my
people, and I am your God," says the Sovereign
Lord.

Ez 34:11-16, 23-31

I Will Bring You Back, My People

"On the mountains of Israel the trees will again
grow leaves and bear fruit for you, my people

Israel. You are going to come home soon. I am on your side, and I will make sure that your land is plowed again and crops are planted on it. I will make your population grow. You will live in the cities and rebuild everything that was left in ruins. I will make people and cattle increase in number. There will be more of you than ever before, and you will have many children. I will let you live there as you used to live, and I will make you more prosperous than ever. Then you will know that I am the Lord. I will bring you, my people Israel, back to live again in the land. It will be your own land, and it will never again let your children starve."

Ez 36:8-12

For the Sake of My Name I Will Wash You Clean

"What I am going to do is not for the sake of you Israelites, but for the sake of my holy name, which you have disgraced in every country where you have gone. . . . I will use you to show the nations that I am holy. I will take you from every nation and country and bring you back to your own land. I will sprinkle clean water on you and make you clean from all your idols and everything else that has defiled you. I will give you a new heart and a new mind, I will take away your stubborn heart of stone and give you an obedient heart. I will put my spirit in you and will see to it that you follow my laws and keep all my commands I have given you. Then you will live in the land I gave your ancestors. You will be my people, and I will be your God.

"When I make you clean from all your sins, I will let you live in your cities again and let you rebuild the ruins. Everyone who used to walk by your fields saw how overgrown and wild they were, but I will let you farm them again. Everyone will talk about how this land, which was once a wilderness, has become a Garden of Eden, and how the cities which were torn down, looted, and left in ruins, are now inhabited and fortified. Then the neighboring nations that have survived will know that I, the Lord, rebuild ruined cities and replant waste fields. I, the Lord, have promised that I would do this — and I will."

Ez 36:22, 24-28, 33-36

Then They Will Know That I Am the Lord

The Valley of Dry Bones

I felt the powerful presence of the Lord, and his spirit took me and set me down in a valley where the ground was covered with bones. He led me all around the valley, and I could see that there were very many bones and that they were very dry. He said to me, "Mortal man, can these bones come back to life?"

I replied, "Sovereign Lord, only you can answer that!"

He said, "Prophesy to the bones. Tell these dry bones to listen to the word of the Lord. Tell them that I, the Sovereign Lord, am saying to them: I am going to put breath into you and bring you back to life. I will give you sinews and muscles, and cover you with skin. I will put breath into you and bring you back to life. Then you will know that I am the Lord."

So I prophesied as I had been told. While I was speaking, I heard a rattling noise, and the bones began to join together. While I watched, the bones were covered with sinews and muscles, and then with skin. But there was no breath in the bodies.

God said to me, "Mortal man, prophesy to the wind. Tell the wind that the Sovereign Lord commands it to come from every direction, to breathe into these dead bodies, and to bring them back to life."

So I prophesied as I had been told. Breath entered the bodies, and they came to life and stood up. There were enough of them to form an army.

God said to me, "Mortal man, the people of Israel are like these bones. They say that they are dried up without any hope and with no future. So prophesy to my people Israel and tell them that I, the Lord God, am going to open their graves. I am going to take them out and bring them back to the land of Israel. When I open the graves where my people are buried and bring them out they will know that I am the Lord. I will put my breath in them, bring them back to life, and let them live in their own land. Then they will know that I am the Lord. I have promised that I would do this—and I will. I, the Lord, have spoken."   *Ez 37:1-14*

*   *   *

Daniel Praises God

Then that same night the mystery was revealed to Daniel in a vision, and he praised the God of heaven:

"God is wise and powerful!
Praise him forever and ever.
He controls the times and the seasons;
he makes and unmakes kings;
it is he who gives wisdom and
understanding.
He reveals things that are deep and secret;
he knows what is hidden in darkness,
and he himself is surrounded by light.
I praise you and honor you, God of my
ancestors.
You have given me wisdom and strength;
you have answered my prayer
and shown us what to tell the king."

Dn 2:19-23

The Prayer of Azariah

"O Lord, the God of our ancestors, we praise and adore you; may your name be honored forever. You have treated us as we deserve. In everything you have done to us you are always honest, and when you bring us to judgment, you are always fair. You did what was right when you brought disaster upon Jerusalem, the holy city of our ancestors. We deserved that judgment because of our sins. We disobeyed you, we turned our backs on you, and we are guilty of every sin. We did not do the things that you commanded us to do.

If we had obeyed your laws, we would have prospered, but now we deserve the judgment and punishment that you have brought upon us. You have handed us over. . . . And now all of us who worship you are humiliated; we are too ashamed to open our mouths.

For the Sake of Your Own Honor

"Yet for the sake of your own honor, do not break your covenant with us and abandon us forever. Do not withhold your mercy from us. Keep your promises to Abraham, whom you loved, to Isaac, your servant, and to Jacob, the father of your holy people Israel. You promised to give them as many descendants as the stars in the sky or as the grains of sand along the seashore. But now, Lord, we are fewer in number than any other nation; wherever we are, we live in disgrace because of our sins. We are left without a king, without any prophets or leaders. There is no longer a temple where we can go to offer you burnt offerings, sacrifices, gifts, or incense, no place where we can make offerings to you and find your mercy.

With Repentant Hearts

"But we come to you with repentant hearts and humble spirits, begging you to accept us just as if we had come with burnt offerings of rams and bulls and thousands of fat lambs. Accept our repentance as our sacrifice to you today, so that we may obey you with all our hearts. No one who trusts you will ever be disappointed. Now with all our hearts we promise to obey you, worship you, and come to you in prayer. Treat us with kindness and mercy, and let us never be put to shame. O Lord, rescue us with one of your miracles; bring honor to your name. Bring disgrace and shame on all who harm us. Take away their might and power and crush their strength. Let them know that you alone are Lord and God and that you rule in majesty over the whole world."

Prayer of Azariah 3-22
(Dn 3:26-45 in JB,NAB)

The Song of the Three Young Men

God of Our Fathers

There in the furnace the three young men again started singing together in praise of God:

"We Praise you, O Lord, the God of our
　　ancestors.
May your glorious, holy name be held in honor
　　and reverence forever.
May hymns be sung to your glory forever
　　and may your holy presence be praised in
　　　that temple,
　　where you sit on your heavenly throne
　　　above the winged creatures
　　and look down to the world of the dead.
　　May you be praised and honored forever.
May you be praised as you sit on your royal
　　throne.
　　May hymns be sung to your glory forever.

May you be praised in the dome of the
    heavens.
May hymns be sung to your glory forever.

Lord of Creation

"Praise the Lord, all creation;
    sing his praise and honor him forever.
Praise the Lord, skies above; . . .
Praise the Lord, all angels of the Lord; . . .
Praise the Lord, all waters above the sky; . . .
Praise the Lord, all heavenly powers; . . .
Praise the Lord, sun and moon; . . .
Praise the Lord, stars of heaven; . . .
Praise the Lord, rain and dew; . . .
Praise the Lord, all winds; . . .
Praise the Lord, fire and heat; . . .
Praise the Lord, bitter cold and scorching
    heat; . . .
Praise the Lord, dews and snows; . . .
Praise the Lord, nights and days; . . .
Praise the Lord, daylight and darkness; . . .
Praise the Lord, ice and cold; . . .
Praise the Lord, frost and snow; . . .
Praise the Lord, lightning and storm
    clouds; . . .

Lord of the Earth

"Let the earth praise the Lord;
    sing his praise and honor him forever.
Praise the Lord, mountains and hills; . . .
Praise the Lord, everything that grows; . . .
Praise the Lord, lakes and rivers; . . .
Praise the Lord, springs of water; . . .

Praise the Lord, whales and sea creatures; . . .
Praise the Lord, all birds; . . .
Praise the Lord, all cattle and wild
    animals; . . .

Lord of All People

"Praise the Lord, all people on earth;
  sing his praise and honor him forever.
Praise the Lord, people of Israel; . . .
Praise the Lord, priests of the Lord; . . .
Praise the Lord, servants of the Lord; . . .
Praise the Lord, all faithful people; . . .
Praise the Lord, all who are humble and holy.

The Lord Has Rescued Us

"Praise the Lord, Hananiah, Azariah, and
    Mishael;
  sing his praise and honor him forever.
He rescued us from the world of the dead
  and saved us from the power of death.
He brought us out of the burning furnace
  and saved us from the fire.
Give thanks to the Lord, for he is good
  and his mercy lasts forever.
Praise the Lord, all who worship him;
  sing praise to the God of gods and give him
    thanks,
  for his mercy lasts forever."

Song of the Three Young Men 28-68
(Dn 3:52-90 in JB,NAB)

The Supreme God

King Nebuchadnezzar sent the following message to the people of all nations, races, and languages in the world: "Greetings! Listen to my account of the wonders and miracles which the Supreme God has shown me.

"How great are the wonders God shows us!
How powerful are the miracles he performs!
God will be king forever; he will rule for all
    time."

Dn 4:1-3

Nebuchadnezzar Praises God

"When the seven years had passed," said the king, "I looked up at the sky, and my sanity returned. I praised the Supreme God and gave honor and glory to the one who lives forever:

"He will rule forever,
    and his kingdom will last for all time.
He looks on the people of the earth as nothing;
    angels in heaven and people on earth
    are under his control.
No one can oppose his will
    or question what he does.

"I, Nebuchadnezzar, praise, honor, and glorify the King of Heaven. Everything he does is right and just, and he can humble anyone who acts proudly." *Dn 4:34-35, 37*

He Is the Living God

King Darius wrote to the people of all nations, races and languages on earth:

"Greetings! I command that throughout my empire everyone should fear and respect Daniel's God.

"He is a living God.
    and he will rule forever.
His kingdom will never be destroyed,
    and his power will never come to an end.
He saves and rescues;
    he performs wonders and miracles
    in heaven and on earth.
He saved Daniel from being killed by the
    lions."

Dn 6:25-28

The Ancient of Days and
One Like the Son of Man

While I was looking, thrones were put in
        place.
One who had been living forever sat down on
        one of the thrones.
His clothes were white as snow,
    and his hair was like pure wool.
His throne, mounted on fiery wheels,
    was blazing with fire,
    and a stream of fire was pouring out of it.
There were many thousands of people there
        to serve him,
    and millions of people stood before him.
The court began its session,
    and the books were opened.

And One Like the Son of Man

During this vision in the night,
I saw what looked like a human being.
    He was approaching me, surrounded by
        clouds,
and he went to the one who had been living
        forever
    and was presented to him.
He was given authority, honor, and royal
        power,
    so that the people of all nations, races, and
        languages would serve him.
His authority would last forever,
    and his kingdom would never end.

Dn 7:9-10, 13-14

Daniel Prays for His People

I prayed to the Lord my God and confessed the sins of my people.

I said, "Lord God, you are great, and we honor you. You are faithful to your covenant and show constant love to those who love you and do what you command.

"We have sinned, we have been evil, we have done wrong. We have rejected what you commanded us to do and have turned away from what you showed us was right. We have not listened to your servants the prophets, who spoke in your name to our kings, our rulers, our ancestors, and our whole nation. You, Lord, always do what is right, but we have always brought disgrace on ourselves. This is true of all of us who live in Judea and in Jerusalem and of all the Israelites whom you scattered in countries near and far because they were unfaithful to you. Our kings, our rulers, and our ancestors have acted shamefully and sinned against you, Lord. You are merciful and forgiving, although we have rebelled against you. We did not listen to you, O Lord our God, when you told us to live according to the laws which you gave us through your servants the prophets. All Israel broke your laws and refused to listen to what you said. We sinned against you, and so you brought on us the curses that are written in the Law of Moses, your servant. You did what you said you would do to us and our rulers. You punished Jerusalem more severely than any other city on earth, giving us all the punishment described in the Law of Moses. But even now, O Lord our God, we have not tried to please you by turning from our sins or by following your truth. You, O Lord our God, were prepared to punish us, and you did, because you always do what is right, and we did not listen to you.

Lord, Forgive Us

"O Lord our God, you showed your power by bringing your people out of Egypt, and your power is still remembered. We have sinned; we have done wrong. You have defended us in the past, so do not be angry with Jerusalem any longer. It is your city, your sacred hill. All the people in the neighboring countries look down on Jerusalem and on your people because of our sins and the evil our ancestors did. O God, hear my prayer and pleading. Restore your Temple, which has been destroyed; restore it so that everyone will know that you are God. Listen to us, O God; look at us and see the trouble we are in and the suffering of the city that bears your name. We are praying to you because you are merciful, not because we have done right. Lord, hear us. Lord, forgive us. Lord, listen to us, and act! In order that everyone will know that you are God, do not delay! This city and these people are yours."

Dn 9:4-19

Minor
Prophets

The Lord's Love for His People

So I am going to take her into the desert again:
    There I will win her back with words of
      love.
I will give back to her the vineyards she had
    and make Trouble Valley a door of hope.
She will respond to me there as she did when
    she was young,
    when she came back from Egypt.
Then once again she will call me her
    husband. . . .

He Will Answer Their Prayers

Israel, I will make you my wife;
    I will be true and faithful;
    I will show you constant love and mercy
    and make you mine forever.
I will keep my promise and make you mine
    and you will acknowledge me as Lord.
At that time I will answer the prayers of my
    people Israel.
    I will make rain fall on the earth,
    and the earth will produce grain and grapes
    and olives.
I will establish my people in the land and make
    them prosper.
I will show love to those who were called
    "Unloved,"
    and to those who were called "Not-My-
    People."
I will say, "You are my people,"
    and they will answer, "You are our God."

Ho 2:14-16, 19-23

What I Want Is Your Constant Love

The people say,
"Let's return to the Lord!
 He has hurt us, but he will be sure to heal
  us;
He has wounded us, but he will bandage our
  wounds,
 won't he?
In two or three days he will revive us,
 and we will live in his presence.
Let us try to know the Lord.
He will come to us as surely as the day dawns,
 as surely as the spring rains fall upon the
  earth."
But the Lord says,
"Israel and Judah, what am I going to do
  with you?
Your love for me disappears as quickly as the
  morning mist;
 it is like dew that vanishes early in the day.
That is why I have sent my prophets to you
 with my message of judgment and
  destruction.
What I want from you is plain and clear:
I want your constant love, not your animal
  sacrifices.
I would rather have my people know me
 than have them burn offerings to me."

Ho 6:1-6

God's Love for His People Endures

The Lord says,
"When Israel was a child, I loved him
 and called him out of Egypt as my son.

But the more I called to him,
   the more he turned away from me.
My people sacrificed to Baal;
   they burned incense to idols.
Yet I was the one who taught Israel to walk.
I took my people up in my arms,
   but they did not acknowledge that I took
      care of them.
I drew them to me with affection and love.
   I picked them up and held them to my
      cheek;
   I bent down and fed them.

"How can I give you up, Israel?
   How can I abandon you? . . .
   My love for you is too strong.
I will not punish you in my anger;
   I will not destroy Israel again.
For I am God, and not man.
   I, the Holy One, am with you.
I will not come to you in anger."

Hosea's Prayer for Israel

Ho 11:1-4, 8-9

Return to the Lord your God, people of Israel.
   Your sin has made you stumble and fall.
Return to the Lord, and let this prayer be our
      offering to him:
"Forgive all our sins and accept our prayer:
   and we will praise you as we have promised.
Assyria can never save us, and war horses
      cannot protect us.
   We will never again say to our idols that
      they are our God.
O Lord, you show mercy to those who have no
      one else to turn to."

The Lord Is Faithful

The Lord says,
"I will bring my people back to me.
I will love them with all my heart;
    no longer am I angry with them.
I will be to the people of Israel
    like rain in a dry land.
They will blossom like flowers;
    they will be firmly rooted like the trees of
        Lebanon.
They will be alive with new growth,
    and beautiful like olive trees.
They will be fragrant
    like the cedars of Lebanon.
Once again they will live under my protection.
They will grow crops of grain
    and be fruitful like a vineyard.
    They will be famous as the wine of
        Lebanon.
The people of Israel will have nothing more to
    do with idols;
    I will answer their prayers and take care of
        them.
Like an evergreen tree I will shelter them;
    I am the source of all their blessings."

Ho 14:1-8

A Summons to Prayer

Pay attention, you older people;
    everyone in Judah, listen.
Has anything like this ever happened
    in your time or the time of your fathers?

Tell your children about it;
    they will tell their children
    who in turn will tell the next generation.

Swarm after swarm of locusts settled on the
        crops;
    what one swarm left, the next swarm
        devoured.
Wake up and weep, you drunkards;
    cry, you wine-drinkers;
    the grapes for making new wine have been
        destroyed.

An army of locusts . . . has destroyed our
        grapevines
    and chewed up our fig trees.
They have stripped off the bark,
    till the branches are white.

Cry, you people, like a girl who mourns the
        death
    of the man she was going to marry.

The Drought

There is no grain or wine to offer in the
        Temple;
    the priests mourn because they have no
        offerings for the Lord.
The fields are bare;
    the ground mourns because the grain is
        destroyed,
    the grapes are dried up, and the olive trees
        are withered.

Grieve, you farmers;
cry, you that take care of the vineyards,
   because the wheat, the barley,
    yes all the crops are destroyed.
The grapevines and the fig trees have
      withered;
   all the fruit trees have wilted and died.

The joy of the people is gone,
Put on sackcloth and weep,
   you priests who serve at the altar!
Go into the Temple and mourn all night!
There is no grain or wine to offer your God.
Give orders for a fast;
   call an assembly!
Gather the leaders
   and all the people of Judah
   into the Temple of the Lord your God
   and cry out to him!
The day of the Lord is near,
   the day when the Almighty brings
    destruction.

Jl 1:2-15

A Call to Repentance

"But even now," says the Lord,
   "repent sincerely and return to me
   with fasting and weeping and mourning.
Let your broken heart show your sorrow;
   tearing your clothes is not enough."

Come back to the Lord your God.
   He is kind and full of mercy;
   he is patient and keeps his promise;
   he is always ready to forgive and not punish.

Perhaps the Lord your God will change his
     mind
   and bless you with abundant crops.
Then you can offer him grain and wine.

Blow the trumpet on Mount Zion;
   give orders for a fast and call an assembly!
Gather the people together;
   prepare them for a sacred meeting;
   bring the old people;
   gather the children and the babies too.
   Even the newly married couples must leave
     their homes and come.
The priests, serving the Lord
   between the altar and the entrance to the
     Temple,
must weep and pray:
  "Have pity on your people, Lord.
   Do not let other nations despise us and
     mock us
   by saying, 'Where is your God?' "

Jl 2:12-17

God Answers the People's Prayer

Then the Lord showed concern for his land;
   he had mercy on his people.
He answered them:
  "Now I am going to give you
     grain and wine
   and olive oil,
   and you will be satisfied.
   Other nations will no longer despise you.

"Fields, don't be afraid, but be joyful and glad
    because of all the Lord has done for you.
Animals, don't be afraid.
    The pastures are green: the trees bear their
        fruit,
    and there are plenty of figs and grapes.

"Be glad, people of Zion,
    rejoice at what the Lord your God has
        done for you. . . .
The threshing places will be full of grain;
    the pits besides the presses will overflow
        with wine and oil. . . .

"You will praise the Lord your God,
    who has done wonderful things for you.
    My people will never be despised again.
Then, Israel, you will know that I am among
        you
and that I, the Lord, am your God
and there is no other. . . .

My Spirit on Everyone

    "Afterward I will pour out my spirit on
        everyone:
    your sons and daughters will proclaim my
        message;
    your old men will have dreams,
    and your young men will see visions.
At that time I will pour out my spirit
    even on servants, both men and women."

Jl 2:18-19, 21-24, 26-29

God Is the One

God is the one who made the mountains
   and created the winds.
He makes his thoughts known to man;
   he changes the day into night.
He walks on the heights of the earth.
This is his name: the Lord God Almighty!

Am 4:13

His Name Is the Lord

The Lord made the stars,
   the Pleiades and Orion.
He turns darkness into daylight
   and day into night.
He calls for the waters of the sea
   and pours them out on the earth.
His name is the Lord.
He brings destruction on the mighty and their
   strongholds.

Am 5:8-9

The Sovereign Lord Almighty

The Sovereign Lord Almighty touches the
      earth,
   and it quakes;
   all who live there mourn.
The whole world rises and falls like the
      Nile River.
The Lord builds his home in the heavens,
   and over the earth he puts the dome of the
      sky.
He calls for the waters of the sea
   and pours them on the earth.
His name is the Lord!

Am 9:5-6

Words of Hope from the Lord

The Lord says,
"A day is coming when I will restore the
        kingdom of David,
    which is like a house fallen into ruins.
I will repair its walls and restore it.
I will rebuild it and make it as it was long ago.

"The day is coming," says the Lord,
    "when grain will grow faster than it can be
        harvested,
    and grapes will grow faster than the wine
        can be made.
The mountains will drip with sweet wine,
    and the hills will flow with it.
I will bring my people back to their land.
    They will rebuild their ruined cities and
        live there;
    they will plant vineyards and drink the
        wine;
    they will plant gardens and eat what they
        grow.
I will plant my people on the land I gave them,
    and they will not be pulled up again."

Am 9:11-15

The Lord Himself Will Be King

The Lord says to Edom,
"Your capital is a fortress of solid rock;
    your home is high in the mountains,
and so you say to yourself,
    'Who can ever pull me down?'

Even though you make your home
    as high as an eagle's nest,
      so that it seems to be among the stars,
yet I will pull you down. . . .

"The victorious men of Jerusalem
    will attack Edom and rule over it.
And the Lord himself will be king."
Ob 2-4, 21

Jonah's Canticle of Thanksgiving

"In my distress, O Lord, I called to you,
    and you answered me.
From deep in the world of the dead
    I cried for help and you heard me.
You threw me down into the depths,
    to the very bottom of the sea,
      where the waters were all around me,
      and all your mighty waves rolled over me.
I thought I had been banished from your
      presence
    and would never see your holy Temple
      again.
The water came over me and choked me;
    the sea covered me completely,
      and seaweed wrapped around my head.
I went down to the very roots of the
      mountains,
    into the land whose gates are shut forever.
But you, O Lord my God,
    brought me back from the depths alive.
When I felt my life slipping away,
    then, O Lord, I prayed to you,
      and in your holy Temple you heard me.

Those who worship worthless idols
 have abandoned their loyalty to you.
But I will sing praises to you;
 I will offer you a sacrifice
 and do what I have promised.
Salvation comes from the Lord!"

Jon 2:2-9

A Song of Universal Peace

In days to come,
 the mountain where the Temple stands
 will be the highest one of all,
 towering above all the hills.
Many nations will come streaming to it,
 and their people will say,
"Let us go up the hills of the Lord,
 to the Temple of Israel's God.
For he will teach us what he wants us to do;
 we will walk in the paths he has chosen.
For the Lord's teaching comes from Jerusalem;
 from Zion he speaks to his people."

He will settle disputes among the nations,
 among the great powers near and far.
They will hammer the swords into plows
 and their spears into pruning knives.
Nations will never again go to war,
 never prepare for battle again.
Everyone will live in peace
 among his vineyards and fig trees,
 and no one will make him afraid.
The Lord Almighty has promised this.

Mic 4:1-4

What the Lord Requires

What shall I bring to the Lord, the God of heaven, when I come to worship him? Will the Lord be pleased if I bring him thousands of sheep or endless streams of olive oil? Shall I offer him my first-born child to pay for my sins? No, the Lord has told us what is good.

What he requires of us is this:
To do what is just,
to show constant love,
and to live in humble fellowship with our God.

Mic 6:6-8

A Prayer to Yahweh

Be a shepherd to your people. Lord, the people you have chosen. Although they live apart in the wilderness, there is fertile land around them. Let them go and feed in the rich pastures of Bashan and Gilead, as they did long ago.

Work miracles for us, Lord, as you did in the days when you brought us out of Egypt. The nations will see this and be frustrated in spite of all their strength. In dismay they will close their mouths and cover their ears. They will crawl in the dust like snakes; they will come from their fortresses, trembling and afraid. They will turn in fear to the Lord our God.

A Prayer for Forgiveness

There is no other god like you, O Lord: you forgive the sins of your people who have survived. You do not stay angry forever, but you take pleasure in showing us your constant love. You will be merciful to us once again. You will trample our sins underfoot and send them to the bottom of the sea! You will show your faithfulness and constant love to your people, the descendants of Abraham and of Jacob as you promised our ancestors long ago.

Mic 7:14-20

Canticle of Nahum

The Lord Tolerates No Rivals

The Lord God tolerates no rivals;
 He punishes those who oppose him.
 In his anger he pays them back.
The Lord does not easily become angry,
 but he is powerful and never lets the guilty
  go unpunished.

Where the Lord walks, storms arise;
 the clouds are the dust raised by his feet!
He commands the sea, and it dries up!
 He makes the rivers go dry.
The fields of Bashan wither, Mount Carmel
  turns brown,
 and the flowers of Lebanon fade.
Mountains quake in the presence of the Lord;
 hills melt before him.
The earth shakes when the Lord appears;
 the world and all its people tremble.
When he is angry, who can survive?
 Who can survive his terrible fury?
He pours out his flaming anger;
 rocks crumble to dust before him.

The Lord is good;
 he protects his people in times of trouble;
 he takes care of those who turn to him.
Like a great rushing flood he completely
  destroys his enemies;
 he sends to their death those who oppose
  him.
What are you plotting against the Lord?
 He will destroy you.
 No one opposes him more than once.
Like tangled thorns and dry straw
 you will be burned up!

Nh 1:2-10

Canticle of Habakkuk

O Lord, I have heard of what you have done,
 and I am filled with awe.
Now do again in our times
 the great deeds you used to do.
Be merciful, even when you are angry.
God is coming again from Edom;
 the holy God is coming from the hills of
  Paran.
His splendor covers the heavens,
 and the earth is full of his praise.
He comes with the brightness of lightning;
 light flashes from his hand,
 there where his power is hidden.
When he stops, the earth shakes;
 at his glance the nations tremble.
The eternal mountains are shattered;
 the everlasting hills sink down,
 the hills where he walked in ancient times.

The Lord Is a Warrior

I saw the people of Cushan afraid
  and the people of Midian tremble.
Was it the rivers that made you angry, Lord?
  Was it the sea that made you furious?
You rode upon the clouds;
  the storm cloud was your chariot,
  as you brought victory to your people.
You got ready to use your bow,
  ready to shoot your arrows. . . .
At the flash of your speeding arrows
  and the gleam of your shining spear,
  the sun and the moon stood still.
You marched across the earth in anger,
  in fury you trampled the nations.
You went out to save your people,
  to save your chosen king.
You struck down the leader of the wicked
  and completely destroyed his followers. . . .
You trampled the sea with your horses,
  and the mighty waters foamed. . . .

The Lord God Is My Savior

I will quietly wait for the time to
    come
  when God will punish those who attack us.
Even though the fig trees have no fruit,
  and no grapes grow on the vines,
even though the olive crop fails
  and the fields produces no grain,
even though the sheep all die
  and the cattle stalls are empty,

I will still be joyful and glad,
    because the Lord God is my savior.
The Sovereign Lord gives me strength.
    He makes me sure-footed as a deer
    and keeps me safe on the mountains.

Hb 3:2-4, 6-9, 11-13, 15-19

The People of All Nations Will Pray to Me

"Then I will change the people of the nations, and they will pray to me alone and not to other gods. They will all obey me. Even from distant Sudan my scattered people will bring offerings to me. At that time you, my people, will no longer need to be ashamed that you rebelled against me. I will remove everyone who is proud and arrogant, and you will never again rebel against me on my sacred hill. I will leave there a humble and lowly people, who will come to me for help. The people of Israel who survive will do no wrong to anyone, tell no lies, nor try to deceive. They will be prosperous and secure, afraid of no one."

Zep 3:9-13

A Song of Joy

Sing and shout for joy, people of Israel!
    Rejoice with all your heart, Jerusalem!
The Lord has stopped your punishment;
    he has removed all your enemies.
The Lord, the king of Israel, is with
        you;
    there is no reason now to be afraid.

The time is coming when they will say to
    Jerusalem,
  "Do not be afraid, city of Zion!
  Do not let your hand hang limp!
The Lord your God is with you;
  his power gives you victory.
The Lord will take delight in you,
  and his love will give you new life.
He will sing and be joyful over you,
  as joyful as people at a festival."

The Lord says,
"I have ended the threat of doom
  and taken away your disgrace.
The time is coming!
I will punish your oppressors;
  I will rescue the lame
  and bring the exiles home.
I will turn their shame into honor,
  and all the world will praise them.
The time is coming!
I will bring your scattered people home;
  I will make you famous throughout
    the world
and make you prosperous once again."

Zep 3:14-20

The Lord's Command

The Lord Almighty said to Haggai, "These people say that this is not the right time to rebuild
the Temple." The Lord then gave this message to
the people through the prophet Haggai. "My
people, why should you be living in well-built

houses while my Temple lies in ruins? Don't you see what is happening to you? You have planted much grain, but have harvested very little. You have food to eat, but not enough to make you full. You have wine to drink, but not enough to get your fill! You have clothing, but not enough to keep you warm. And the working man cannot earn enough to live on. Can't you see why this has happened? Now go up into the hills, get lumber, and rebuild the Temple; then I will be pleased and will be worshiped as I should be."

Hg 1:2-8

The Lord's Blessing

The Lord says, "Can't you see what has happened to you? Before you started to rebuild the Temple, you would go to a pile of grain expecting to find twenty bushels, but there would be only ten. You would go to draw fifty gallons of wine from a vat, but find only twenty. I sent scorching winds and hail to ruin everything you tried to grow, but still you did not repent. Today is the twenty-fourth day of the ninth month, the day that the foundation of the Temple has been completed. See what is going to happen from now on. Although there is no grain left, and the grapevines, fig trees, pomegranates, and olive trees have not yet produced, yet from now on I will bless you."

Hg 2:15-19

A Song of Rejoicing about the Future King

Rejoice, rejoice, people of Zion!
   Shout for joy, you people of Jerusalem!
   Look, your king is coming to you!
He comes triumphant and victorious,
   but humble and riding on a donkey—
   on a colt, the foal of a donkey.
The Lord says,
"I will remove the war chariots from Israel
   and take the horses from Jerusalem;
   the bows used in battle will be destroyed.
Your king will make peace among the nations;
   he will rule from sea to sea,
   from the Euphrates River to the ends of the
      earth."

The Lord will save his people,
   as a shepherd saves his flock from danger.
They will shine in his land
   like the jewels of a crown.
How good and beautiful the land will be!
   The young people will grow strong on its
      grain and wine.   *Zec 9:9-10, 16-17*

A Song of Mourning

"I will fill the descendants of David and the other people of Jerusalem with the spirit of mercy and the spirit of prayer. They will look at the one whom they stabbed to death, and they will mourn for him like those who mourn for an only child. They will mourn bitterly, like those who have lost their first-born son. At that time the mourning in Jerusalem will be great."

Zec 12:10-11

God's Promise of Mercy

The people who feared the Lord spoke to one another, and the Lord listened and heard what they said. In his presence, there was written down in a book a record of those who feared the Lord and respected him. "They will be my people," says the Lord Almighty. "On the day when I act, they will be my very own. I will be merciful to them as a father is merciful to the son who serves him. Once again my people will see the difference between what happens to the righteous and to the wicked, to the person who serves me and the one who does not."

Ml 3:16-18

Psalms

Introduction

The Psalms are the collected prayers of the people of God going back to ancient times. They are the religious poetry of Israel. They are the prayer book of the Bible. In this book they are a prayer book within a prayer book. Composed by different authors over a long period of time, they are hymns of praise and of thanksgiving, songs of lament and confession, prayers of supplication and entreaty.

"The Psalms were used by Jesus, quoted by the writers of the New Testament, and became the treasured book of worship of the Christian church from its beginning" (GNB). They are thus also called the prayer book of the church.

It is significant that beyond being a grand collection of Hebrew prayers and poems, the Psalms are a prayer book "full of the incarnate Word" (Merton). They speak of Christ, are most intelligible in terms of Christ, and attain their deepest meaning only in Christ.

For the purposes of this book, they have been somewhat edited for prayer. Because they are collections, the Psalms often change subject abruptly, and there are sections that seem out of place for prayer; for example, statements about sinners, evil men, and enemies that exhort the Lord to violence. These don't seem quite to fit in since Jesus came and revealed God more clearly. A small example might be verses 19-22 in Psalm 139. The most radical shortening has been done on Psalm 119, a 22-stanza, alphabet psalm.

Even after an explanation, editing the Psalms

seems a presumptuous thing to do and one would dare to do it only because unexcerpted versions are everywhere available in literally millions of Bibles.

It has been mentioned that the Psalms are a collection of a variety of prayers: hymns of praise, songs of thanksgiving, individual cries for help and community laments (also called entreaties), prayers of trust and confidence, and minor and overlapping groups of psalms, such as: messianic psalms, penitential psalms, etc. Below are listed the numbers of psalms in various groups, without the listings being either complete or exclusive. Certain psalms, especially more lengthy and complex ones could well be listed under several categories, and others fit none of the categories below.

Hymns of Praise: 8, 19, 29, 33, 46, 47, 48, 76, 84, 87, 89, 93, 96, 97, 98, 99, 100, 104, 111, 113, 114, 117, 122, 135, 136, 145, 146, 147, 148, 149, 150

Songs of Thanksgiving: 18, 21, 30, 40, 66, 92, 116, 138

Individual Cries for Help: 3, 5, 6, 7, 10, 12, 13, 17, 22, 25, 28, 35, 38, 39, 42, 43, 51, 54, 55, 56, 57, 59, 63, 64, 69, 70, 71, 77, 86, 88, 102, 120, 140, 141, 142, 143

Community Laments: 44, 60, 74, 79, 80, 83, 85, 123, 129, 137

Prayers of Trust and Confidence: 11, 16, 23, 31, 56, 62, 71, 91, 121, 131, 139

Messianic Psalms: 2, 16, 22, 35, 45, 69, 72,
110, 118
Penitential Psalms: 6, 32, 38, 51, 102, 130,
143

Book One

1 True Happiness

Happy are those who reject the advice of evil
men
   who do not follow the example of sinners
   or join those who have no use for God.
Instead, they find joy in obeying the Law of
the Lord,
   and they study it day and night.
They are like trees that grow beside a stream,
   that bear fruit at the right time,
   and whose leaves do not dry up.
They succeed in everything they do.

But evil men are not like this at all;
   they are like straw that the wind blows
   away.
Sinners will be condemned by God
   and kept apart from God's own people.
The righteous are guided and protected by the
Lord,
   but the evil are on the way to their doom.
Ps 1:1-6

2 God's Chosen King

Why do the nations plan rebellion?
   Why do people make their useless plots?
Their kings revolt,
   their rulers plot together against the Lord
   and against the king he chose.
"Let us free ourselves from their rule," they
   say;
   "let us throw off their control."

From his throne in heaven the Lord laughs
    and mocks their feeble plans. . . .
"On Zion, my sacred hill," he says,
    "I have installed my king."

"I will announce," says the king, "what the
       Lord has declared.
    He said to me: 'You are my son;
    today I have become your father.
Ask, and I will give you all the nations;
    the whole earth will be yours.
You will break them with an iron rod;
    you will shatter them in pieces like a clay
       pot.' "

Now listen to this warning, you kings;
    learn this lesson, you rulers of the world;
Serve the Lord with fear;
    tremble and bow down to him; . . .
Happy are all who go to him for protection.
Ps 2:1-4, 6-11

3 Morning Prayer for Help

I have so many enemies, Lord,
    so many who turn against me!
They talk about me and say,
    "God will not help him."

But you, O Lord, are always my shield
       from danger;
    you give me victory
    and restore my courage.
I call to the Lord for help,
    and from his sacred hill he answers me.

I lie down and sleep,
    and all night long the Lord protects me.
I am not afraid of the thousands of
        enemies
    who surround me on every side.

Come, Lord! Save me, my God!
You punish all my enemies
    and leave them powerless to harm me.
Victory comes from the Lord—
    may he bless his people.

Ps 3:1-8

4 Evening Prayer for Help

Answer me when I pray,
    O God, my defender!
When I was in trouble, you helped me.
    Be kind to me now and hear my prayer.

How long will you people insult me?
    How long will you love what is worthless
    and go after what is false?

Remember that the Lord has chosen the
        righteous for his own,
    and he hears me when I call to him.

Tremble with fear and stop sinning;
    think deeply about this,
    when you lie in silence on your beds.
Offer the right sacrifices to the Lord,
    and put your trust in him.

There are many who pray;
    "Give us more blessings, O Lord.
    Look on us with kindness!"

But the joy that you have given me
    is more than they will ever have
    with all their grain and wine.

When I lie down, I go to sleep in peace;
    you alone, O Lord, keep me perfectly safe.
                                            Ps 4:1-8

5 A Prayer for Protection

Listen to my words, O Lord,
    and hear my sighs.
Listen to my cry for help,
    my God and king!

I pray to you, O Lord;
    you hear my voice in the morning;
at sunrise I offer my prayer
    and wait for your answer.

You are not a God who is pleased with
        wrongdoing;
    you allow no evil in your presence.

But because of your great love
    I can come into your house;
I can worship in your holy Temple
    and bow down to you in reverence.
Lord, I have so many enemies!
    Lead me to do your will;
    make your way plain for me to follow.

But all who find safety in you will rejoice;
    they can always sing for joy.

Protect those who love you;
>because of you they are truly happy.
You bless those who obey you, Lord;
>your love protects them like a shield.

>>>>*Ps 5:1-4, 7-8, 11-12*

6 A Prayer for Help in Time of Trouble

Lord, don't be angry and rebuke me!
>Don't punish me in your anger!
I am worn out, O Lord; have pity on me!
>Give me strength; I am completely
>>exhausted
>and my whole being is deeply troubled.
How long, O Lord, will you wait to help me?

Come and save me, Lord;
>in your mercy rescue me from death.
In the world of the dead you are not
>>remembered;
>no one can praise you there.

I am worn out with grief;
>every night my bed is damp from my
>>weeping;
>my pillow is soaked with tears.
I can hardly see;
>my eyes are so swollen
>from the weeping caused by my
>>enemies. . . .
The Lord hears my weeping;
>he listens to my cry for help
>and will answer my prayer.

>>>>*Ps 6:1-9*

7 A Prayer for Justice

O Lord, my God, I come to you for protection;
    rescue me and save me from all who pursue
        me,
or else like a lion they will carry me off
    where no one can save me,
        and there they will tear me to pieces.

Rise in your anger, O Lord!
    Stand up against the fury of my enemies;
    rouse yourself and help me!
Justice is what you demand,
    so bring together all the peoples around you,
    and rule over them from above.
You are the judge of all mankind.
    Judge in my favor, O Lord;
    you know that I am innocent.
You are a righteous God
    and judge our thoughts and desires.
Stop the wickedness of evil men
    and reward those who are good.

God is my protector;
    he saves those who obey him.
God is a righteous judge
    and always condemns the wicked.

I thank the Lord for his justice;
    I sing praises to the Lord, the Most High.
                            Ps 7:1-2, 6-11, 17

8 God's Glory and Man's Dignity

O Lord, our Lord,
    your greatness is seen in all the world!

Your praise reaches up to the heavens;
  it is sung by children and babies.
You are safe and secure from all your enemies;
  you stop anyone who opposes you.

When I look at the sky, which you have made,
  at the moon and the stars, which you set in
    their places—
what is man, that you think of him;
  mere man, that you care for him?

Yet you made him inferior only to yourself;
  you crowned him with glory and honor.
You appointed him ruler over everything you
  made;
  you placed him over all creation:
  sheep and cattle, and the wild animals too;
  the birds and the fish
  and the creatures in the seas.

O Lord, our Lord,
  your greatness is seen in all the world!

Ps 8:1-9

9 Thanksgiving to God for His Justice

I will praise you, Lord, with all my
    heart;
I will tell of all the wonderful
  things you have done.
I will sing with joy because of you.
  I will sing praise to you, Almighty God.

The Lord is king forever;
  he has set up his throne for judgment.
He rules the world with righteousness;
  he judges the nations with justice.

242 Psalms

The Lord is a refuge for the oppressed,
    a place of safety in times of trouble.
Those who know you, Lord, will trust
      you;
    you do not abandon anyone who comes
      to you.

Sing praise to the Lord, who rules in Zion!
    Tell every nation what he has done!
God remembers those who suffer;
    he does not forget their cry,
    and he punishes those who wrong them.

Be merciful to me, O Lord!
    See the sufferings my enemies cause me!
Rescue me from death, O Lord,
    that I may stand before the people of
      Jerusalem
    and tell them all the things for which I
      praise you.
I will rejoice because you saved me.

The needy will not always be neglected;
    the hope of the poor will not be crushed
      forever.

Ps 9:1-2, 7-14, 18

10 A Prayer for the Needy

Why are you so far away, O Lord?
Why do you hide yourself
    when we are in trouble?
The wicked are proud and persecute the poor.

The helpless victims lie crushed;
    brute strength has defeated them.

The wicked man says to himself, "God doesn't
   care!
   He has closed his eyes and will never see
   me!"

But you do see; you take notice of trouble and
   suffering
   and are always ready to help.
The helpless man commits himself to you;
   you have always helped the needy.

The Lord is king forever and ever.
   Those who worship other gods
   will vanish from his land.

You will listen, O Lord, to the prayers of the
   lowly;
   you will give them courage.
You will hear the cries of the oppressed and the
   orphans;
   you will judge in their favor,
   so that mortal men may cause terror no
   more.

Ps 10:1-2, 10-11, 14, 16-18

11 Confidence in the Lord

I trust in the Lord for safety.
   How foolish of you to say to me,
"Fly away like a bird to the mountains,
   because the wicked have drawn their
      bows and aimed their arrows
   to shoot at good men in the darkness.
There is nothing a good man can do
   when everything falls apart."

The Lord is in his holy temple;
    he has his throne in heaven.
He watches people everywhere
    and knows what they are doing.
He examines the good and the wicked
    alike.

The Lord is righteous and loves good
      deeds;
    those who do them will live in his
    presence.

Ps 11:1-5, 7

12 A Prayer for Help

Help us, Lord!
    There is not a good man left;
    honest men can no longer be found.
All of them lie to one another;
    they deceive each other with flattery.

"But now I will come," says the Lord,
    "because the needy are oppressed
    and the persecuted groan in pain.
I will give them the security they long for."

The promises of the Lord can be trusted;
    they are as genuine as silver
    refined seven times in the furnace.

Wicked men are everywhere,
    and everyone praises what is evil.
Keep us always safe, O Lord,
    and preserve us from such people.

Ps 12:1-2, 5-8

13 A Cry for Help

How much longer will you forget me, Lord?
  Forever?
  How much longer will you hide yourself
  from me?
How long must I endure trouble?
  How long will sorrow fill my heart day and
  night?
  How long will my enemies triumph over
  me?

Look at me, O Lord my God, and answer me.
  Restore my strength; don't let me die.
Don't let my enemies say, "We have defeated
  him."
  Don't let them gloat over my downfall.

I rely on your constant love;
  I will be glad, because you will rescue me.
I will sing to you, O Lord,
  because you have been good to me.

Ps 13:1-6

14 The Wickedness of Men

Fools say to themselves,
  "There is no God!"
They are all corrupt,
  and they have done terrible things;
  there is no one who does what is right.

The Lord looks down from heaven at
    mankind
  to see if there are any who are wise,
  any who worship him.

But they have all gone wrong;
    they are all equally bad.
Not one of them does what is right,
    not a single one.

"Don't they know?" asks the Lord.
    "Are all these evildoers ignorant?
They live by robbing my people,
    and they never pray to me."

But then they will be terrified,
    for God is with those who obey him.
Evildoers frustrate the plans of the humble
       man,
    but the Lord is his protection.

Ps 14:1-6

15 What God Requires

Lord, who may enter your Temple?
    Who may worship on Zion, your sacred
       hill?
A person who obeys God in everything
    and always does what is right,
whose words are true and sincere,
    and who does not slander others.
He does no wrong to his friends
    and does not spread rumors about his
       neighbors.
He despises those whom God rejects,
    but honors those who obey the Lord.
He always does what he promises,
    no matter how much it may cost.

He makes loans without charging interest
    and cannot be bribed to testify against the
        innocent.

Whoever does these things will always be
    secure.

Ps 15:1-5

16 A Prayer of Confidence

Protect me, O God; I trust in you for safety.
I say to the Lord, "You are my Lord;
    all the good things I have come from you."

How excellent are the Lord's faithful people!
    My greatest pleasure is to be with them.

You, Lord, are all I have,
    and you give me all I need;
    my future is in your hands.
How wonderful are your gifts to me;
    how good they are!

I praise the Lord, because he guides me.
    and in the night my conscience warns me.
I am always aware of the Lord's presence;
    he is near, and nothing can shake me.

And so I am thankful and glad,
    and because I feel completely secure,
because you protect me from the power of
        death.
I have served you faithfully,
    and you will not abandon me to the world
        of the dead.

You will show me the path that leads to life;
    your presence fills me with joy
    and brings me pleasure forever.

Ps 16:1-3, 5-11

17 The Prayer of an Innocent Man

Listen, O Lord, to my plea for justice;
    pay attention to my cry for help!
    Listen to my honest prayer.
You will judge in my favor,
    because you know what is right.

You know my heart.
    You have come to me at night;
    you have examined me completely
    and found no evil desire in me.
I speak no evil, as others do;
    I have obeyed your command
    and have not followed paths of violence.
I have always walked in your way
    and have never strayed from it.

I pray to you, O God, because you answer me;
    so turn to me and listen to my words.
Reveal your wonderful love and save me;
    at your side I am safe from my enemies.

Protect me as you would your very eyes;
    hide me in the shadow of your wings
    from the attacks of the wicked.

But I will see you, because I have done no
        wrong;
    and when I awake, your presence will fill
    me with joy.

Ps 17:1-9, 15

18 David's Song of Victory

How I love you, Lord!
 You are my defender.

The Lord is my protector;
 he is my strong fortress.
My God is my protection,
 and with him I am safe.
He protects me like a shield;
 he defends me and keeps me safe.
I call to the Lord,
 and he saves me from my enemies.
Praise the Lord!

The danger of death was all around me;
 the waves of destruction rolled over me.
The danger of death was around me,
 and the grave set its trap for me.
In my trouble I called to the Lord;
 I called to my God for help.
In his temple he heard my voice;
 he listened to my cry for help.

The Lord reached down from above and took
   hold of me;
 he pulled me out of the deep waters.
He rescued me from my powerful enemies
 and from all those who hate me—
 they were too strong for me.
When I was in trouble, they attacked
   me,
 but the Lord protected me.
He helped me out of danger;
 he saved me because he was pleased with
   me.

O Lord, you give me light;
   you dispel my darkness.
You give me strength to attack my enemies
   and power to overcome their defenses.

This God—how perfect are his deeds.
   How dependable his words!
He is like a shield
   for all who seek his protection.
The Lord alone is God;
   God alone is our defense.
He is the God who makes me strong.
   who makes my pathway safe.
He makes me sure-footed as a deer;
   he keeps me safe on the mountains.
He trains me for battle,
   so that I can use the strongest bow.

O Lord, you protect me and save me;
   your care has made me great,
   and your power has kept me safe.
You have kept me from being captured,
   and I have never fallen.

The Lord lives! Praise my defender!
   Proclaim the greatness of the God who saves
      me.
He gives me victory over my enemies;
   he subdues the nations under me
   and saves me from my foes.

O Lord, you give me victory over my enemies
   and protect me from violent men.
And so I praise you among the nations;
   I sing praises to you.

God gives great victories to his king;
    he shows constant love to the one he has
      chosen,
    to David and his descendants forever.
Ps 18:1-6, 16-19, 28-36, 46-50

19 God's Glory in Creation and the Law of the Lord

How clearly the sky reveals God's glory!
    How plainly it shows what he has done!
Each day announces it to the following day;
    each night repeats it to the next.
No speech or words are used,
    no sound is heard;
yet their voice goes out to all the world
    and is heard to the ends of the earth.
God made a home in the sky for the sun;
    it comes out in the morning like a happy
      bridegroom,
    like an athlete eager to run a race.
It starts at one end of the sky
    and goes across to the other.
    Nothing can hide from its heat.

The Law of the Lord

The law of the Lord is perfect;
    it gives new strength.
The commands of the Lord are trustworthy,
    giving wisdom to those who lack it.
The laws of the Lord are right,
    and those who obey them are happy.
The commands of the Lord are just
    and give understanding to the mind.

The worship of the Lord is good;
    it will continue forever.
The judgments of the Lord are just;
    they are always fair.
They are more desirable than the finest gold;
    they are sweeter than the purest honey.
They give knowledge to me, your servant;
    I am rewarded for obeying them.

No one can see his own errors;
    deliver me, Lord, from hidden faults!
Keep me safe, also, from willful sins;
    don't let them rule over me.
Then I shall be perfect
    and free from the evil of sin.

May my words and my thoughts be
      acceptable to you.
    O Lord, my refuge and my redeemer!

Ps 19:1-14

20 A Prayer for Victory

May the Lord answer you when you are in
      trouble!
    May the God of Jacob protect you!
May he send you help from his Temple
    and give you aid from Mount Zion.
May he accept all your offerings
    and be pleased with all your sacrifices.
May he give you what you desire
    and make all your plans succeed.
Then we will shout for joy over your victory
    and celebrate your triumph by praising
      our God.
May the Lord answer all your requests.

Now I know that the Lord gives victory to
     his chosen king;
    he answers him from his holy heaven
    and by his power gives him great victories.
Some trust in their war chariots
    and others in their horses,
    but we trust in the power of the Lord
     our God.
Such people will stumble and fall,
    but we will rise and stand firm.

Give victory to the king, O Lord:
    answer us when we call.

Ps 20:1-9

21 Praise for Victory

The king is glad, O Lord, because you gave
     him strength;
    he rejoices because you made him
     victorious.
You have given him his heart's desire;
    you have answered his request.

You came to him with great blessings
    and set a crown of gold on his head.
He asked for life, and you gave it,
    a long and lasting life.

His glory is great because of your help;
    you have given him fame and majesty.
Your blessings are with him forever,
    and your presence fills him with joy.

The king trusts in the Lord Almighty;
 and because of the Lord's constant love
 he will always be secure.

We praise you Lord, for your great strength!
We will sing and praise your power.

Ps 21:1-7, 13

22 A Cry of Anguish and a Song of Praise

My God, my God, why have you abandoned
 me?
I have cried desperately for help,
 but still it does not come.
During the day I call to you, my God,
 but you do not answer;
I call at night,
 but get no rest.
But you are enthroned as the Holy One.
 the one whom Israel praises.
Our ancestors put their trust in you;
 they trusted you, and you saved them.
They called to you and escaped from danger;
 they trusted you and were not disappointed.

But I am no longer a man; I am a worm,
 despised and scorned by everyone!
All who see me make fun of me;
 they stick out their tongues and shake
  their heads.
"You relied on the Lord," they say.
 "Why doesn't he save you?
If the Lord likes you,
 why doesn't he help you?"

It was you who brought me safely through
   birth,
   and when I was a baby, you kept me safe.
I have relied on you since the day I was born,
   and you have always been my God.
Do not stay away from me!
   Trouble is near,
   and there is no one to help.

My strength is gone,
   gone like water spillled on the ground.
All my bones are out of joint;
   my heart is like melted wax.
My throat is as dry as dust,
   and my tongue sticks to the roof of my
      mouth.
You have left me for dead in the dust.

A gang of evil men is around me;
   like a pack of dogs they close in on me;
   they tear at my hands and feet.
All my bones can be seen.
   My enemies look at me and stare.
They gamble for my clothes
   and divide them among themselves.

O Lord, don't stay away from me!
   Come quickly to my rescue!
Save me from the sword;
   save my life from these dogs.

A Song of Praise
   I will tell my people what you have done;
   I will praise you in their assembly:

"Praise him, you servants of the Lord!
　　Honor him, you descendants of Jacob!
　　Worship him, you people of Israel!
He does not neglect the poor or ignore their
　　　suffering;
　　he does not turn away from them,
　　but answers when they call for help."

In the full assembly I will praise
　　　you for what you have done;
　　in the presence of those who worship you
　　I will offer the sacrifices I promised.
The poor will eat as much as they want;
　　those who come to the Lord will praise him.
May they prosper forever!

All nations will remember the Lord.
　　From every part of the world they will
　　　turn to him;
　　all races will worship him.
The Lord is king,
　　and he rules the nations.

All proud men will bow down to him,
　　all mortal men will bow down before him.
Future generations will serve him;
　　men will speak of the Lord to the coming
　　　generation.
People not yet born will be told:
　　"The Lord saved his people."

Ps 22:1-11, 14-31

23 The Lord Is My Shepherd

The Lord is my shepherd;
　　I have everything I need.

He lets me rest in fields of green grass
    and leads me to quiet pools of fresh water.
He gives me new strength.
He guides me in the right paths,
    as he has promised,
Even if I go through the deepest darkness,
    I will not be afraid, Lord,
    for you are with me.
Your shepherd's rod and staff protect me.

You prepare a banquet for me,
    where all my enemies can see me;
you welcome me as an honored guest
    and fill my cup to the brim.
I know that your goodness and love will be
      with me all my life;
    and your house will be my home as long as I
      live.

Ps 23:1-6

24 The Great King

The world and all that is in it belong to the
      Lord;
    the earth and all who live on it are his.
He built it on the deep waters beneath the
      earth
    and laid its foundations in the ocean depths.

Who has the right to go up the Lord's hill?
    Who may enter his holy Temple?
Those who are pure in act and in thought,
    who do not worship idols
    or make false promises.

The Lord will bless them and save them;
    God will declare them innocent.
Such are the people who come to God,
    who come into the presence of the God of
        Jacob.

Fling wide the gates,
    open the ancient doors,
    and the great king will come in.
Who is this great king?
He is the Lord, strong and mighty,
    the Lord, victorious in battle.

Fling wide the gates,
    open the ancient doors,
    and the great king will come in.
Who is this great king?
The triumphant Lord—he is the great king!
                                    Ps 24:1-10

25 A Prayer for Guidance and Protection

To you, O Lord, I offer my prayer;
    in you, my God, I trust.
Save me from the shame of defeat;
    don't let my enemies gloat over me!
Defeat does not come to those who trust in
        you,
    but to those who are quick to rebel against
        you.

Teach me your ways, O Lord;
    make them known to me.
Teach me to live according to your truth,
    for you are my God, who saves me.
    I always trust in you.

Remember, O Lord, your kindness and
    constant love
  which you have shown from long ago.
Forgive the sins and errors of my youth.
In your constant love and goodness,
    remember me, Lord!

Because the Lord is righteous and good,
    he teaches sinners the path they should
        follow.
He leads the humble in the right way
    and teaches them his will.
With faithfulness and love he leads
    all who keep his covenant and obey his
        commands.

Keep your promise, Lord, and forgive my sins,
    for they are many.
Those who obey the Lord
    will learn from him the path they should
        follow.
They will always be prosperous,
    and their children will possess the land.
The Lord is the friend of those who obey him
    and he affirms his covenant with them.

I look to the Lord for help at all times,
    and he rescues me from danger.
Turn to me, Lord, and be merciful to me,
    because I am lonely and weak.
Relieve me of my worries
    and save me from all my troubles.
Consider my distress and suffering
    and forgive all my sins.

See how many enemies I have;
    see how much they hate me.
Protect me and save me;
    keep me from defeat.
    I come to you for safety.
May my goodness and honesty preserve me,
    because I trust in you.

Ps 25:1-21

26 The Prayer of a Good Man

Declare me innocent, O Lord,
    because I do what is right
    and trust you completely.
Examine me and test me, Lord;
    judge my desires and thoughts.

Lord, I wash my hands to show that I am
      innocent
    and march in worship around your altar.
I sing a hymn of thanksgiving
    and tell of all your wonderful deeds.

I love the house where you live, O Lord,
    the place where your glory dwells.
Do not destroy me with the sinners;
    spare me from the fate of murderers—
    men who do evil all the time
    and are always ready to take bribes.

As for me, I do what is right;
    be merciful to me and save me!

I am safe from all dangers;
    in the assembly of his people I praise the
      Lord.

Ps 26:1-2, 6-12

27 A Prayer of Praise

The Lord is my light and my salvation;
    I will fear no one.
The Lord protects me from all danger;
    I will never be afraid.

When evil men attack me and try to kill me,
    they stumble and fall.
Even if a whole army surrounds me,
    I will not be afraid;
even if enemies attack me,
    I will still trust God.

I have asked the Lord for one thing;
    one thing only do I want:
to live in the Lord's house all my life,
    to marvel there at his goodness,
    and to ask for his guidance.
In times of trouble he will shelter me;
    he will keep me safe in his Temple
    and make me secure on a high rock.
So I will triumph over my enemies around me.
    With shouts of joy I will offer sacrifices in
        his Temple;
I will sing, I will praise the Lord.

Hear me, Lord, when I call to you!
    Be merciful and answer me!
When you said, "Come worship me,"
I answered, "I will come, Lord."
    Don't hide yourself from me!

Don't be angry with me;
    don't turn your servant away.

You have been my help;
    don't leave me, don't abandon me,
    O God, my savior.
My father and mother may abandon me,
    but the Lord will take care of me.

Teach me, Lord, what you want me to do,
    and lead me along a safe path,
    because I have many enemies.
Don't abandon me to my enemies,
    who attack me with lies and threats.

I know that I will live to see
    the Lord's goodness in this present life.
Trust in the Lord.
    Have faith, do not despair.
Trust in the Lord.

Ps 27:1-14

28 A Call for Help

O Lord, my defender, I call to you.
    Listen to my cry!
If you do not answer me,
    I will be amongst those who go down to the
        world of the dead.
Hear me when I cry to you for help,
    when I lift my hands toward your holy
        Temple.
Do not condemn me with the wicked,
    with those who do evil—
    men whose words are friendly,
    but who have hatred in their hearts.

Give praise to the Lord;
   he has heard my cry for help.
The Lord protects and defends me;
   I trust in him.
He gives me help and makes me glad;
   I praise him with joyful songs.

The Lord protects his people;
   he defends and saves his chosen king.
Save your people, Lord,
   and bless those who are yours.
Be their shepherd,
   and take care of them forever.

Ps 28:1-3, 6-9

29 The Voice of the Lord

Praise the Lord, you heavenly beings;
   praise his glory and power.
Praise the Lord's glorious name;
   bow down before the Holy One when he
      appears.

The voice of the Lord is heard on the seas;
   the glorious God thunders,
   and his voice echoes over the ocean.
The voice of the Lord is heard
   in all its might and majesty.

The voice of the Lord breaks the cedars,
   even the cedars of Lebanon.
He makes the mountains of Lebanon jump
      like calves
   and makes Mount Hermon leap like a young
      bull.

The voice of the Lord makes the lightning
    flash.
His voice makes the desert shake;
    he shakes the desert of Kadesh.
The Lord's voice shakes the oaks
    and strips the leaves from the trees
    while everyone in his Temple shouts, "Glory
    to God!"

The Lord rules over the deep waters;
    he rules as king forever.
The Lord gives strength to his people
    and blesses them with peace.

Ps 29:1-11

30 A Prayer of Thanksgiving

I praise you, Lord, because you have saved me
    and kept my enemies from gloating over me.
I cried to you for help, O Lord my God,
    and you healed me;
    you kept me from the grave.
I was on my way to the depths below,
    but you restored my life.

Sing praise to the Lord,
    all his faithful people!
Remember what the Holy One has done,
    and give him thanks!
His anger lasts only a moment,
    his goodness for a lifetime.
Tears may flow in the night,
    but joy comes in the morning.

I felt secure and said to myself,
  "I will never be defeated."
You were good to me, Lord;
  you protected me like a mountain fortress.
But then you hid yourself from me,
  and I was afraid.

I called to you, Lord;
  I begged for your help:
"What will you gain from my death?
  What profit from my going to the grave?
Are dead people able to praise you?
  Can they proclaim your unfailing goodness?
Hear me, Lord, and be merciful!
  Help me, Lord!"

You have changed my sadness into a joyful
    dance;
  you have taken away my sorrow
  and surrounded me with joy.
So I will not be silent;
  I will sing praise to you.
Lord, you are my God;
  I will give you thanks forever.

Ps 30:1-12

31 A Prayer of Trust in God

I come to you, Lord, for protection;
  never let me be defeated.
You are a righteous God;
  save me, I pray!
Hear me! Save me now!
Be my refuge to protect me;
  my defense to save me.

You are my refuge and defense;
  guide me and lead me as you have promised.
Keep me safe from the trap that has been set
      for me;
  shelter me from danger.
I place myself in your care.
You will save me, Lord;
  you are a faithful God.

I will be glad and rejoice
  because of your constant love.
You see my suffering;
  you know my trouble.

Be merciful to me, Lord,
  for I am in trouble;
my eyes are tired from so much crying;
  I am completely worn out.
I am exhausted by sorrow,
  and weeping has shortened my life.
I am weak from all my troubles;
  even my bones are wasting away.

All my enemies, and especially my neighbors,
  treat me with contempt;
Those who know me are afraid of me;
  when they see me in the street, they run
      away.
Everyone has forgotten me, as though I were
    dead;
  I am like something thrown away.
I hear many enemies whispering;
  terror is all around me.
They are making plans against me,
  plotting to kill me.

But my trust is in you, O Lord;
  you are my God.
I am always in your care;
  save me from my enemies,
  from those who persecute me.

Look on your servant with kindness;
  save me in your constant love.
I call to you, Lord;
  don't let me be disgraced.

How wonderful are the good things
  you keep for those who honor you!
Everyone knows how good you are,
  how securely you protect those who trust
    you.

Praise the Lord!
How wonderfully he showed his love for me
  when I was surrounded and attacked!
I was afraid and thought
  that he had driven me out of his presence.
But he heard my cry,
  when I called to him for help.

Love the Lord, all his faithful people.
The Lord protects the faithful,
  but punishes the proud as they deserve.
Be strong, be courageous,
  all you that hope in the Lord.

Ps 31:1-5, 7, 9-17, 19, 21-24

32 Confession and Forgiveness

Happy are those whose sins are forgiven,
  whose wrongs are pardoned.
Happy is the man whom the Lord does not
    accuse of doing wrong
  and who is free from all deceit.

When I did not confess my sins,
  I was worn out from crying all day long.
Day and night you punished me, Lord;
  my strength was completely drained,
  as moisture is dried up by the summer heat.

Then I confessed my sins to you;
  I did not conceal my wrongdoings.
I decided to confess them to you,
  and you forgave all my sins.

So all your loyal people should pray to you in
    times of need;
  when a great flood of trouble comes rushing
    in,
  it will not reach them.
You are my hiding place;
  you will save me from trouble.
I sing aloud of your salvation,
  because you protect me.

The Lord says, "I will teach you the way you
    should go;
  I will instruct you and advise you.
Don't be stupid like a horse or a mule,
  which must be controlled with a bit and
    bridle
  to make it submit."

The wicked will have to suffer,
    but those who trust in the Lord
    are protected by his constant love.
You that are righteous, be glad and rejoice
    because of what the Lord has done.
You that obey him, shout for joy!

Ps 32:1-11

33 A Hymn of Praise

All you that are righteous,
    shout for joy for what the Lord has done;
    praise him, all you that obey him.
Give thanks to the Lord with harps,
    sing to him with stringed instruments.
Sing a new song to him,
    play the harp with skill, and shout for joy!

The words of the Lord are true,
    and all his works are dependable.
The Lord loves what is righteous and just;
    his constant love fills the earth.

The Lord created the heavens by his
    command,
    the sun, moon, and stars by his spoken
    word.
He gathered all the seas into one place;
    he shut up the ocean depths in storerooms.

Have reverence for the Lord, all the earth!
    Honor him, all peoples of the world!
When he spoke, the world was created;
    at his command everything appeared.

The Lord frustrates the purposes of the
   nations;
   he keeps them from carrying out their plans.
But his plans endure forever;
   his purposes last eternally.
Happy is the nation whose God is the Lord;
   happy are the people he has chosen for his
      own!

The Lord looks down from heaven
   and sees all mankind.
From where he rules, he looks down
   on all who live on earth.
He forms all their thoughts
   and knows everything they do.

A king does not win because of his powerful
   army;
   a soldier does not triumph because of his
      strength.
War horses are useless for victory;
   their great strength cannot save.

The Lord watches over those who have
   reverence for him,
   those who trust in his constant love.
He saves them from death;
   he keeps them alive in time of famine.

We put our hope in the Lord;
   he is our protector and our help.
We are glad because of him;
   we trust in his holy name.

May your constant love be with us, Lord,
   as we put our hope in you.
                                    Ps 33:1-22

34 In Praise of God's Goodness

I will always thank the Lord;
   I will never stop praising him.
I will praise him for what he has done;
   may all who are oppressed listen and be
      glad!
Proclaim with me the Lord's greatness;
   let us praise his name together!

I prayed to the Lord, and he answered me;
   he freed me from all my fears.
The oppressed look to him and are glad;
   they will never be disappointed.
The helpless call to him, and he answers;
   he saves them from all their troubles.
His angel guards those who have reverence
      for the Lord
   and rescues them from danger.

Find out for yourself how good the Lord is
   Happy are those who find safety with him.
Have reverence for the Lord, all his people;
   those who obey him have all they need.
Even lions go hungry for lack of food,
   but those who obey the Lord lack nothing
      good.

Come, my young friends, and listen to me,
   and I will teach you to have reverence for
      the Lord.
Would you like to enjoy life?
   Do you want long life and happiness?
Then keep from speaking evil and from telling
   lies.

Turn away from evil and do good;
  strive for peace with all your heart.

The Lord watches over the righteous
  and listens to their cries;
but he opposes those who do evil,
  so that when they die, they are soon
    forgotten.
The righteous call to the Lord, and he listens;
  he rescues them from all their troubles.
The Lord is near to those who are discouraged;
  he saves those who have lost all hope.

The good man suffers many troubles,
  but the Lord saves him from them all;
the Lord preserves him completely;
  not one of his bones is broken.

The Lord will save his people;
  those who go to him for protection will be
    spared.

Ps 34:1-20, 22

35 Lord, Come to My Rescue

Oppose those who oppose me, Lord,
  and fight those who fight against me!
Take your shield and armor
  and come to my rescue.
Lift up your spear and war ax
  against those who pursue me.
Promise that you will save me.

Then I will be glad because of the Lord;
  I will be happy because he saved me.

With all my heart I will say to the Lord,
  "There is no one like you.
  You protect the weak from the strong,
  the poor from the oppressor."

Evil men testify against me
  and accuse me of crimes I know nothing
    about.
They pay me back evil for good,
  and I sink in despair.
But when they were sick, I dressed in
    mourning;
  I deprived myself of food;
I prayed with my head bowed low,
  as I would pray for a friend or a brother.
I went around bent over in mourning,
  as one who mourns for his mother.

But when I was in trouble, they were all glad
  and gathered around me to make fun of me;
strangers beat me
  and kept striking me.
Like men who would mock a cripple,
  they glared at me with hate.

How much longer, Lord, will you just look on?
  Rescue me from their attacks;
  save my life from these lions!
Then I will thank you in the assembly of your
    people;
  I will praise you before them all.

May those who want to see me acquitted
  shout for joy and say again and again,

"How great is the Lord!
    He is pleased with the success of his
        servant."
Then I will proclaim your righteousness,
    and I will praise you all day long.

Ps 35:1-3, 9-18, 27-28

36 The Goodness of God

Lord, your constant love reaches the heavens;
    your faithfulness extends to the skies.
Your righteousness is towering like the
        mountains;
    your justice is like the depths of the sea.
Men and animals are in your care.

How precious, O God. is your constant love!
    We find protection under the shadow of
        your wings.
We feast on the abundant food you provide;
    you let us drink from the river of your
        goodness.
You are the source of all life,
    and because of your light we see the light.

Continue to love those who know you
    and to do good to those who are righteous.

Ps 36:5-10

37 The Destiny of the Wicked and
of the Good

Trust in the Lord and do good;
    live in the land and be safe.

Seek your happiness in the Lord,
and he will give you your heart's desire.

Give yourself to the Lord;
    trust in him, and he will help you;
he will make your righteousness shine like the
    noonday sun.

Be patient and wait for the Lord to act;
    don't be worried about those who prosper
    or those who succeed in their evil plans.

Those who trust in the Lord will possess the
    land,
    but the wicked will be driven out.

The little that a good man owns
    is worth more than the wealth of all the
    wicked,
because the Lord will take away the strength
    of the wicked,
    but protect those who are good.

The Lord takes care of those who obey him,
    and the land will be theirs forever.
They will not suffer when times are bad;
    they will have enough in time of famine.

The Lord guides a man in the way he should
    go
    and protects those who please him.
If they fall, they will not stay down,
    because the Lord will help them up.

I am an old man now; I have lived a long time,
    but I have never seen a good man
    abandoned by the Lord
    or his children begging for food.

At all times he gives freely and lends to others,
  and his children are a blessing.

Turn away from evil and do good,
  and your descendants will always live in the
    land;
for the Lord loves what is right
  and does not abandon his faithful people.
He protects them forever,
  but the descendants of the wicked will be
    driven out.
The righteous will possess the land
  and live in it forever.

A good man's words are wise,
  and he is always fair.
He keeps the law of his God in his heart
  and never departs from it.

I once knew a wicked man who was a tyrant;
  he towered over everyone like a cedar of
    Lebanon;
but later I passed by, and he wasn't there;
  I looked for him, but couldn't find him.

Notice the good man, observe the righteous
    man;
  a peaceful man has descendants,
but sinners are completely destroyed,
  and their descendants are wiped out.

The Lord saves righteous men
  and protects them in times of trouble.
He helps them and rescues them;
  he saves them from the wicked,
    because they go to him for protection.

Ps 37:3-7, 9, 16-19, 23-31, 35-40

38 The Prayer of a Suffering Man

O Lord, don't punish me in your anger!
You have wounded me with your arrows;
   you have struck me down.

Because of your anger, I am in great pain;
   my whole body is diseased because of my
      sins.
I am drowning in the flood of my sins;
   they are a burden too heavy to bear.

O Lord, you know what I long for;
   you hear all my groans.
My heart is pounding, my strength is gone,
   and my eyes have lost their brightness.
My friends and neighbors will not come near
      me,
   because of my sores;
   even my family keeps away from me.

I am like a deaf man and cannot hear,
   like a dumb man and cannot speak.
I am like a man who does not answer,
   because he cannot hear.
But I trust in you, O Lord;
   and you, O Lord my God, will answer me.
Don't let my enemies gloat over my distress;
   don't let them boast about my downfall!
I am about to fall
   and am in constant pain.

I confess my sins;
   they fill me with anxiety.
My enemies are healthy and strong;
   there are many who hate me for no reason.

Do not abandon me, O Lord;
    do not stay away, my God!
Help me now, O Lord my savior!
Ps 38:1-4, 9-11, 13-19, 21-22

39 The Confession of a Suffering Man

I said, "I will be careful about what I do
    and will not let my tongue make me sin;
I will not say anything
    while evil men are near."
I kept quiet, not saying a word,
    not even about anything good!
But my suffering only grew worse,
    and I was overcome with anxiety.
The more I thought, the more troubled I
      became;
    I could not keep from asking:
"Lord, how long will I live?
    When will I die?
    Tell me how soon my life will end."

How short you have made my life!
    In your sight my lifetime seems nothing.
Indeed every living man is no more than a
      puff of wind,
    no more than a shadow.
All he does is for nothing;
    he gathers wealth, but doesn't know who
      will get it.

What, then, can I hope for, Lord?
    I put my hope in you.
Save me from all my sins,
    and don't let fools make fun of me.

I will keep quiet, I will not say a word,
  for you are the one who made me suffer like
    this.
Don't punish me any more!
I am about to die from your blows.

Hear my prayer, Lord,
  and listen to my cry;
  come to my aid when I weep.
Like all my ancestors
  I am only your guest for a little while.
Leave me alone so that I may have some
    happpiness
  before I go away and am no more.

Ps 39:1-10, 12-13

40 A Song of Praise

I waited patiently for the Lord's help;
  then he listened to me and heard my cry.
He pulled me out of a dangerous pit,
  out of the deadly quicksand.
He set me safely on a rock
  and made me secure.
He taught me to sing a new song,
  a song of praise to our God.
Many who see this will take warning
  and will put their trust in the Lord.

Happy are those who trust the Lord,
  who do not turn to idols
  or join those who worship false gods.

You have done many things for us, O Lord
 our God;
  there is no one like you!
  You have made many wonderful plans for
  us.
I could never speak of them all—
  their number is so great!

In the assembly of all your people, Lord,
  I told the good news that you save us.
  You know that I will never stop telling it.
I have not kept the news of salvation to myself;
  I have always spoken of your faithfulness
  and help.
In the assembly of all your people I have not
  been silent
  about your loyalty and constant love.

Lord, I know you will never stop being
  merciful to me.
  Your love and loyalty will always keep me
  safe.   Ps 40:1-5, 9-11

41 The Prayer of a Sick Man

Happy are those who are concerned for the
  poor;
  the Lord will help them when they are in
  trouble.
The Lord will protect them and preserve
  their lives;
  he will make them happy in the land;
  he will not abandon them to the power of
  their enemies.
The Lord will help them when they are sick
  and will restore them to health.

I said, "I have sinned against you, Lord;
  be merciful to me and heal me."
My enemies say cruel things about me.
  They want me to die and be forgotten.

They say, "He is fatally ill;
  he will never leave his bed again."
Even my best friend, the one I trusted most,
  the one who shared my food,
  has turned against me.

Be merciful to me, Lord, and restore my
    health,
  and I will pay my enemies back.
They will not triumph over me,
  and I will know that you are pleased with
    me.
You will help me, because I do what is right;
  you will keep me in your presence forever.

Praise the Lord, the God of Israel!
Praise him now and forever!

    Amen! Amen!

Ps 41:1-5, 8-13

Book Two

42 The Prayer of a Man in Exile

As a deer longs for a stream of cool water,
  so I long for you, O God.
I thirst for you, the living God.
  When can I go and worship in your
    presence?
Day and night I cry,
  and tears are my only food;
all the time my enemies ask me,
  "Where is your God?"

My heart breaks when I remember the past,
  when I went with the crowds to the house of
    God
  and led them as they walked along,
  a happy crowd, singing and shouting praise
    to God.
Why am I so sad?
  Why am I so troubled?
I will put my hope in God,
  and once again I will praise him,
  my savior and my God.

Here in exile my heart is breaking,
  and so I turn my thoughts to him.
He has sent waves of sorrow over my soul; . . .
  from Mount Hermon and Mount Mizar.
May the Lord show his constant love during
    the day,
  so that I may have a song at night,
  a prayer to the God of my life.

Ps 42:1-8

43 The Prayer of a Homesick Man

O God, declare me innocent,
    and defend my cause against the ungodly;
    deliver me from lying and evil men!
You are my protector;
    why have you abandoned me?
Why must I go on suffering
    from the cruelty of my enemies?

Send your light and your truth;
    may they lead me
    and bring me back to Zion, your sacred hill,
    and to your Temple, where you live.
Then I will go to your altar, O God;
    you are the source of my happiness.
I will play my harp and sing praise to you,
    O God, my God.

Why am I so sad?
    Why am I so troubled?
I will put my hope in God,
    and once again I will praise him,
    my savior and my God.

Ps 43:1-5

44 A Prayer for Protection

With our own ears we have heard it, O God—
    our ancestors have told us about it,
about the great things you did in their time,
    in the days of long ago:
how you yourself drove out the heathen
    and established your people in their land;
how you punished the other nations
    and caused your own to prosper.

Your people did not conquer the land with
    their swords;
  they did not win it by their own power;
it was by your power and your strength,
    by the assurance of your presence,
    which showed that you loved them.

You are my king and my God;
  you give victory to your people,
  and by your power we defeat our enemies.
I do not trust in my bow
  or in my sword to save me;
but you have saved us from our enemies
  and defeated those who hate us.
We will always praise you
  and give thanks to you forever.

But now you have rejected us and let us be
    defeated;
  you no longer march out with our armies.

Wake up, Lord! Why are you asleep?
  Rouse yourself! Don't reject us forever!

Why are you hiding from us?
  Don't forget our suffering and trouble!

We fall crushed to the ground;
  we lie defeated in the dust.
Come to our aid!
  Because of your constant love save us!

Ps 44:1-9, 23-26

45 A Royal Wedding Song

You are the most handsome of men;
    you are an eloquent speaker.
    God has always blessed you.
Buckle on your sword, mighty king;
    you are glorious and majestic.

Ride on in majesty to victory
    for the defense of truth and justice!
    Your strength will win you great victories!

The kingdom that God has given you
    will last forever and ever.
You rule over your people with justice;
    you love what is right and hate what is evil.
That is why God, your God, has chosen you
    and has poured out more happiness on you
    than on any other king.

Among the ladies of your court are daughters
    of kings,
    and at the right of your throne stands the
    queen,
    wearing ornaments of finest gold.

The princess is in the palace—how beautiful
    she is!
    Her gown is made of gold thread.
In her colorful gown she is led to the king,
    followed by her bridesmaids,
    and they also are brought to him.
With joy and gladness they come
    and enter the king's palace.

You, my king, will have many sons
  to succeed your ancestors as kings,
  and you will make them rulers over the
    whole earth.

Ps 45:2-4, 6-7, 9, 13-16

46 God Is with Us

God is our shelter and strength,
  always ready to help in times of trouble.
So we will not be afraid, even if the earth is
    shaken
  and mountains fall into the ocean depths;
even if the seas roar and rage,
  and the hills are shaken by the violence.

There is a river that brings joy to the city of
    God,
  to the sacred house of the Most High.
God is in that city, and it will never be
    destroyed;
  at early dawn he will come to its aid.

The Lord Almighty is with us;
  the God of Jacob is our refuge.

Come and see what the Lord has done.
  See what amazing things he has done on
    earth.
He stops wars all over the world;
  he breaks bows, destroys spears,
  and sets shields on fire.
"Stop fighting," he says, "and know that I am
    God,
  supreme among the nations,
  supreme over the world."

The Lord Almighty is with us;
the God of Jacob is our refuge.

Ps 46:1-5, 7-11

47 The Supreme Ruler

Clap your hands for joy, all peoples!
Praise God with loud songs!
The Lord, the Most High, is to be feared,
he is a great king, ruling over all the world.
He gave us victory over the peoples;
he made us rule over the nations.
He chose for us the land where we live,
the proud possession of his people, whom he
loves.

God goes up to his throne.
There are shouts of joy and the blast of
trumpets,
as the Lord goes up.
Sing praise to God;
sing praise to our king!
God is king over all the world;
praise him with songs!

God sits on his sacred throne;
he rules over the nations.
The rulers of the nations assemble
with the people of the God of Abraham.
More powerful than all armies is he;
he rules supreme.

Ps 47:1-9

48 Zion, the City of God

The Lord is great and is to be highly praised
  in the city of our God, on his sacred hill.
Zion, the mountain of God, is high and
      beautiful;
    the city of the great king brings joy to all the
      world.
God has shown that there is safety with him
  inside the fortresses of the city.

The kings gathered together
  and came to attack Mount Zion.
But when they saw it, they were amazed;
  they were afraid and ran away.
They were seized with fear and anguish
  like a woman about to bear a child,
  like ships tossing in a furious storm.

We have heard what God has done,
  and now we have seen it
  in the city of our God, the Lord Almighty;
he will keep the city safe forever.

Inside your Temple, O God,
  we think of your constant love.
You are praised by people everywhere,
  and your fame extends over all the earth.
You rule with justice;
  let the people of Zion be glad!
You give right judgments;
  let there be joy in the cities of Judah!

People of God, walk around Zion and count
      the towers;
    take notice of the walls and examine the
      fortresses,

so that you may tell the next generation:
"This God is our God forever and ever;
he will lead us for all time to come."

Ps 48:1-14

49 The Foolishness of Trusting in Riches

Hear this, everyone!
Listen, all people everywhere,
great and small alike
rich and poor together.
My thoughts will be deep;
I will speak words of wisdom.
I will turn my attention to proverbs
and explain their meaning as I play the
harp.

I am not afraid in times of danger
when I am surrounded by enemies,
by evil men who trust in their riches
and boast of their great wealth.
A person can never redeem himself;
he cannot pay God the price for his life,
because the payment for a human life is
too great.
What he could pay would never be enough
to keep him from the grave,
to let him live forever.

Anyone can see that even wise men die,
as well as foolish and stupid men.
They all leave their riches to their
descendants.
Their graves are their homes forever;
there they stay for all time,
though they once had lands of their own.

A man's greatness cannot keep him from
    death;
    he will still die like the animals.

See what happens to those who trust in
    themselves,
    the fate of those who are satisfied with
    their wealth—
they are doomed to die like sheep,
    and Death will be their shepherd.
The righteous will triumph over them,
    as their bodies quickly decay
    in the world of the dead far from their
    homes.
But God will rescue me;
    he will save me from the power of death.

Ps 49:1-15

50 True Worship

The Almighty God, the Lord, speaks;
    he calls to the whole earth from east to west.
God shines from Zion,
    the city perfect in its beauty.

Our God is coming, but not in silence;
    a raging fire is in front of him,
    a furious storm around him.
He calls heaven and earth as witnesses
    to see him judge his people.
He says, "Gather my faithful people to me,
    those who made a covenant with me by
    offering a sacrifice."
The heavens proclaim that God is righteous,
    that he himself is judge.

"Listen, my people, and I will speak;
  I will testify against you, Israel.
  I am God, your God.
I do not reprimand you because of your
    sacrifices
  and the burnt offerings you always bring
    me.
And yet I do not need bulls from your farms
  or goats from your flocks;
all the animals in the forest are mine
  and the cattle on thousands of hills.
All the wild birds are mine
  and all living things in the fields.

"If I were hungry, I would not ask you for
    food,
  for the world and everything in it is mine.
Do I eat the flesh of bulls
  or drink the blood of goats?
Let the giving of thanks be your sacrifice to
    God,
  and give the Almighty all that you
    promised.
Call to me when trouble comes;
  I will save you,
  and you will praise me.
Giving thanks is the sacrifice that honors me,
  and I will surely save all who obey me."

Ps 50:1-15, 23

51 A Prayer for Forgiveness

Be merciful to me, O God,
  because of your constant love.
Because of your great mercy
  wipe away my sins!

Wash away all my evil
and make me clean from my sin!

I recognize my faults;
I am always conscious of my sins.
I have sinned against you—only against you—
and done what you consider evil.
So you are right in judging me;
you are justified in condemning me.
I have been evil from the time I was born;
from the day of my birth I have been sinful.

Sincerity and truth are what you require;
fill my mind with your wisdom.
Remove my sin, and I will be clean;
wash me, and I will be whiter than snow.
Let me hear the sounds of joy and gladness;
and though you have crushed me and
broken me,
I will be happy once again.
Close your eyes to my sins
and wipe out all my evil.

Create a pure heart in me, O God,
and put a new and loyal spirit in me.
Do not banish me from your presence;
do not take your holy spirit away from me.
Give me again the joy that comes from your
salvation,
and make me willing to obey you.
Then I will teach sinners your commands,
and they will turn back to you.

Spare my life, O God, and save me,
and I will gladly proclaim your
righteousness.

Help me to speak, Lord,
  and I will praise you.

You do not want sacrifices,
  or I would offer them;
you are not pleased with burnt offerings.
My sacrifice is a humble spirit, O God;
  you will not reject a humble and repentant
    heart.

Ps 51:1-17

52 God's Judgment and Grace

Why do you boast, great man, of your evil?
  God's faithfulness is eternal.
You make plans to ruin others;
  your tongue is like a sharp razor.
  You are always inventing lies.
You love evil more than good
  and falsehood more than truth.
You love to hurt people with your words, you
    liar!

So God will ruin you forever;
  he will take hold of you and snatch you from
    your home;
  he will remove you from the world of the
    living.

Righteous people will see this and be afraid;
  Then they will laugh at you and say,
"Look, here is a man who did not depend on
    God for safety,
  but trusted instead in his great wealth
  and looked for security in being wicked."

But I am like an olive tree growing in the house
of God;
  I trust in his constant love forever and ever.
I will always thank you, God, for what you
have done;
  in the presence of your people
  I will proclaim that you are good.

Ps 52:1-9

53 The Godlessness of Men

Fools say to themselves,
  "There is no God."
They are all corrupt,
  and they have done terrible things;
  there is no one who does what is right.

God looks down from heaven at mankind
  to see if there are any who are wise,
  and who worship him.
But they have all turned away;
  they are all equally bad,
Not one of them does what is right,
  not a single one.

God has rejected them,
  and so Israel will totally defeat them.

How I pray that victory
  will come to Israel from Zion.
How happy the people of Israel will be
  when God makes them prosperous again!

Ps 53:1-3, 5-6

54 A Prayer in Time of Trouble

Save me by your power, O God;
  set me free by your might!
Hear my prayer, O God;
  listen to my words!
Proud men are coming to attack me;
  cruel men are trying to kill me—
  men who do not care about God.

But God is my helper.
  The Lord is my defender.
May God use their own evil to punish my
    enemies.
  He will destroy them because he is faithful.

I will gladly offer you a sacrifice, O Lord;
  I will give you thanks
  because you are good.
You have rescued me from all my troubles,
  and I have seen my enemies defeated.
                                    Ps 54:1-7

55 Prayer of a Persecuted Man

Hear my prayer, O God;
  don't turn away from my plea!
Listen to me and answer me;
  I am worn out by my worries.
I am terrified by the threats of my enemies,
  crushed by the oppression of the wicked.
They bring trouble on me;
  they are angry with me and hate me.

I am terrified,
    and the terrors of death crush me.
I am gripped by fear and trembling;
    I am overcome with horror.
I wish I had wings like a dove.
    I would fly away and find rest.
I would fly far away
    and make my home in the desert.
I would hurry and find myself a shelter
    from the raging wind and the storm.
Confuse the speech of my enemies, O Lord!

If it were an enemy making fun of me,
    I could endure it;
if it were an opponent boasting over me,
    I could hide myself from him.
But it is you, my companion,
    my colleague and close friend.
We had intimate talks with each other
    and worshiped together in the Temple.

But I call to the Lord God for help,
    and he will save me.
Morning, noon, and night
    my complaints and groans go up to him,
    and he will hear my voice.
He will bring me safely back
    from the battles that I fight against so many
        enemies.

Leave your troubles with the Lord,
    and he will defend you;
    he never lets honest men be defeated.

Ps 55:1-9, 12-14, 16-18, 22

56 A Prayer of Trust in God

Be merciful to me, O God,
  because I am under attack;
  my enemies persecute me all the time.
All day long my opponents attack me.
  There are so many who fight against me.
When I am afraid, O Lord Almighty,
  I put my trust in you.
I trust in God and am not afraid;
  I praise him for what he has promised.
What can a mere human being do to me?

You know how troubled I am;
  you have kept a record of my tears.
  Aren't they listed in your book?
The day I call to you,
  my enemies will be turned back.
I know this: God is on my side —
  the Lord, whose promises I praise.
In him I trust, and I will not be afraid.
  What can a mere human being do to me?

O God, I will offer you what I have promised;
  I will give you my offering of thanksgiving,
because you have rescued me from death
  and kept me from defeat.
And so I walk in the presence of God,
  in the light that shines on the living.

Ps 56:1-4, 8-13

57 A Prayer for Help

Be merciful to me, O God, be merciful,
  because I come to you for safety.
In the shadow of your wings I find protection
  until the raging storms are over.

I call to God, the Most High,
to God, who supplies my every need.
He will answer from heaven and save me;
he will defeat my oppressors.
God will show me his constant love and
faithfulness.

I am surrounded by enemies,
who are like man-eating lions.
Their teeth are like spears and arrows:
their tongues are like sharp swords.

Show your greatness in the sky, O God,
and your glory over all the earth.

I have complete confidence, O God;
I will sing and praise you!
Wake up, my soul!
Wake up, my harp and lyre!
I will wake up the sun.
I will thank you, O Lord, among the
nations.
I will praise you among the peoples.
Your constant love reaches the heavens;
your faithfulness touches the skies.
Show your greatness in the sky, O God,
and your glory over all the earth.

Ps 57: 1-5, 7-11

58 A Plea for Justice

Do you rulers ever give a just decision?
Do you judge all men fairly?
No! You think only of the evil you can do,
and commit crimes of violence in the land.

Evil men go wrong all their lives;
    they tell lies from the day they are born.

They are full of poison like snakes;
    they stop up their ears like a deaf cobra,
which does not hear the voice of the snake
      charmer,
    or the chant of the clever magician.

Break the teeth of these fierce lions, O God.
May they disappear like water draining away;
    may they be crushed like weeds on a path.

The righteous will be glad when they see
    sinners punished. . . .
People will say, "The righteous are indeed
    rewarded;
    there is indeed a God who judges the
      world."   *Ps 58:1-7, 10-11*

59 A Prayer for Safety

Save me from my enemies, my God;
    protect me from those who attack me!
Save me from those evil men;
    rescue me from those murderers!

Look! They are waiting to kill me;
    cruel men are gathering against me.
It is not because of any sin or wrong I have
    done,
    nor because of any fault of mine, O Lord,
    that they hurry to their places.

Rise, Lord God Almighty, and come to my
    aid;
    see for yourself, God of Israel!

They come back in the evening,
    snarling like dogs as they go about the city.
Listen to their insults and threats.
Their tongues are like swords in their mouths,
    yet they think that no one hears them.

But you laugh at them, Lord;
    you mock all the heathen.
I have confidence in your strength;
    you are my refuge, O God.
My God loves me and will come to me;
    he will let me see my enemies defeated.

I will sing about your strength;
    every morning I will sing aloud of your
        constant love.
You have been a refuge for me,
    a shelter in my time of trouble.
I will praise you, my defender.
    My refuge is God,
    the God who loves me.

Ps 59:1-10, 16-17

60 A Prayer for Deliverance

You have rejected us, God, and defeated us;
    you have been angry with us—but now turn
        back to us.
You have made the land tremble, and you
        have cut it open;
    now heal its wounds, because it is falling
        apart.
You have made your people suffer greatly;
    we stagger around as though we were
        drunk.

You have warned those who have reverence
  for you,
    so that they might escape destruction.
Save us by your might; answer our prayer,
    so that the people you love may be rescued.
Ps 60:1-5

61 A Prayer for Protection

Hear my cry, O God;
  listen to my prayer!
In despair and far from home
  I call to you!

Take me to a safe refuge,
    for you are my protector,
    my strong defense against my enemies.

Let me live in your sanctuary all my life;
    let me find safety under your wings.
You have heard my promises, O God,
    and you have given me what belongs to
      those who honor you.

Add many years to the king's life;
    let him live on and on!
May he rule forever in your presence, O
  God;
    protect him with your constant love and
      faithfulness.

So I will always sing praises to you,
    as I offer you daily what I have promised.
Ps 61:1-8

62 Confidence in God's Protection

I wait patiently for God to save me;
   I depend on him alone.
He alone protects and saves me;
   he is my defender,
   and I shall never be defeated.

How much longer will all of you attack a man
   who is no stronger than a broken-down
      fence?
You only want to bring him down from his
     place of honor;
   you take pleasure in lies.
You speak words of blessing,
   but in your heart you curse him.

I depend on God alone;
   I put my hope in him.
He alone protects and saves me;
   he is my defender,
   and I shall never be defeated.
My salvation and honor depend on God;
   he is my strong protector;
   he is my shelter.

Trust in God at all times, my people.
   Tell him all your troubles,
   for he is our refuge.

More than once I have heard God say
   that power belongs to him
   and that his love is constant.
You yourself, O Lord, reward everyone
   according to his deeds.

Ps 62:1-8, 11-12

63 Longing for God

O God, you are my God,
    and I long for you.
My whole being desires you;
    like a dry, worn-out, and waterless land,
    my soul is thirsty for you.
Let me see you in the sanctuary;
    let me see how mighty and glorious you are.
Your constant love is better than life itself,
    and so I will praise you.
I will give you thanks as long as I live;
    I will raise my hands to you in prayer.
My soul will feast and be satisfied.
    and I will sing glad songs of praise to you.

As I lie in bed, I remember you;
    all night long I think of you,
    because you have always been my help.
In the shadow of your wings I sing for joy.
I cling to you,
    and your hand keeps me safe.

Ps 63:1-8

64 A Prayer for Protection
Against Enemies

I am in trouble, God—listen to my prayer!
    I am afraid of my enemies—save my life!
Protect me from the plots of the wicked,
    from mobs of evil men.
They sharpen their tongues like swords
    and aim cruel words like arrows.

But God shoots his arrows at them,
  and suddenly they are wounded.
He will destroy them because of their words;
  all who see them will shake their heads.
They will all be afraid;
  they will think about what God has done
  and tell about his deeds.
All righteous people will rejoice
  because of what the Lord has done.
They will find safety in him;
  all good people will praise him.

Ps 64:1-3, 7-10

65 A Hymn of Praise

O God, it is right for us to praise you in Zion
  and keep our promises to you,
  because you answer prayers.
People everywhere will come to you
  on account of their sins.
Our faults defeat us,
  but you forgive them.
Happy are those whom you choose,
  whom you bring to live in your sanctuary.
We shall be satisfied with the good things of
    your house,
  the blessings of your sacred Temple.

You answer us by giving us victory,
  and you do wonderful things to save us.
People all over the world
  and across the distant seas trust in you.
You set the mountains in place by your
    strength,
  showing your mighty power.

You calm the roar of the seas
  and the noise of the waves;
    you calm the uproar of the peoples.
The whole world stands in awe
  of the great things that you have done.
Your deeds bring shouts of joy
  from one end of the earth to the other.

You show your care for the land by sending
    rain;
  you make it rich and fertile.
You fill the streams with water;
  you provide the earth with crops.

What a rich harvest your goodness provides!
  Wherever you go there is plenty.
The pastures are filled with flocks;
  the hillsides are full of joy.
The fields are covered with sheep;
  the valleys are full of wheat.
Everything shouts and sings for joy.

Ps 65:1-9, 11-13

66 A Song of Praise and Thanksgiving

Praise God with shouts of joy, all people!
Sing to the glory of his name;
  offer him glorious praise!
Say to God, "How wonderful are the things
    you do!
  Your power is so great
  that your enemies bow down in fear before
    you.
Everyone on earth worships you;
  they sing praises to you,
  they sing praises to your name."

Come and see what God has done,
   his wonderful acts among men.
He changed the sea into dry land;
   our ancestors crossed the river on foot.
There we rejoiced because of what he did.
He rules forever by his might
   and keeps his eyes on the nations.
   Let no rebels rise against him.
Praise our God, all nations;
   let your praise be heard.
He has kept us alive
   and has not allowed us to fall.

You have put us to the test, God;
   as silver is purified by fire,
   so you have tested us.
You let us fall into a trap
   and placed heavy burdens on our backs.
You let our enemies trample us;
   we went through fire and flood,
but now you have brought us to a place of
      safety.

Come and listen, all who honor God,
   and I will tell you what he has done for me.
I cried to him for help;
   I praised him with songs.
If I had ignored my sins,
   the Lord would not have listened to me.
But God has indeed heard me;
   he has listened to my prayer.

I praise God,
   because he did not reject my prayer
   or keep back his constant love from me.

Ps 66:1-12, 16-20

67 A Song of Thanksgiving

God, be merciful to us and bless us;
   look on us with kindness,
so that the whole world may know your will;
   so that all nations may know your salvation.

May the peoples praise you, O God;
   may all the peoples praise you!

May the nations be glad and sing for joy,
   because you judge the peoples with justice
   and guide every nation on earth.

May the peoples praise you, O God;
   may all the peoples praise you!

The land has produced its harvest;
   God, our God, has blessed us.
God has blessed us;
   may all people everywhere honor him.

Ps 67:1-7

68 A National Song of Triumph

Sing to God, sing praises to his name;
   prepare a way for him who rides on the
      clouds.
   His name is the Lord—be glad in his
      presence!

God, who lives in his sacred Temple,
   cares for orphans and protects widows.
He gives the lonely a home to live in
   and leads prisoners out into happy freedom,
   but rebels will have to live in a desolate
      land.

O God, when you led your people,
   when you marched across the desert,
the earth shook, and the sky poured down
      rain,
      because of the coming of the God of Sinai,
      the coming of the God of Israel;
You caused abundant rain to fall
      and restored your worn-out land;
your people made their home there;
      in your goodness you provided for the poor.

Praise the Lord,
      who carries our burdens day after day;
      he is the God who saves us.

Our God is a God who saves;
      he is the Lord, our Lord,
      who rescues us from death.

O God, your march of triumph is seen by all,
      the procession of God, my king, into his
         sanctuary.
The singers are in front, the musicians are
         behind,
      in between are the girls beating the
         tambourines.
"Praise God in the meeting of his people;
      praise the Lord, all you descendants of
         Jacob!"

Show your power, O God,
      the power you have used on our behalf
      from your Temple in Jerusalem,
      where kings bring gifts to you.

Sing to God, kingdoms of the world,
    sing praise to the Lord,
    to him who rides in the sky,
    the ancient sky.
Listen to him shout with a mighty roar.
Proclaim God's power;
    his majesty is over Israel,
    his might is in the skies.
How awesome is God as he comes from his
      sanctuary—
    the God of Israel!
He gives strength and power to his people.

Praise God!

Ps 68:4-10, 19-20, 24-26, 28-29, 32-35

69 A Cry for Help

Save me, O God!
    The water is up to my neck;
I am sinking in deep mud,
    and there is no solid ground;
I am out in deep water,
    and the waves are about to drown me.
I am worn out from calling for help,
    and my throat is aching.
I have strained my eyes,
    looking for your help.

Those who hate me for no reason
    are more numerous than the hairs on my
      head.
My enemies tell lies against me;
    they are strong and want to kill me.

Don't let me bring shame on those who trust
   in you,
      Sovereign Lord Almighty!
Don't let me bring disgrace to those who
      worship you,
      O God of Israel!
It is for your sake that I have been insulted
   and that I am covered with shame.

As for me, I will pray to you, Lord;
   answer me, God, at a time you choose.
Answer me because of your great love,
   because you keep your promise to save.
Save me from sinking in the mud;
   keep me safe from my enemies,
   safe from the deep water.
Don't let the flood come over me;
   don't let me drown in the depths
   or sink into the grave.

Answer me, Lord, in the goodness of your
      constant love;
   in your great compassion turn to me!
Don't hide yourself from your servant;
   I am in great trouble—answer me now!
Come to me and save me;
   rescue me from my enemies.

You know how I am insulted,
   how I am disgraced and dishonored;
   you see all my enemies.
Insults have broken my heart,
   and I am in despair.
I had hoped for sympathy, but there was none;
   for comfort, but I found none.

When I was hungry, they gave me poison;
  when I was thirsty, they offered me
    vinegar.

I am in pain and despair;
  lift me up, O God, and save me!

I will praise God with a song;
  I will proclaim his greatness by giving
    thanks.

Ps 69:1-4, 6-7, 13-21, 29-30

70 A Prayer for Help

Save me, O God!
  Lord, help me now!
May those who try to kill me
  be defeated and confused.
May those who are happy because of my
    troubles
  be turned back and disgraced.
May those who make fun of me
  be dismayed by their defeat.

May all who come to you
  be glad and joyful.
May all who are thankful for your salvation
  always say, "How great is God!"

I am weak and helpless;
  come to me quickly, O God.
You are my savior and my Lord—
  hurry to my aid!

Ps 70:1-5

71 An Old Man's Prayer

Lord, I have come to you for protection;
    never let me be defeated!
Because you are righteous, help me and rescue
    me.
    Listen to me and save me!
Be my secure shelter
    and a strong fortress to protect me;
    you are my refuge and defense.

My God, rescue me from wicked men,
    from the power of cruel and evil men.
Sovereign Lord, I put my hope in you;
    I have trusted in you since I was young.
I have relied on you all my life;
    you have protected me since the day I was
      born.
    I will always praise you.

My life has been an example to many,
    because you have been my strong defender.
All day long I praise you
    and proclaim your glory.
Do not reject me now that I am old;
    do not abandon me now that I am feeble.

I will always put my hope in you;
    I will praise you more and more.
I will tell of your goodness;
    all day long I will speak of your salvation,
    though it is more than I can understand.
I will praise your power, Sovereign Lord;
    I will proclaim your goodness, yours alone.

You have taught me ever since I was young,
　　and I still tell of your wonderful acts.
Now that I am old and my hair is gray,
　　do not abandon me, O God!
Be with me while I proclaim your power and
　　　　might
　　to all generations to come.

Your righteousness, God, reaches the skies.
　　You have done great things;
　　there is no one like you.
You have sent troubles and suffering on me,
　　but you will restore my strength;
　　you will keep me from the grave.
You will make me greater than ever;
　　you will comfort me again.

I will indeed praise you with the harp;
　　I will praise your faithfulness, my God.
On my harp I will play hymns to you,
　　the Holy One of Israel.
I will shout for joy as I play for you;
　　with my whole being I will sing
　　because you have saved me.
I will speak of your righteousness all day long,
　　because those who tried to harm me
　　have been defeated and disgraced.

Ps 71:1-9, 14-24

72 A Prayer for the King

May the land enjoy prosperity;
　　may it experience righteousness.
May the king judge the poor fairly;
　　may he help the needy
　　and defeat their oppressors.

May your people worship you as long as the
    sun shines,
  as long as the moon gives light for ages to
  come.

May the king be like rain on the fields,
  like showers falling on the land.
May righteousness flourish in his lifetime,
  and may prosperity last as long as the moon
  gives light.

His kingdom will reach from sea to sea,
  from the Euphrates to the ends of the earth.
The peoples of the desert will bow down
    before him;
  his enemies will throw themselves to the
  ground.
The kings of Spain and of the islands will offer
    him gifts;
  the kings of Arabia and Ethiopia will bring
  him offerings.
All kings will bow down before him;
  all nations will serve him.

May the king's name never be forgotten;
  may his fame last as long as the sun.
May all nations praise him,
  may they ask God to bless them
  and may they wish happiness for the king.

Praise the Lord, the God of Israel!
He alone does these wonderful things.
Praise his glorious name forever!
May his glory fill the whole world.

    Amen! Amen!

Ps 72:3-11, 17-19

Book Three

73 The Justice of God

God is indeed good to Israel,
    to those who have pure hearts.
But I had nearly lost confidence;
    my faith was almost gone
because I was jealous of the proud
    when I saw that things go well for the
        wicked.

Is it for nothing, then, that I have kept myself
        pure
    and have not committed sin?
O God, you have made me suffer all day long;
    every morning you have punished me.

I tried to think this problem through,
    but it was too difficult for me
until I went into your Temple.
Then I understood what will happen to the
        wicked.

You will put them in slippery places
    and make them fall to destruction!
They are like a dream that goes away in the
        morning;
    when you rouse yourself, O Lord, they
        disappear.

When my thoughts were bitter
    and my feelings were hurt,
I was as stupid as an animal;
    I did not understand you.
Yet I always stay close to you,
    and you hold me by the hand.

You guide me with your instruction
and at the end you will receive me with
honor.
What else do I have in heaven but you?
Since I have you, what else could I want on
earth?
My mind and my body may grow weak,
but God is my strength;
he is all I ever need.

Ps 73:1-3, 13-14, 16-18, 20-26

74 A Prayer for National Deliverance

Why have you abandoned us like this, O God?
Will you be angry with your own people
forever?
Remember your people, whom you chose for
yourself long ago,
whom you brought out of slavery to be your
own tribe.
Remember Mount Zion, where once you
lived.
Walk over these total ruins;
our enemies have destroyed everything in
the Temple.

All our sacred symbols are gone;
there are no prophets left,
and no one knows how long this will last.
How long, O God, will our enemies laugh at
you?
Will they insult your name forever?
Why have you refused to help us?
Why do you keep your hands behind you?

But you have been our king from the
    beginning, O God;
      you have saved us many times.

But remember, O Lord, that your enemies
    laugh at you,
      that they are godless and despise you.
Don't abandon your helpless people to their
    cruel enemies;
      don't forget your persecuted people!

Remember the covenant you made with us.
    There is violence in every dark corner of
    the land.
Don't let the oppressed be put to shame;
    let those poor and needy people praise you.

Rouse yourself, God, and defend your cause!
Ps 74:1-3, 9-12, 18-22

75 God the Judge

We give thanks to you, O God, we give
    thanks to you!
    We proclaim how great you are
    and tell of the wonderful things you have
    done.

"I have set a time for judgment," says God,
    "and I will judge with fairness.
Though every living creature tremble
    and the earth itself be shaken,
    I will keep its foundations firm.
I tell the wicked not to be arrogant;
    I tell them to stop their boasting."

Judgment does not come from the east or
     from the west,
  from the north or from the south;
it is God who is the judge,
  condemning some and acquitting others.
The Lord holds a cup in his hand,
  filled with the strong wine of his anger.

He pours it out, and all the wicked drink it;
  they drink it down to the last drop.

But I will never stop speaking of the God of
     Jacob
  or singing praises to him.
He will break the power of the wicked,
  but the power of the righteous will be
     increased.

Ps 75:1-10

76 God the Victor

God is known in Judah;
  his name is honored in Israel.
He has his home in Jerusalem;
  he lives on Mount Zion.
There he broke the arrows of the enemy,
  their shields and swords, yes, all their
     weapons.

How glorious you are, O God!
  How majestic, as you return from the
     mountains
  where you defeated your foes.

Their brave soldiers have been stripped of all
    they had
   and now are sleeping the sleep of death;
   all their strength and skill was useless.

But you, Lord, are feared by all.
   No one can stand in your presence
   when you are angry.
You made your judgment known from heaven;
   the world was afraid and kept silent,
when you rose up to pronounce judgment,
   to save all the oppressed on earth.

Men's anger only results in more praise for
    you;
   those who survive the wars will keep your
   festivals.

Give the Lord your God what you promised
    him;
   bring gifts to him, all you nearby nations.
Ps 76:1-5, 7-11

77 Comfort in Time of Distress

I cry aloud to God;
   I cry aloud, and he hears me.
In times of trouble I pray to the Lord;
   all night long I lift my hands in prayer,
   but I cannot find comfort.
When I think of God, I sigh;
   when I meditate, I feel discouraged.

He keeps me awake all night;
   I am so worried that I cannot speak.
I think of days gone by
   and remember years of long ago.
I spend the night in deep thought;
   I meditate, and this is what I ask myself:
"Will the Lord always reject us?
   Will he never again be pleased with us?
Has he stopped loving us?
   Does his promise no longer stand?
Has God forgotten to be merciful?
   Has anger taken the place of his
      compassion?"
Then I said, "What hurts me most is this—
   that God is no longer powerful."

I will remember your great deeds, Lord;
   I will recall the wonders you did in the past.
I will think about all that you have done;
   I will meditate on all your mighty acts.

Everything you do, O God, is holy.
   No god is as great as you.
You are the God who works miracles;
   you showed your might among the nations.
By your power you saved your people,
   the descendants of Jacob and Joseph.
                                          Ps 77:1-15

78 God and His People

Listen, my people, to my teaching,
  and pay attention to what I say.
I am going to use wise sayings
  and explain mysteries from the past,
  things we have heard and known,
  things that our fathers told us.
We will not keep them from our children;
  we will tell the next generation
  about the Lord's power and his great deeds
  and the wonderful things he has done.

He gave laws to the people of Israel
  and commandments to the descendants
    of Jacob.
He instructed our ancestors
  to teach his laws to their children,
so that the next generation might learn them
  and in turn should tell their children.
In this way they also will put their trust in God
  and not forget what he has done,
  but always obey his commandments.

He divided the sea and took them through it;
  he made the waters stand like walls.
By day he led them with a cloud
  and all night long with the light of a fire.
He split rocks open in the desert
  and gave them water from the depths.
He caused a stream to come out of the rock
    and made water flow like a river.

He gave them grain from heaven,
  by sending down manna for them to eat.

So they ate the food of angels,
    and God gave them all they wanted.
Then he led his people out like a shepherd
    and guided them through the desert.
He led them safely, and they were not afraid;
    but the sea came rolling over their enemies.
He brought them to his holy land,
    to the mountains which he himself
        conquered.

He chose his servant David;
    he took him from the pastures,
    where he looked after his flocks,
    and he made him king of Israel,
    the shepherd of the people of God.
        Ps 78:1-7, 13-16, 24-25, 52-54, 70-71

79 A Prayer for the Nation's Deliverance

O God, the heathen have invaded your land.
They have desecrated your holy Temple
and left Jerusalem in ruins.

Lord, will you be angry with us forever?
    Will your anger continue to burn like fire?
Turn your anger on the nations that do not
        worship you,
    on the people who do not pray to you.
For they have killed your people;
    they have ruined your country.

Do not punish us for the sins of our ancestors.
    Have mercy on us now;
    we have lost all hope.

Help us, O God, and save us;
  rescue us and forgive our sins
  for the sake of your own honor.
Why should the nations ask us,
  "Where is your God?"
Let us see you punish the nations
  for shedding the blood of your servants.

Listen to the groans of the prisoners,
  and by your great power free
    those who are condemned to die.
Lord, pay the other nations back seven times
  for all the insults they have hurled at you.
Then we, your people, the sheep of your flock,
  will thank you forever
  and praise you for all time to come.

Ps 79:1, 5-13

80 A Prayer for the Nation's Restoration

Listen to us, O Shepherd of Israel;
  hear us, leader of your flock.
Show us your strength;
  come and save us!

How much longer, Lord God Almighty,
  will you be angry with your people's
    prayers?
You have given us sorrow to eat,
  a large cup of tears to drink.
You let the surrounding nations fight over our
    land;
  our enemies insult us.

Bring us back, Almighty God!
   Show us your mercy, and we will be saved!

You brought a grapevine out of Egypt;
   you drove out other nations and planted it
      in their land.

You cleared a place for it to grow;
   its roots went deep, and it spread out over
      the whole land.
It covered the hills with its shade;
   its branches overshadowed the giant cedars.
It extended its branches to the Mediterranean
      Sea
   and as far as the Euphrates River.
Why did you break down the fences around it?
   Now anyone passing by can steal its grapes;
   wild hogs trample it down,
   and wild animals feed on it.

Turn to us, Almighty God!
   Look down from heaven at us;
   come and save your people!
Come and save this grapevine that you
      planted,
   this young vine you made grow so strong!

Preserve and protect the people you have
      chosen,
   the nation you made so strong.
We will never turn away from you again;
   keep us alive, and we will praise you.

Ps 80:1-2, 4-15, 17-18

81 A Song for a Festival

Shout for joy to God our defender;
  sing praise to the God of Jacob!
Start the music and beat the tambourines;
  play pleasant music on the harps and the
    lyres.
Blow the trumpet for the festival.

I hear an unknown voice saying,
"I took the burdens off your backs;
  I let you put down your loads of bricks.
When you were in trouble, you called to me,
    and I saved you.
  From my hiding place in the storm, I
    answered you.
  I put you to the test at the springs of
    Meribah.
Listen, my people, to my warning;
  Israel, how I wish you would listen to me!
You must never worship another god.
I am the Lord your God,
  who brought you out of the land of Egypt.
Open your mouth, and I will feed you.

"But my people would not listen to me;
  Israel would not obey me.
  So I let them go their stubborn ways
    and do whatever they wanted.
How I wish my people would listen to me;
  how I wish they would obey me!
I would quickly defeat their enemies
  and conquer all their foes.

Those who hate me would bow in fear before
    me;
    their punishment would last forever.
But I would feed you with the finest wheat
    and satisfy you with wild honey."

Ps 81:1-3, 6-16

82 God the Supreme Ruler

God presides in the heavenly council;
    in the assembly of the gods he gives his
        decision:
"You must stop judging unjustly;
    you must no longer be partial to the wicked!
Defend the rights of the poor and the orphans;
    be fair to the needy and the helpless.
Rescue them from the power of evil men.

"How ignorant you are! How stupid!
    You are completely corrupt,
    and justice has disappeared from the world.
'You are gods,' I said;
    'all of you are sons of the Most High.'
But you will die like men;
    your life will end like that of any prince."

Come, O God, and rule the world;
    all the nations are yours.

Ps 82:1-8

83 A Prayer Against Israel's Enemies

O God, do not keep silent;
    do not be still, do not be quiet!
Look! Your enemies are in revolt,
    and those who hate you are rebelling.

They are making secret plans against your
  people;
  they are plotting against those you protect.
"Come," they say, "let us destroy their nation,
  so that Israel will be forgotten forever."

They agree on their plan
  and form an alliance against you.

Scatter them like dust, O God,
  like straw blown away by the wind.
As fire burns the forest,
  as flames set the hills on fire,
chase them away with your storm
  and terrify them with your fierce winds.
Cover their faces with shame, O Lord,
  and make them acknowledge your power.
May they be defeated and terrified forever;
  may they die in complete disgrace.
May they know that you alone are the Lord,
  supreme ruler over all the earth.

Ps 83:1-5, 13-18

84 Longing for God's House

How I love your Temple, Lord Almighty!
  How I want to be there!
  I long to be in the Lord's Temple.

With my whole being I sing for joy
  to the living God.
Even the sparrows have built a nest,
  and the swallows have their own home;

they keep their young near your altars,
    Lord Almighty, my king and my God.
How happy are those who live in your Temple,
    always singing praise to you.

How happy are those whose strength comes
      from you,
    who are eager to make the pilgrimage to
      Mount Zion.
As they pass through the dry valley of Baca,
    it becomes a place of springs;
    the early rain fills it with pools.
They grow stronger as they go;
    they will see the God of gods on Zion.

One day spent in your Temple
    is better than a thousand anywhere else;

I would rather stand at the gate of the house of
      my God
    than live in the homes of the wicked.
The Lord is our protector and glorious king,
    blessing us with kindness and honor.
He does not refuse any good thing
    to those who do what is right.
Almighty God, how happy are those who trust
      in you!

Ps 84:1-7, 10-12

85 A Prayer for the Nation's Welfare

Lord, you have been merciful to your land;
    you have made Israel prosperous again.
You have forgiven your people's sins
    and pardoned all their wrongs.

You stopped being angry with them
and held back your furious rage.

Bring us back, O God our saviour,
and stop being displeased with us!
Will you be angry with us forever?
Will your anger never cease?
Make us strong again,
and we, your people, will praise you.
Show us your constant love, O Lord,
and give us your saving help.

I am listening to what the Lord God is saying;
he promises peace to us, his own people,
if we do not go back to our foolish ways.
Surely he is ready to save those who honor
him,
and his saving presence will remain in our
land.

Love and faithfulness will meet;
righteousness and peace will embrace.
Man's loyalty will reach up from the earth,
and God's righteousness will look down
from heaven.
The Lord will make us prosperous,
and our land will produce rich harvests.
Righteousness will go before the Lord
and prepare the path for him.

Ps 85:1-13

86 A Prayer for Help

Listen to me, Lord, and answer me,
    for I am helpless and weak.
Save me from death, because I am loyal to
        you;
    save me, for I am your servant and I trust in
        you.

You are my God, so be merciful to me;
    I pray to you all day long.
Make your servant glad, O Lord,
    because my prayers go up to you.
You are good to us and forgiving,
    full of constant love for all who pray to you.

Listen, Lord, to my prayer;
    hear my cries for help.
I call to you in times of trouble,
    because you answer my prayers.

There is no god like you, O Lord,
    not one has done what you have done.
All the nations that you have created
    will come and bow down to you;
    they will praise your greatness.
You are mighty and do wonderful things;
    you alone are God.

Teach me, Lord, what you want me to do,
    and I will obey you faithfully;
    teach me to serve you with complete
        devotion.
I will praise you with all my heart, O Lord
        my God;
    I will proclaim your greatness forever.

How great is your constant love for me!
    You have saved me from the grave itself.

You, O Lord, are a merciful and loving God,
    always patient, always kind and faithful.
Turn to me and have mercy on me;
    strengthen me and save me,
    because I serve you just as my mother did.
Show me proof of your goodness, Lord;
    those who hate me will be ashamed
    when they see that you have given me
        comfort and help.   *Ps 86:1-13, 15-17*

87 In Praise of Jerusalem

The Lord built his city on the sacred hill;
    more than any other place in Israel
    he loves the city of Jerusalem.
Listen, city of God,
    to the wonderful things he says about you:

"I will include Egypt and Babylonia
    when I list the nations that obey me;
the people of Philistia, Tyre, and Sudan
    I will number among the inhabitants of
        Jerusalem."

Of Zion it will be said
    that all nations belong there
    and that the Almighty will make her strong.
The Lord will write a list of the peoples
    and include them all as citizens of
        Jerusalem.
They dance and sing,
    "In Zion is the source of all our blessings."
                                    Ps 87:1-7

88 A Cry for Help

Lord God, my savior, I cry out all day,
and at night I come before you.
Hear my prayer;
listen to my cry for help!

So many troubles have fallen on me
that I am close to death.
I am like all others who are about to die;
all my strength is gone.
Your anger lies heavy on me,
and I am crushed beneath its waves.

You have caused my friends to abandon me;
you have made me repulsive to them.
I am closed in and cannot escape;
my eyes are weak from suffering.
Lord, every day I call to you
and lift my hands to you in prayer.

Do you perform miracles for the dead?
Do they rise up and praise you?
Is your constant love spoken of in the grave
or your faithfulness in the place of
destruction?
Are your miracles seen in that place of
darkness
or your goodness in the land of the
forgotten?

Lord, I call to you for help;
every morning I pray to you.
Why do you reject me, Lord?
Why do you turn away from me?

Ever since I was young, I have suffered and
    been near death;
  I am worn out from the burden of your
    punishments.
Your furious anger crushes me;
  your terrible attacks destroy me.
All day long they surround me like a flood;
  they close in on me from every side.
You have made even my closest friends
    abandon me,
  and darkness is my only companion.

Ps 88:1-4, 7-18

89 A Hymn to God's Faithfulness

O Lord, I will always sing of your constant
    love;
  I will proclaim your faithfulness forever.
I know that your love will last for all time,
  that your faithfulness is as permanent as the
    sky.
You said, "I have made a covenant with the
    man I chose;
  I have promised my servant David,
'A descendant of yours will always be king;
  I will preserve your dynasty forever.' "

The heavens sing of the wonderful things
    you do;
  the holy ones sing of your faithfulness,
    Lord.
No one in heaven is like you, Lord;
  none of the heavenly beings is your equal.
You are feared in the council of the holy ones;
  they all stand in awe of you.

Lord God Almighty, none is as mighty as you;
   in all things you are faithful, O Lord.

Your kingdom is founded on righteousness
      and justice;
   love and faithfulness are shown in all you do.
How happy are the people who worship you
      with songs,
   who live in the light of your kindness!
Because of you they rejoice all day long,
   and they praise you for your goodness.
You give us great victories;
   in your love you make us triumphant.
You, O Lord, chose our protector;
   you, the Holy God of Israel, gave us our
      king.

God's Promise to David

In a vision long ago you said to your faithful
      servants,
   "I have given help to a famous soldier;
   I have given the throne to one I chose from
      the people.
I have made my servant David king
   by anointing him with holy oil.
My strength will always be with him,
   my power will make him strong.
His enemies will never succeed against him;
   the wicked will not defeat him.
I will love him and be loyal to him;
   I will make him always victorious.
I will extend his kingdom
   from the Mediterranean to the Euphrates
      River.

He will say to me,
'You are my father and my God;
you are my protector and savior.'
I will make him my first-born son,
the greatest of all kings.
I will always keep my promise to him,
and my covenant with him will last forever.
His dynasty will be as permanent as the sky;
a descendant of his will always be king."

Ps 89:1-8, 14-22, 24-29

Book Four

90 Of God and Man

O Lord, you have always been our home.
Before you created the hills
    or brought the world into being,
    you were eternally God,
    and will be God forever.

You tell man to return to what he was;
    you change him back to dust.
A thousand years to you are like one day;
    they are like yesterday, already gone,
    like a short hour in the night.
You carry us away like a flood;
    we last no longer than a dream.
We are like weeds that sprout in the morning,
    that grow and burst into bloom,
    then dry up and die in the evening.

Seventy years is all we have—
    eighty years, if we are strong;
yet all they bring us is trouble and sorrow;
    life is soon over, and we are gone.

Teach us how short our life is,
    so that we may become wise.
    Have pity, O Lord, on your servants!

Fill us each morning with your constant love,
    so that we may sing and be glad all our life.
Give us now as much happiness as the sadness
      you gave us
    during all our years of misery.
Let us, your servants, see your mighty deeds;
    let our descendants see your glorious might.
Lord our God, may your blessings be with us.
    Give us success in all we do!   *Ps 90:1-6, 10, 12, 14-17*

91 God Our Protector

Whoever goes to the Lord for safety,
   whoever remains under the protection of
      the Almighty,
can say to him,
   "You are my defender and protector.
   You are my God; in you I trust."
He will cover you with his wings;
   you will be safe in his care;
   his faithfulness will protect and defend you.
You need not fear any dangers at night
   or sudden attacks during the day
   or the plagues that strike in the dark
   or the evils that kill in daylight.

A thousand may fall dead beside you,
   ten thousand all around you,
   but you will not be harmed.
You will look and see
   how the wicked are punished.

You have made the Lord your defender,
   the Most High your protector,
and so no disaster will strike you,
   no violence will come near your home.
God will put his angels in charge of you
   to protect you wherever you go.
They will hold you up with their hands
   to keep you from hurting your feet on the
      stones.

God says, "I will save those who love me
   and will protect those who acknowledge me
      as Lord.

When they call to me, I will answer them;
when they are in trouble, I will be with
them.
I will rescue them and honor them.
I will reward them with long life;
I will save them."

Ps 91:1-2, 4-12, 14-16

92 A Song of Praise

How good it is to give thanks to you, O Lord,
to sing in your honor, O Most High God,
to proclaim your constant love every morning
and your faithfulness every night,
with the music of stringed instruments
and with melody on the harp.
Your mighty deeds, O Lord, make me glad;
because of what you have done, I sing for
joy.

How great are your actions, Lord!
How deep are your thoughts!
This is something a fool cannot know;
a stupid man cannot understand:
the wicked may grow like weeds,
those who do wrong may prosper;
yet they will be totally destroyed,
because you, Lord, are supreme forever.

The righteous will flourish like palm trees;
they will grow like the cedars of Lebanon.

They are like trees planted in the house of the
    Lord,
    that flourish in the Temple of our God,
    that still bear fruit in old age
    and are always green and strong.
This shows that the Lord is just,
    that there is no wrong in my protector.

Ps 92:1-8, 12-15

93 God the King

The Lord is king.
    He is clothed with majesty and strength.
The earth is set firmly in place
    and cannot be moved.
Your throne, O Lord, has been firm from
    the beginning,
    and you existed before time began.

The ocean depths raise their voice, O Lord;
    they raise their voice and roar.
The Lord rules supreme in heaven,
    greater than the roar of the ocean,
    more powerful than the waves of the sea.

Your laws are eternal, Lord,
    and your Temple is holy indeed,
    forever and ever.

Ps 93:1-5

94 God the Judge of All

How much longer will the wicked be glad?
    How much longer, Lord? . . .

They crush your people, Lord;
    they oppress those who belong to you.

They kill widows and orphans,
  and murder the strangers who live in our
  land.
They say, "The Lord does not see us;
  the God of Israel does not notice."

My people, how can you be such stupid fools?
  When will you ever learn?
God made our ears—can't he hear?
  He made our eyes—can't he see?
He scolds the nations—won't he punish
  them?
  He is the teacher of all men—hasn't he any
  knowledge?
The Lord knows what they think;
  he knows how senseless their reasoning is.

Lord, how happy is the person you instruct,
  the one to whom you teach your law!
You give him rest from days of trouble
  until a pit is dug to trap the wicked.
The Lord will not abandon his people;
  he will not desert those who belong to him.
Justice will again be found in the courts,
  and all righteous people will support it.

Who stood up for me against the wicked?
  Who took my side against the evildoers?
If the Lord had not helped me,
  I would have gone quickly to the land of
  silence.
I said, "I am falling";
  but your constant love, O Lord, held me up.
Whenever I am anxious and worried,
  you comfort me and make me glad.

Ps 94:3-19

95 Come, Let Us Praise the Lord

Come, let us praise the Lord!
   Let us sing for joy to God, who protects us!
Let us come before him with thanksgiving
   and sing joyful songs of praise.
For the Lord is a mighty God,
   a mighty king over all the gods.
He rules over the whole earth,
   from the deepest caves to the highest hills.
He rules over the sea, which he made;
   the land also, which he himself formed.

Come, let us bow down and worship him;
   let us kneel before the Lord, our Maker!
He is our God;
   we are the people he cares for,
   the flock for which he provides.

Ps 95:1-7

96 God the Supreme King

Sing a new song to the Lord!
   Sing to the Lord, all the world!
Sing to the Lord, and praise him!
   Proclaim every day the good news that he
      has saved us.
Proclaim his glory to the nations,
   his mighty acts to all peoples.

The Lord is great and is to be highly praised;
   he is to be honored more than all the gods.
The gods of all other nations are only idols,
   but the Lord created the heavens.
Glory and majesty surround him;
   power and beauty fill his Temple.

Praise the Lord, all people on earth;
     praise his glory and might.
Praise the Lord's glorious name;
     bring an offering and come into his Temple.
Bow down before the Holy One when he
          appears;
     tremble before him, all the earth!

Say to all the nations, "The Lord is king!
     The earth is set firmly in place and cannot
          be moved;
     he will judge the peoples with justice."
Be glad, earth and sky!
     Roar, sea, and every creature in you;
     be glad, fields, and everything in you!
The trees in the woods will shout for joy
     when the Lord comes to rule the earth.
He will rule the peoples of the world
     with justice and fairness.

Ps 96:1-13

97 God the Supreme Ruler

The Lord is king! Earth, be glad!
     Rejoice, you islands of the seas!
Clouds and darkness surround him;
     he rules with righteousness and justice.
His lightning lights up the world;
     the earth sees it and trembles.
The hills melt like wax before the Lord,
     before the Lord of all the earth.
The heavens proclaim his righteousness,
     and all the nations see his glory.

Everyone who worships idols is put to shame;
   all the gods bow down before the Lord.

The people of Zion are glad,
   and the cities of Judah rejoice
   because of your judgments, O Lord.
Lord Almighty, you are ruler of all the earth;
   you are much greater than all the gods.

The Lord loves those who hate evil;
   he protects the lives of his people;
   he rescues them from the power of the
      wicked.
Light shines on the righteous,
   and gladness on the good.
All you that are righteous be glad
   because of what the Lord has done!
Remember what the holy God has done,
   and give thanks to him.

Ps 97:1-2, 4-12

98 God the Ruler of the World

Sing a new song to the Lord;
   he has done wonderful things!
By his own power and holy strength
   he has won the victory.
The Lord announced his victory;
   he made his saving power known to the
      nations.
He kept his promise to the people of Israel
   with loyalty and constant love for them.
All people everywhere have seen the victory
   of our God.

Sing for joy to the Lord, all the earth;
  praise him with songs and shouts of joy!
Sing praises to the Lord!
  Play music on the harps!
Blow trumpets and horns,
  and shout for joy to the Lord, our king.

Roar, sea, and every creature in you;
  sing, earth, and all who live on you!
Clap your hands, you rivers;
  you hills, sing together with joy before the
    Lord,
  because he comes to rule the earth.
He will rule the peoples of the world
  with justice and fairness.

Ps 98:1-9

99 The Lord Is King

The Lord is king. . . .
He sits on his throne above the winged
    creatures. . . .
The Lord is mighty in Zion;
  he is supreme over all the nations.
Everyone will praise his great and majestic
    name.
  Holy is he!

Mighty king, you love what is right;
  you have established justice in Israel;
  you have brought righteousness and
    fairness.
Praise the Lord our God;
  worship before his throne!
  Holy is he!

Moses and Aaron were his priests,
  and Samuel was one who prayed to him;
  they called to the Lord, and he answered
    them.
He spoke to them from the pillar of cloud;
  they obeyed the laws and commands that he
    gave them.

O Lord, our God, you answered your people;
  you showed them that you are a God who
    forgives,
  even though you punished them for their
    sins.
Praise the Lord our God,
  and worship at his sacred hill!
The Lord our God is holy.

Ps 99:1-9

100 A Hymn of Praise

Sing to the Lord, all the world!
Worship the Lord with joy;
  come before him with happy songs!

Never forget that the Lord is God.
  He made us, and we belong to him;
  we are his people, we are his flock.

Enter the Temple gates with thanksgiving;
  go into its courts with praise.
  Give thanks to him and praise him.

The Lord is good;
  his love is eternal
  and his faithfulness lasts forever.

Ps 100:1-5

101 A Song of Loyalty to God

My song is about loyalty and justice,
    and I sing it to you, O Lord.
My conduct will be faultless.
    When will you come to me?

I will live a pure life in my house
    and will never tolerate evil.
I hate the actions of those who turn away
        from God;
    I will have nothing to do with them.
I will not be dishonest,
    and will have no dealings with evil.
I will get rid of anyone
    who whispers evil things about someone
        else;
I will not tolerate a man
    who is proud and arrogant.

I will approve of those who are faithful to
        God
    and will let them live in my palace.
Those who are completely honest
    will be allowed to serve me.

No liar will live in my palace;
    no hypocrite will remain in my presence.
Day after day I will destroy
    the wicked in our land;
I will expel all evil men
    from the city of the Lord.

Ps 101:1-8

102 The Prayer of a Troubled Young Man

Listen to my prayer, O Lord,
   and hear my cry for help!
When I am in trouble,
   don't turn away from me!
Listen to me,
   and answer me quickly when I call!

My life is disappearing like smoke;
   my body is burning like fire.
I am beaten down like dry grass;
   I have lost my desire for food.
I groan aloud;
   I am nothing but skin and bones.
I am like a wild bird in the desert,
   like an owl in abandoned ruins.
I lie awake;
   I am like a lonely bird on a housetop.

Because of your anger and fury,
   ashes are my food,
   and my tears are mixed with my drink.
You picked me up and threw me away.
My life is like the evening shadows;
   I am like dry grass.
But you, O Lord, are king forever;
   all generations will remember you.
You will rise and take pity on Zion;
   the time has come to have mercy on her;
   this is the right time.
Your servants love her,
   even though she is destroyed;
they have pity on her,
   even though she is in ruins.

Write down for the coming generation what
     the Lord has done,
  so that people not yet born will praise him.
The Lord looked down from his holy place on
     high,
  he looked down from heaven to earth.
He heard the groans of prisoners
  and set free those who were condemned to
    die.
And so his name will be proclaimed in Zion,
  and he will be praised in Jerusalem
  when nations and kingdoms come together
  and worship the Lord.

The Lord has made me weak while I am still
     young;
  he has shortened my life.
O God, do not take me away now
  before I grow old.

O Lord, you live forever;
  long ago you created the earth,
  and with your own hands you made the
    heavens.
They will disappear, but you will remain;
  they will all wear out like clothes.
You will discard them like clothes,
  and they will vanish.
But you are always the same,
  and your life never ends.
Our children will live in safety,
  and under your protection
  their descendants will be secure.

Ps 102:1-7, 9-14, 18-28

103 The Love of God

Praise the Lord, my soul!
    All my being, praise his holy name!
Praise the Lord, my soul,
    and do not forget how kind he is.
He forgives all my sins
    and heals all my diseases.
He keeps me from the grave
    and blesses me with love and mercy.
He fills my life with good things,
    so that I stay young and strong like an
       eagle.

The Lord judges in favor of the oppressed
    and gives them their rights.
He revealed his plans to Moses
    and let the people of Israel see his mighty
       deeds.
The Lord is merciful and loving,
    slow to become angry and full of constant
       love.
He does not keep on rebuking;
    he is not angry forever.
He does not punish us as we deserve
    or repay us according to our sins and
       wrongs.
As high as the sky is above the earth,
    so great is his love for those who have
       reverence for him.
As far as the east is from the west,
    so far does he remove our sins from us.

As a father is kind to his children,
  so kind is the Lord to those who honor him.
He knows what we are made of;
  he remembers that we are dust.

As for us, our life is like grass.
We grow and flourish like a wild flower;
  then the wind blows on it, and it is gone —
  no one sees it again.
But for those who honor the Lord, his love
    lasts forever,
  and his goodness endures for all
    generations
of those who are true to his covenant
  and who faithfully obey his commands.

The Lord placed his throne in heaven;
  he is king over all.
Praise the Lord, you strong and mighty
    angels,
  who obey his commands,
  who listen to what he says.
Praise the Lord, all you heavenly powers,
  you servants of his, who do his will!
Praise the Lord, all his creatures
  in all the places he rules.
Praise the Lord, my soul!

Ps 103:1-22

104 In Praise of the Creator

Praise the Lord, my soul!
  O Lord, my God, how great you are!
You are clothed with majesty and glory;
  you cover yourself with light.

You spread out the heavens like a tent
    and built your home on the waters above.
You use the clouds as your chariot
    and ride on the wings of the wind.
You use the winds as your messengers
    and flashes of lightning as your servants.

You make springs flow in the valleys,
    and rivers run between the hills.
They provide water for the wild animals;
    there the wild donkeys quench their thirst.
In the trees near by,
    the birds make their nests and sing.

From the sky you send rain on the hills,
    and the earth is filled with your blessings.
You make grass grow for the cattle
    and plants for man to use,
so that he can grow his crops
    and produce wine to make him happy,
    olive oil to make him cheerful,
    and bread to give him strength.

Lord, you have made so many things!
    How wisely you made them all!
    The earth is filled with your creatures

All of them depend on you
    to give them food when they need it.
You give it to them, and they eat it;
    you provide food, and they are satisfied.
When you turn away, they are afraid;
    when you take away their breath, they die
    and go back to the dust from which they
        came.

But when you give them breath, they are
created;
you give new life to the earth.

May the glory of the Lord last forever!
May the Lord be happy with what he has
made!

I will sing to the Lord all my life;
as long as I live I will sing praises to my
God.

Praise the Lord, my soul!
Praise the Lord!

Ps 104:1-4, 10-15, 24, 27-31, 33

105 God and His People

Give thanks to the Lord, proclaim his
greatness;
tell the nations what he has done.
Sing praise to the Lord;
tell the wonderful things he has done.
Be glad that we belong to him;
let all who worship him rejoice.
Go to the Lord for help;
and worship him continually.
You descendants of Abraham, his servant;
you descendants of Jacob, the man he chose:
remember the miracles that God performed
and the judgments that he gave.

The Lord is our God;
his commands are for all the world.
He will keep his covenant forever,
his promises for a thousand generations.

He will keep the agreement he made with
    Abraham
  and his promise to Isaac.
The Lord made a covenant with Jacob,
  one that will last forever.
"I will give you the land of Canaan," he said.
  "It will be your own possession."

So he led his chosen people out,
  and they sang and shouted for joy.
He gave them the lands of other peoples
  and let them take over their fields,
so that his people would obey his laws
  and keep all his commands.

Praise the Lord!

Ps 105:1-11, 43-45

106 The Lord's Goodness to His People

Praise the Lord!

Give thanks to the Lord, because he is good;
  his love is eternal.
Who can tell all the great things he has done?
  Who can praise him enough?
Happy are those who obey his commands,
  who always do what is right.
Remember me, Lord, when you help your
    people;
  include me when you save them.
Let me see the prosperity of your people
  and share in the happiness of your nation,
  in the glad pride of those who belong to you.

We have sinned as our ancestors did;
  we have been wicked and evil.
Our ancestors in Egypt did not understand
    God's wonderful acts;
  they forgot the many times he showed them
    his love,
  and they rebelled against the Almighty at
    the Red Sea.
But he saved them, as he had promised,
  in order to show his great power.
He gave a command to the Red Sea,
  and it dried up;
  he led his people across on dry land.
He saved them from those who hated them;
  he rescued them from their enemies.
But the water drowned their enemies;
  not one of them was left.
Then his people believed his promises
  and sang praises to him.

Many times the Lord rescued his people,
  but they chose to rebel against him
  and sank deeper into sin.
Yet the Lord heard them when they cried out,
  and he took notice of their distress.
For their sake he remembered his covenant,
  and because of his great love he relented.
He made all their oppressors feel sorry for
    them.

Save us, O Lord our God,
  and bring us back from among the nations,
  so that we may be thankful
  and praise your holy name.

Praise the Lord, the God of Israel;
  praise him now and forever!
  Let everyone say, "Amen!"

Praise the Lord!

Ps 106:1-12, 43-48

107 In Praise of God's Goodness

"Give thanks to the Lord, because he is good;
  his love is eternal!"
Repeat these words in praise to the Lord,
  all you whom he has saved.
He has rescued you from your enemies
  and has brought you back from foreign
    countries,
  from east and west, from north and south.

Some wandered in the trackless desert
  and could not find their way to a city to live
    in.
They were hungry and thirsty
  and had given up all hope.

Then in their trouble they called to the Lord,
  and he saved them from their distress.
He led them by a straight road
  to a city where they could live.
They must thank the Lord for his constant
    love,
  for the wonderful things he did for them.
He satisfies those who are thirsty
  and fills the hungry with good things.

Some were living in gloom and darkness,
  prisoners suffering in chains.

They were worn out from hard work;
    they would fall down, and no one would
      help.
Then in their trouble they called to the Lord,
    and he saved them from their distress.
He brought them out of their gloom and
      darkness
    and broke their chains in pieces.
They must thank the Lord for his constant
      love,
    for the wonderful things he did for them.
He breaks down doors of bronze
    and smashes iron bars.

Some were fools, suffering because of their sins
    and because of their evil;
they couldn't stand the sight of food
    and were close to death.
Then in their trouble they called to the Lord,
    and he saved them from their distress.
He healed them with his command
    and saved them from the grave.
They must thank the Lord for his constant
      love,
    for the wonderful things he did for them.
They must thank him with sacifices,
    and with songs of joy must tell all that he
      has done.

Some sailed over the ocean in ships,
    earning their living on the seas.
They saw what the Lord can do,
    his wonderful acts on the seas.

He commanded, and a mighty wind began to
    blow
  and stirred up the waves.
The ships were lifted high in the air
  and plunged down into the depths.
Then in their trouble they called to the Lord,
  and he saved them from their distress.
He calmed the raging storm,
  and the waves became quiet.
They were glad because of the calm,
  and he brought them safe to the port they
    wanted.
They must thank the Lord for his constant
    love,
  for the wonderful things he did for them.
They must proclaim his greatness in the
    assembly of the people
  and praise him before the council of the
    leaders.

Ps 107:1-10, 12-26, 28-32

108 Morning Prayer for Help

I have complete confidence, O God!
  I will sing praise to you!
Wake up, my soul!
  Wake up, my harp and lyre!
  I will wake up the sun.
I will thank you, O Lord, among the nations.
  I will praise you among the peoples.
Your constant love reaches above the heavens;
  your faithfulness touches the skies.

Show your greatness in the sky, O God,
　　and your glory over all the earth.
Save us by your might; answer my prayer,
　　so that the people you love may be rescued.

Who, O God, will take me into the fortified
　　city?
　　Who will lead me to Edom?
Have you really rejected us?
　　Aren't you going to march out with our
　　　armies?
Help us against the enemy;
　　human help is worthless.
With God on our side we will win;
　　he will defeat our enemies.

Ps 108:1-6, 10-13

109 Lament of a Man in Trouble

I praise you, God; don't remain silent!
Wicked men and liars have attacked me.
They tell lies about me,
　　and they say evil things about me,
　　attacking me for no reason.
They oppose me, even though I love them
　　and have prayed for them.
They pay me back evil for good
　　and hatred for love.

But Lord, my God, help me as you have
　　promised,
　　and rescue me because of the goodness of
　　　your love.
I am poor and needy;
　　I am hurt to the depths of my heart.

Like an evening shadow I am about to vanish;
    I am blown away like an insect.
My knees are weak from lack of food;
    I am nothing but skin and bones.
When people see me, they laugh at me;
    they shake their heads in scorn.

Help me, O Lord my God;
    because of your constant love, save me!
Make my enemies know
    that you are the one who saves me.
They may curse me, but you will bless me.

I will give loud thanks to the Lord;
    I will praise him in the assembly of the
        people,
because he defends the poor man
    and saves him from those who condemn him
        to death.

Ps 109:1-5, 21-28, 30-31

110 The Lord and His Chosen King

The Lord said to my lord, the king,
    "Sit here at my right side
    until I put your enemies under your feet."
From Zion the Lord will extend your royal
        power.
    "Rule over your enemies," he says.
On the day you fight your enemies,
    your people will volunteer.
Like the dew of early morning
    your young men will come to you on the
        sacred hills.

The Lord made a solemn promise and will not
    take it back:
    "You will be a priest forever
    in the line of succession to Melchizedek."

The Lord is at your right side;
    when he becomes angry, he will defeat
      kings.
He will pass judgment on the nations; . . .
    he will defeat kings all over the earth.
The king will drink from the stream by the
    road,
    and strengthened, he will stand victorious.
                            Ps 110:1-7

111 In Praise of the Lord

Praise the Lord!

With all my heart I will thank the Lord
    in the assembly of his people.
How wonderful are the things the Lord does!
    All who are delighted with them want to
      understand them.
All he does is full of honor and majesty;
    his righteousness is eternal.

The Lord does not let us forget his wonderful
    actions;
    he is kind and merciful.
He provides food for those who have reverence
    for him;
    he never forgets his covenant.
He has shown his power to his people
    by giving them the lands of foreigners.

In all he does he is faithful and just;
    all his commands are dependable.
They last for all time;
    they were given in truth and righteousness.
He set his people free
    and made an eternal covenant with them.
    Holy and mighty is he!

Ps 111:1-9

112 In Praise of the Good Person

Praise the Lord!

Happy is the person who has reverence for the
    Lord,
    who takes pleasure in obeying his
    commands.
The good man's children will be powerful in
    the land;
    his descendants will be blessed.
His family will be wealthy and rich,
    and he will be prosperous forever.

Light shines in the darkness for good men,
    for those who are merciful, kind, and just.
Happy is the person who is generous with his
    loans,
    who runs his business honestly.
A good person will never fail;
    he will always be remembered.

He is not afraid of receiving bad news;
    his faith is strong, and he trusts in the Lord.
He is not worried or afraid;
    he is certain to see his enemies defeated.

He gives generously to the needy,
and his kindness never fails;
he will be powerful and respected.
The wicked see this and are angry;
they glare in hate and disappear;
their hopes are gone forever.

Ps 112:1-10

113 In Praise of the Lord's Goodness

Praise the Lord!

You servants of the Lord,
praise his name!
His name will be praised,
now and forever.
From the east to the west
praise the name of the Lord!
The Lord rules over all nations;
his glory is above the heavens.

There is no one like the Lord our God.
He lives in the heights above,
but he bends down
to see the heavens and the earth.
He raises the poor from the dust;
he lifts the needy from their misery
and makes them companions of princes,
the princes of his people.
He honors the childless wife in her home;
he makes her happy by giving her children.

Praise the Lord!

Ps 113:1-9

114 A Passover Song

When the people of Israel left Egypt,
    when Jacob's descendants left that foreign
        land,
Judah became the Lord's holy people,
    Israel became his own possession.

The Red Sea looked and ran away;
    the Jordan River stopped flowing.
The mountains skipped like goats;
    the hills jumped around like lambs.

What happened, Sea, to make you run
        away?
    And you, O Jordan, why did you stop
        flowing?
You mountains, why did you skip like goats?
    You hills, why did you jump around like
        lambs?

Tremble, earth, at the Lord's coming,
    at the presence of the God of Jacob,
who changes rocks into pools of water
    and solid cliffs into flowing springs.

Ps 114:1-8

115 The One True God

To you alone, O Lord, to you alone,
    and not to us, must glory be given
    because of your constant love and
        faithfulness.

Why should the nations ask us,
    "Where is your God?"
Our God is in heaven;
    he does whatever he wishes.

Their gods are made of silver and gold,
    formed by human hands.
They have mouths, but cannot speak,
    and eyes, but cannot see.
They have ears, but cannot hear,
    and noses, but cannot smell.
They have hands, but cannot feel,
    and feet, but cannot walk;
    they cannot make a sound.
May all who made them and who trust in them
    become like the idols they have made.

Trust in the Lord, you people of Israel.
    He helps you and protects you.
Trust in the Lord, you priests of God.
    He helps you and protects you.
Trust in the Lord, all you that worship him.
    He helps you and protects you.
The Lord remembers us and will bless us;
    he will bless the people of Israel
    and all the priests of God.
He will bless everyone who honors him,
    the great and the small alike.

May the Lord give you children—
    you and your descendants!
May you be blessed by the Lord,
    who made heaven and earth!

Heaven belongs to the Lord alone,
    but he gave the earth to man.
The Lord is not praised by the dead,
    by any who go down to the land of silence.
But we, the living, will give thanks to him
    now and forever.

Praise the Lord!   *Ps 115:1-18*

116 Thanks to the God Who Saves

I love the Lord, because he hears me;
   he listens to my prayers.
He listens to me
   every time I call to him.
The danger of death was all around me;
   the horrors of the grave closed in on me;
   I was filled with fear and anxiety.
Then I called to the Lord,
   "I beg you, Lord, save me!"

The Lord is merciful and good;
   our God is compassionate.
The Lord protects the helpless;
   when I was in danger, he saved me.
Be confident, my heart,
   because the Lord has been good to me.

The Lord saved me from death;
   he stopped my tears
   and kept me from defeat.
And so I walk in the presence of the Lord
   in the world of the living.
I kept on believing, even when I said,
   "I am completely crushed."
even when I was afraid and said,
   "No one can be trusted."

What can I offer the Lord
   for all his goodness to me?
I will bring a wine offering to the Lord,
   to thank him for saving me.
In the assembly of all his people
   I will give him what I have promised.

How painful it is to the Lord
    when one of his people dies!
I am your servant, Lord;
    I serve you just as my mother did.
You have saved me from death.
I will give you a sacrifice of thanksgiving
    and offer my prayer to you.
In the assembly of all your people,
    in the sanctuary of your Temple in
        Jerusalem,
    I will give you what I have promised.

Praise the Lord!

Ps 116:1-19

117 Praise the Lord, All Nations

Praise the Lord, all nations!
    Praise him, all peoples!
His love for us is strong,
    and his faithfulness is eternal.

Praise the Lord!

Ps 117:1-2

118 A Prayer of Thanks for Victory

Give thanks to the Lord, because he is good,
    and his love is eternal.
Let the people of Israel say,
    "His love is eternal."
Let the priests of God say,
    "His love is eternal."
Let all who worship him say,
    "His love is eternal."

In my distress I called to the Lord;
  he answered me and set me free.
The Lord is with me, I will not be afraid;
  what can anyone do to me?
It is the Lord who helps me,
  and I will see my enemies defeated.
It is better to trust in the Lord
  than to depend on man.
It is better to trust in the Lord
  than to depend on human leaders.

Many enemies were around me;
  but I destroyed them by the power of the
    Lord!
They were around me on every side;
  but I destroyed them by the power of the
    Lord!
They swarmed around me like bees,
  but they burned out as quickly as a brush
    fire;
  by the power of the Lord I destroyed them.
I was fiercely attacked and was being
    defeated,
  but the Lord helped me.
The Lord makes me powerful and strong;
  he has saved me.

Listen to the glad shouts of victory in the
    tents of God's people:
  "The Lord's mighty power has done it!
  His power has brought us victory—
  his mighty power in battle!"
I will not die; instead, I will live
  and proclaim what the Lord has done.

He has punished me severely,
    but he has not let me die.

Open to me the gates of the Temple;
    I will go in and give thanks to the Lord!

This is the gate of the Lord;
    only the righteous can come in.

I praise you, Lord, because you heard me,
    because you have given me victory.

The stone which the builders rejected as
      worthless
    turned out to be the most important of all.
This was done by the Lord;
    what a wonderful sight it is!
This is the day of the Lord's victory;
    let us be happy, let us celebrate!
Save us, Lord, save us!
Give us success, O Lord!

May God bless the one who comes in the name
      of the Lord!
    From the Temple of the Lord we bless you.
The Lord is God; he has been good to us.
With branches in your hands, start the festival
    and march around the altar.

You are my God, and I give you thanks;
    I will proclaim your greatness.

Give thanks to the Lord, because he is good,
    and his love is eternal.

Ps 118:1-29

119 The Law of the Lord

Happy are those whose lives are faultless,
  who live according to the law of the Lord.
Happy are those who follow his commands,
  who obey him with all their heart.
They never do wrong;
  they walk in the Lord's ways.
Lord, you have given us your laws
  and told us to obey them faithfully.
How I hope that I shall be faithful
  in keeping your instructions!
If I pay attention to all your commands,
  then I will not be put to shame.
As I learn your righteous judgments,
  I will praise you with a pure heart.
I will obey your laws;
  never abandon me!

Obedience to the Law of the Lord

How can a young man keep his life pure?
  By obeying your commands.
With all my heart I try to serve you;
  keep me from disobeying your
    commandments.
I keep your law in my heart,
  so that I will not sin against you.
I praise you, O Lord;
  teach me your ways.
I will repeat aloud
  all the laws you have given.
I delight in following your commands
  more than in having great wealth.

I study your instructions;
  I examine your teachings.
I take pleasure in your laws;
  your commands I will not forget.

Love for the Law of the Lord

How I love your law!
  I think about it all day long.
Your commandment is with me all the time
  and makes me wiser than my enemies.
I understand more than all my teachers,
  because I meditate on your instructions.
I have greater wisdom than old men,
  because I obey your commands.

Light from the Law of the Lord

Your word is a lamp to guide me
  and a light for my path.
I will keep my solemn promise
  to obey your just instructions.
Your commandments are my eternal
    possession;
  they are the joy of my heart.
I have decided to obey your laws
  until the day I die.

A Prayer for Help

Let my cry for help reach you, Lord!
  Give me understanding, as you have
    promised.
Listen to my prayer,
  and save me according to your promise!

I will always praise you,
    because you teach me your laws.
I will sing about your law,
    because your commands are just.
Always be ready to help me,
    because I follow your commands.
How I long for your saving help, O Lord!
    I find happiness in your law.
Give me life, so that I may praise you;
    may your instructions help me.
I wander about like a lost sheep;
    so come and look for me, your servant,
    because I have not neglected your laws.

Ps 119:1-16, 97-100, 105-106, 111-112, 169-176

120 A Prayer for Help

When I was in trouble, I called to the Lord,
    and he answered me.
Save me, Lord,
    from liars and deceivers.

You liars, what will God do to you?
    How will he punish you?
With a soldier's sharp arrows,
    with red-hot coals!

Living among you is as bad as living in
    Meshech
    or among the people of Kedar.
I have lived too long
    with people who hate peace!
When I speak of peace,
    they are for war.

Ps 120:1-7

121 The Lord Our Protector

I look to the mountains;
  where will my help come from?
My help will come from the Lord,
  who made heaven and earth.

He will not let you fall;
  your protector is always awake.

The protector of Israel
  never dozes or sleeps.
The Lord will guard you;
  he is by your side to protect you.
The sun will not hurt you during the day,
  nor the moon during the night.

The Lord will protect you from all danger;
  he will keep you safe.
He will protect you as you come and go
  now and forever.   *Ps 121:1-8*

122 In Praise of Jerusalem

I was glad when they said to me,
  "Let us go to the Lord's house."
And now we are here,
  standing inside the gates of Jerusalem!

Jerusalem is a city restored
  in beautiful order and harmony.
This is where the tribes come,
  the tribes of Israel,
to give thanks to the Lord
  according to his command.
Here the kings of Israel
  sat to judge their people.

Pray for the peace of Jerusalem:
    "May those who love you prosper.
    May there be peace inside your walls
    and safety in your palaces."
For the sake of my relatives and friends
    I say to Jerusalem, "Peace be with you!"
For the sake of the house of the Lord our God
    I pray for your prosperity.

Ps 122:1-9

123 A Prayer for Mercy

Lord, I look up to you,
    up to heaven, where you rule.
As a servant depends on his master,
    as a maid depends on her mistress,
so we will keep looking to you,
        O Lord our God,
    until you have mercy on us.

Be merciful to us, Lord, be merciful;
    we have been treated with so much
        contempt.
We have been mocked too long by the rich
    and scorned by proud oppressors.

Ps 123:1-4

124 God Protects His People

What if the Lord had not been on our side?
    Answer, O Israel!
"If the Lord had not been on our side
    when our enemies attacked us,
then they would have swallowed us alive
    in their furious anger against us;

then the flood would have carried us away,
  the water would have covered us,
  the raging torrent would have drowned us."

Let us thank the Lord,
  who has not let our enemies destroy us.
We have escaped like a bird from a hunter's
      trap;
  the trap is broken, and we are free!
Our help comes from the Lord,
  who made heaven and earth.

Ps 124:1-8

125 The Security of God's People

Those who trust in the Lord are like Mount
      Zion,
  which can never be shaken, never be
      moved.
As the mountains surround Jerusalem,
  so the Lord surrounds his people,
  now and forever.

The wicked will not always rule over the land
      of the righteous;
  if they did, the righteous themselves might
      do evil.
Lord, do good to those who are good,
  to those who obey your commands.
But when you punish the wicked,
  punish also those who abandon your ways.

Peace be with Israel!

Ps 125:1-5

126 A Prayer for Deliverance

When the Lord brought us back to Jerusalem,
   it was like a dream!
How we laughed, how we sang for joy!
   Then the other nations said about us,
   "The Lord did great things for them."
Indeed he did great things for us;
   how happy we were!

Lord, take us back to our land,
   just as the rain brings water back to dry
      riverbeds.
Let those who wept as they planted their
      crops,
   gather the harvest with joy!

Those who wept as they went out carrying
      the seed
   will come back singing for joy,
   as they bring in the harvest.

                                    Ps 126:1-6

127 In Praise of God's Goodness

If the Lord does not build the house,
   the work of the builders is useless;
if the Lord does not protect the city,
   it does no good for the sentries to stand
      guard.
It is useless to work so hard for a living,
   getting up early and going to bed late.
For the Lord provides for those he loves,
   while they are asleep.

Children are a gift from the Lord;
  they are a real blessing.
The sons a man has when he is young
  are like arrows in a soldier's hand.
Happy is the man who has many such
    arrows.
He will never be defeated
  when he meets his enemies in the place
    of judgment.

Ps 127:1-5

128 The Reward of Obedience

Happy are those who obey the Lord,
  who live by his commands.

Your work will provide for your needs;
  you will be happy and prosperous.
Your wife will be like a fruitful vine in your
    home,
  and your sons will be like young olive trees
    around your table.
A man who obeys the Lord
  will surely be blessed like this.

May the Lord bless you from Zion!
  May you see Jerusalem prosper
  all the days of your life!
May you live to see your grandchildren!

Peace be with Israel!

Ps 128:1-6

129 A Prayer Against Enemies

Israel, tell us how your enemies have
    persecuted you
  ever since you were young.

"Ever since I was young,
  my enemies have persecuted me cruelly,
  but they have not overcome me.
They cut deep wounds in my back
  and made it like a plowed field.
But the Lord, the righteous one.
  has freed me from slavery."

May everyone who hates Zion
  be defeated and driven back.
May they all be like grass growing on the
    housetops,
  which dries up before it can grow;
  no one gathers it up
  or carries it away in bundles.
No one who passes by will say to them,
  "May the Lord bless you!
  We bless you in the name of the Lord."

Ps 129:1-8

130 A Cry for Help

From the depths of my despair I call to you,
    Lord.
Hear my cry, O Lord;
  listen to my call for help!
If you kept a record of our sins,
  who could escape being condemned?
But you forgive us,
  so that we should reverently obey you.

I wait eagerly for the Lord's help,
    and in his word I trust.
I wait for the Lord
    more eagerly than watchmen wait for the
        dawn—
    than watchmen wait for the dawn.

Israel, trust in the Lord,
    because his love is constant
    and he is always willing to save.
He will save his people Israel
    from all their sins.

Ps 130:1-8

131 A Prayer of Humble Trust

Lord, I have given up my pride
    and turned away from my arrogance.
I am not concerned with great matters
    or with subjects too difficult for me.
Instead, I am content and at peace.
As a child lies quietly in its mother's arms,
    so my heart is quiet within me.
Israel, trust in the Lord
    now and forever!

Ps 131:1-3

132 In Praise of the Temple

Lord, do not forget David
    and all the hardships he endured.
Remember, Lord, what he promised,
    the vow he made to you, the Mighty God of
        Jacob:

"I will not go home or go to bed;
   I will not rest or sleep,
   until I provide a place for the Lord,
   a home for the Mighty God of Jacob."

In Bethlehem we heard about the Covenant
     Box,
   and we found it in the fields of Jearim.
We said, "Let us go to the Lord's house;
   let us worship before his throne."

Come to the Temple, Lord, with the Covenant
     Box,
   the symbol of your power,
   and stay here forever.
May your priests do always what is right;
   may your people shout for joy!

You made a promise to your servant David;
   do not reject your chosen king, Lord.
You made a solemn promise to David—
   a promise you will not take back:
"I will make one of your sons king,
   and he will rule after you.
If your sons are true to my covenant
   and to the commands I give them,
   their sons, also, will succeed you for all time
     as kings."

The Lord has chosen Zion;
   he wants to make it his home:
"This is where I will live forever;
   this is where I want to rule.
I will richly provide Zion with all she needs;
   I will satisfy her poor with food.

I will bless her priests in all they do,
  and her people will sing and shout for joy.
Here I will make one of David's descendants
    a great king;
  here I will preserve the rule of my chosen
    king.
I will cover his enemies with shame,
  but his kingdom will prosper and flourish."

Ps 132:1-18

133 In Praise of Brotherly Love

How wonderful it is, how pleasant,
  for God's people to live together in
    harmony!
It is like the precious anointing oil
  running down from Aaron's head and
    beard,
  down to the collar of his robes.
It is like the dew on Mount Hermon,
  falling on the hills of Zion.

That is where the Lord has promised his
    blessing—
  life that never ends.

Ps 133:1-3

134 A Call to Praise God

Come, praise the Lord,
  all his servants,
  all who serve in his Temple at night.
Raise your hands in prayer in the Temple,
  and praise the Lord!

May the Lord, who made heaven and earth,
  bless you from Zion!

Ps 134:1-3

135 A Hymn of Praise

Praise the Lord!

Praise his name, you servants of the Lord,
   who stand in the Lord's house,
   in the Temple of our God.
Praise the Lord, because he is good;
   sing praises to his name, because he is kind.
He chose Jacob for himself,
   the people of Israel for his own.

I know that our Lord is great,
   greater than all the gods.
He does whatever he wishes
   in heaven and on earth,
   in the seas and in the depths below.

Lord, you will always be proclaimed as God;
   all generations will remember you.
The Lord will defend his people;
   he will take pity on his servants.

The gods of the nations are made of silver and
      gold;
   they are formed by human hands.
They have mouths, but cannot speak,
   and eyes, but cannot see.
They have ears, but cannot hear;
   they are not even able to breathe.
May all who made them and who trust in them
   become like the idols they have made!

Praise the Lord, people of Israel;
   praise him, you priests of God!
Praise the Lord, you Levites;
   praise him, all you that worship him!

Praise the Lord in Zion,
   in Jerusalem, his home.

Praise the Lord!

Ps 135:1-6, 13-21

136 A Hymn of Thanksgiving

Give thanks to the Lord, because he is good;
   his love is eternal.
Give thanks to the greatest of all gods;
   his love is eternal.
Give thanks to the mightiest of all lords;
   his love is eternal.

He alone performs great miracles;
   his love is eternal.
By his wisdom he made the heavens;
   his love is eternal;
he built the earth on the deep waters;
   his love is eternal.
He made the sun and the moon;
   his love is eternal;
the sun to rule over the day;
   his love is eternal;
the moon and the stars to rule over the night;
   his love is eternal.

He led the people of Israel out of Egypt;
   his love is eternal;
with his strong hand, his powerful arm;
   his love is eternal.
He divided the Red Sea;
   his love is eternal;

he led his people through it;
   his love is eternal;
but he drowned the king of Egypt and his
    army;
   his love is eternal.

He led his people through the desert;
   his love is eternal.
He killed powerful kings;
   his love is eternal;·
he killed famous kings;
   his love is eternal.
He gave their lands to his people;
   his love is eternal;
he gave them to Israel, his servant;
   his love is eternal.

He did not forget us when we were defeated;
   his love is eternal;
he freed us from our enemies;
   his love is eternal.

He gives food to every living creature;
   his love is eternal.

Give thanks to the God of heaven;
   his love is eternal.

Ps 136:1-9, 11-18, 21-26

137 A Lament in Exile

By the rivers of Babylon we sat down;
   there we wept when we remembered Zion.
On the willows near by
   we hung up our harps.

Those who captured us told us to sing;
    they told us to entertain them:
    "Sing us a song about Zion."

How can we sing a song to the Lord
    in a foreign land?
May I never be able to play the harp again
    if I forget you, Jerusalem!
May I never be able to sing again
    if I do not remember you,
    if I do not think of you as my greatest joy!

Remember, Lord, what the Edomites did
    the day Jerusalem was captured.
Remember how they kept saying,
    "Tear it down to the ground!"

Babylon, you will be destroyed.
Happy is the man who pays you back
    for what you have done to us.

Ps 137:1-8

138 A Prayer of Thanksgiving

I thank you, Lord, with all my heart;
    I sing praise to you before the gods.

I face your holy Temple,
    bow down, and praise your name
because of your constant love and faithfulness,
    because you have shown that your name
        and your commands are supreme.
You answered me when I called to you;
    with your strength you strengthened me.

All the kings in the world will praise you,
    Lord,
  because they have heard your promises.
They will sing about what you have done
  and about your great glory.
Even though you are so high above,
  you care for the lowly,
  and the proud cannot hide from you.

When I am surrounded by troubles,
  you keep me safe.
You oppose my angry enemies
  and save me by your power.
You will do everything you have promised;
  Lord, your love is eternal.
  Complete the work that you have begun.
                              Ps 138:1-8

139 God's Knowledge and Care

Lord, you have examined me and you
    know me.
You know everything I do;
  from far away you understand all my
    thoughts.
You see me, whether I am working or resting;
  you know all my actions.
Even before I speak,
  you already know what I will say.
You are all around me on every side;
  you protect me with your power.
Your knowledge of me is too deep;
  it is beyond my understanding.

Where could I go to escape from you?
Where could I get away from your
presence?
If I went up to heaven, you would be there;
if I lay down in the world of the dead, you
would be there.
If I flew away beyond the east
or lived in the farthest place in the west,
you would be there to lead me,
you would be there to help me.
I could ask the darkness to hide me
or the light around me to turn into night,
but even darkness is not dark for you,
and the night is as bright as the day.
Darkness and light are the same to you.

You created every part of me;
you put me together in my mother's womb.
I praise you because you are to be feared;
all you do is strange and wonderful.
I know it with all my heart.
When my bones were being formed,
carefully put together in my mother's
womb,
when I was growing there in secret,
you knew that I was there—
you saw me before I was born.
The days allotted to me
had all been recorded in your book,
before any of them ever began.
O God, how difficult I find your thoughts;
how many of them there are!
If I counted them, they would be more than
the grains of sand.
When I awake, I am still with you.

Examine me, O God, and know my mind;
    test me, and discover my thoughts.
Find out if there is any evil in me
    and guide me in the everlasting way.
        Ps 139:1-18, 23-24

140 A Prayer for Protection

Save me, Lord, from evil men;
    keep me safe from violent men.
They are always plotting evil,
    always stirring up quarrels.
Their tongues are like deadly snakes;
    their words are like a cobra's poison.

Protect me, Lord, from the power of the
    wicked;
    keep me safe from violent men
    who plot my downfall.
Proud men have set a trap for me;
    they have laid their snares,
    and along the path they have set traps to
    catch me.

I say to the Lord, "You are my God,"
    Hear my cry for help, Lord!
Lord, my God, my strong defender,
    you have protected me in battle.
Lord, don't give the wicked what they want;
    don't let their plots succeed.

Lord, I know that you defend the cause of the
    poor
    and the rights of the needy.
The righteous will praise you indeed;
    they will live in your presence. *Ps 140:1-8, 12-13*

141 An Evening Prayer

I call to you, Lord; help me now!
Listen to me when I call to you.
Receive my prayer as incense,
my uplifted hands as an evening sacrifice.

Lord, place a guard at my mouth,
a sentry at the door of my lips.
Keep me from wanting to do wrong
and from joining evil men in their
wickedness.
May I never take part in their feasts.

A good man may punish me and rebuke me in
kindness,
but I will never accept honor from evil men,
because I am always praying against their
evil deeds.

But I keep trusting in you, my Sovereign Lord.
I seek your protection;
don't let me die!
Protect me from the traps they have set for me,
from the snares of those evildoers.

Ps 141:1-5, 8-9

142 A Prayer for Help

I call to the Lord for help;
I plead with him.
I bring him all my complaints;
I tell him all my troubles.
When I am ready to give up,
he knows what I should do.

In the path where I walk,
  my enemies have hidden a trap for me.
When I look beside me,
  I see that there is no one to help me,
  no one to protect me.
No one cares for me.

Lord, I cry to you for help;
  you, Lord, are my protector;
  you are all I want in this life.
Listen to my cry for help,
  for I am sunk in despair.
Save me from my enemies;
  they are too strong for me.
Set me free from my distress;
  then in the assembly of your people I will
    praise you
  because of your goodness to me.

Ps 142:1-7

143 A Humble Prayer for Help

Lord, hear my prayer!
In your righteousness listen to my plea;
  answer me in your faithfulness!
Don't put me, your servant, on trial;
  no one is innocent in your sight.

My enemy has hunted me down
  and completely defeated me.
He has put me in a dark prison,
  and I am like those who died long ago;
So I am ready to give up;
  I am in deep despair.

I remember the days gone by;
  I think about all that you have done,
  I bring to mind all your deeds.
I lift up my hands to you in prayer;
  like dry ground my soul is thirsty for you.

Answer me now, Lord!
  I have lost all hope.
Don't hide yourself from me,
  or I will be among those who go down to
    the world of the dead.
Remind me each morning of your constant
    love,
  for I put my trust in you.
My prayers go up to you;
  show me the way I should go.

I go to you for protection, Lord;
  rescue me from my enemies.
You are my God;
  teach me to do your will.
Be good to me, and guide me on a safe path.

Rescue me, Lord, as you have promised;
  in your goodness save me from my troubles!
I am your servant.   *Ps 143:1-11*

144 A King Thanks God for Victory

Praise the Lord, my protector!
He trains me for battle
  and prepares me for war.
He is my protector and defender,
  my shelter and savior,
  in whom I trust for safety.
He subdues the nations under me.

Lord, what is man, that you notice him;
　　mere man, that you pay attention to him?
He is like a puff of wind;
　　his days are like a passing shadow.

O Lord, tear the sky open and come down;
　　touch the mountains, and they will pour
　　　out smoke.
Send flashes of lightning and scatter your
　　enemies;
　　shoot your arrows and send them running.
Reach down from above,
　　pull me out of the deep water, and rescue
　　　me.

I will sing you a new song, O God;
　　I will play the harp and sing to you.
You give victory to kings
　　and rescue your servant David.

May our sons in their youth
　　be like plants that grow up strong.
May our daughters be like stately columns
　　which adorn the corners of a palace.
May our barns be filled
　　with crops of every kind.
May the sheep in our fields
　　bear young by the tens of thousands.

May our cattle reproduce plentifully
　　without miscarriage or loss.
May there be no cries of distress in our streets.

Happy is the nation of whom this is true;
　　happy are the people whose God is the
　　　Lord!

Ps 144:1-7, 9-10, 12-15

145 A Hymn of Praise

I will proclaim your greatness, my God and
    king;
  I will thank you forever and ever.
Every day I will thank you;
  I will praise you forever and ever.
The Lord is great and is to be highly praised;
  his greatness is beyond understanding.

What you have done will be praised from one
    generation to the next;
  they will proclaim your mighty acts.
They will speak of your glory and majesty,
  and I will meditate on your wonderful
    deeds.
People will speak of your mighty deeds,
  and I will proclaim your greatness.
They will tell about all your goodness
  and sing about your kindness.
The Lord is loving and merciful,
  slow to become angry and full of constant
    love.
He is good to everyone
  and has compassion on all he made.

All your creatures, Lord, will praise you,
  and all your people will give you thanks.
They will speak of the glory of your royal
    power
  and tell of your might,
so that everyone will know your mighty deeds
  and the glorious majesty of your kingdom.
Your rule is eternal,
  and you are king forever.

The Lord is faithful to his promises;
    he is merciful in all his acts.
He helps those who are in trouble;
    he lifts those who have fallen.

All living things look hopefully to you,
    and you give them food when they need it.
You give them enough
    and satisfy the needs of all.

The Lord is righteous in all he does,
    merciful in all his acts.
He is near to those who call to him,
    who call to him with sincerity.
He supplies the needs of those who honor him;
    he hears their cries and saves them.
He protects everyone who loves him,
    but he will destroy the wicked.

I will always praise the Lord;
    let all his creatures praise his holy name
        forever.

Ps 145:1-21

146 In Praise of God the Savior

Praise the Lord!
    Praise the Lord, my soul!
I will praise him as long as I live;
    I will sing to my God all my life.

Don't put your trust in human leaders;
    no human being can save you.
When they die, they return to the dust;
    on that day all their plans come to an end.

Happy is the man who has the God of Jacob to
    help him
  and who depends on the Lord his God,
  the Creator of heaven, earth, and sea,
  and all that is in them.
He always keeps his promises;
  he judges in favor of the oppressed
  and gives food to the hungry.

The Lord sets prisoners free
  and gives sight to the blind.
He lifts those who have fallen;
  he loves his righteous people.
He protects the strangers who live in our land;
  he helps widows and orphans,
  but takes the wicked to their ruin.

The Lord is king forever.
  Your God, O Zion, will reign for all time.

Praise the Lord!

Ps 146:1-10

147 In Praise of God the Almighty

Praise the Lord!

It is good to sing praise to our God;
  it is pleasant and right to praise him.
The Lord is restoring Jerusalem;
  he is bringing back the exiles.
He heals the broken-hearted
  and bandages their wounds.

He has decided the number of the stars
  and calls each one by name.

Great and mighty is our Lord;
   his wisdom cannot be measured.
He raises the humble,
   but crushes the wicked to the ground.

Sing hymns of praise to the Lord;
   play music on the harp to our God.
He spreads clouds over the sky;
   he provides rain for the earth
   and makes grass grow on the hills.
He gives animals their food
   and feeds the young ravens when they call.
His pleasure is not in strong horses,
   nor his delight in brave soldiers;
but he takes pleasure in those who honor him,
   in those who trust in his constant love.

Praise the Lord, O Jerusalem!
   Praise your God, O Zion!
He keeps your gates strong;
   he blesses your people.
He keeps your borders safe
   and satisfies you with the finest wheat.

Praise the Lord!

Ps 147:1-14

148 All the Earth Praises God

Praise the Lord!

Praise the Lord from heaven,
   you that live in the heights above.
Praise him, all his angels,
   all his heavenly armies.

Praise him, sun and moon;
    praise him, shining stars.
Praise him, highest heavens,
    and the waters above the sky.

Let them all praise the name of the Lord!
He commanded, and they were created;
    by his command they were fixed in their
      places forever,
    and they cannot disobey.

Praise the Lord from the earth,
    sea monsters and all ocean depths;
lightning and hail, snow and clouds,
    strong winds that obey his command.

Praise him, hills and mountains,
    fruit trees and forests;
all animals, tame and wild,
    reptiles and birds.

Praise him, kings and all peoples,
    princes and all other rulers;
girls and young men,
    old people and children too.

Let them all praise the name of the Lord!
His name is greater than all others;
    his glory is above earth and heaven.
He made his nation strong,
    so that all his people praise him—
    the people of Israel, so dear to him.

Praise the Lord!

Ps 148:1-14

149 A Hymn of Praise

Praise the Lord!

Sing a new song to the Lord;
> praise him in the assembly of his faithful
> people!
Be glad, Israel, because of your Creator;
> rejoice, People of Zion, because of your
> king!
Praise his name with dancing;
> play drums and harps in praise of him.
The Lord takes pleasure in his people;
> he honors the humble with victory.
Let God's people rejoice in their triumph
> and sing joyfully all night long.
Let them shout aloud as they praise God,
> with their sharp swords in their hands
> to defeat the nations.

Praise the Lord!

Ps 149:1-7

150 Praise the Lord!

Praise the Lord!

Praise God in his Temple!
> Praise his strength in heaven!
Praise him for the mighty things he has done.
> Praise his supreme greatness.

Praise him with trumpets.
> Praise him with harps and lyres.
Praise him with drums and dancing.
> Praise him with harps and flutes.

Praise him with cymbals.
   Praise him with loud cymbals.
Praise the Lord, all living creatures!

Praise the Lord!

Ps 150:1-6

Prayers and Praying

In the
New Testament

Introduction

Prayer in the New Testament is of a different kind and style than prayer in the Old Testament. It does not have the same prominence, it does not achieve the same eminence. There really is no new body of prayer as such. Jesus gave us only the Our Father . . . and a number of teachings about prayer. The explanation seems to be that Jesus gave himself and his Spirit, that God himself is with us now. Emmanuel is his name. Christ is alive and his Spirit is among us and within us.

At the very beginning there are the canticles of Zechariah and Mary. They have the Old Testament touch, but hardly anything after that has, except here and there where the Old Testament is quoted as being fulfilled now. Actually, something new is going on, with such passages as the Beatitudes, a new commandment, John's Canticle of the Word, Jesus' eucharistic prayer, Paul's Canticle to Love, Paul's raptures about Christ, and the new heaven and the new earth.

It is not the same. Still, it adds up to its own kind of prayer book. There is no room for doubt that the presence of Jesus as the Son of Man, and later the Spirit of Jesus, inspires a new form of conversation with God.

Some special notes: In the Gospels there are two collections of teachings about prayer that cross over gospel lines. The first is gathered together early in Matthew and the second in Luke. These teachings urge on man the conversation with God. They also teach us that Jesus prayed more often than it might at first glance be supposed. Also gathered together in one place at the end of Matthew are the seven last words of Jesus.

Acts does not give us many prayers as such. What it does give us are many instances of prayer and praying. In his epistles Paul seems to be always praying; his epistles begin and end with a blessing. Still, his prayers within the texts are bursts of rapture on the wings of the Spirit, rather than manmade prayers. It seems better to think of them as songs, hymns and canticles, as for instance: "A Hymn to God's Love," "A Hymn to God's Wisdom," "Canticle of Love," "A Hymn of Triumph Over Death," "A Pauline Hymn to Christ." He exhorts all Christians to "sing psalms, hymns, and sacred songs." Indeed, he gives us a considerable number of them.

What we have from John in his first epistle reflects a heart filled with the love of God. In his Revelation he gives us prayers unlike any others. Whatever else about Revelation, it is about the victory of God through Christ over all his enemies, including Satan. It is also the triumph of the people of God. There are "Blessings on Those Who Win the Victory"; there are songs of "Glory, Honor, and Thanks" to God and to the Lamb; there are songs of worship in the heavenly court; there is a new song of a new heaven and earth; and there is a final invitation to all from the Spirit and the Bride who say, "Come."

Gospels

Acts

Not by Bread Alone

"Man does not live by bread alone, but by every
word that proceeds from the mouth of God."

Mt 4:4 (RSV)

The Beatitudes

"How happy are the poor in spirit;
   theirs is the kingdom of heaven.
Happy the gentle:
   they shall have the earth for their heritage.
Happy those who mourn:
   they shall be comforted.
Happy those who hunger and thirst for what is
      right:
   they shall be satisfied.
Happy the merciful:
   they shall have mercy shown them.
Happy the pure in heart:
   they shall see God.
Happy the peacemakers:
   they shall be called sons of God.
Happy those who are persecuted in the
      cause of right:
   theirs is the kingdom of heaven."

Mt 5:3-10 (JB)

"Happy are you poor;
   the Kingdom of God is yours!
Happy are you who are hungry now;
   you will be filled!
Happy are you who weep now;
   you will laugh!
Happy are you when people hate you, reject you,

insult you, and say that you are evil, all because of the Son of Man! Be glad when that happens and dance for joy, because a great reward is kept for you in heaven."

Lk 6:20-23

Love Your Enemies

"You have heard that it was said, 'Love your friends, hate your enemies.' But now I tell you: love your enemies and pray for those who persecute you, so that you may become the sons of your Father in heaven. For he makes his sun to shine on bad and good people alike, and gives rain to those who do evil. Why should God reward you if you love only the people who love you? Even the tax collectors do that! And if you speak only to your friends, have you done anything out of the ordinary? Even pagans do that! You must be perfect — just as your Father in heaven is perfect."

Mt 5:43-48
(Lk 6:27-31)

Teaching About Prayer

"When you pray, do not be like the hypocrites! They love to stand up and pray in the houses of worship and on the street corners, so that everyone will see them. I assure you they have already been paid in full. But when you pray, go to your room, close the door, and pray to your Father, who is unseen. And your Father, who sees what you do in private, will reward you.

"When you pray, do not use a lot of meaningless words, as the pagans do, who think that God will hear them because their prayers are long. Do not be like them. Your Father already knows what you need before you ask him. This is how you should pray:

The Our Father

'Our Father in heaven:
    May your holy name be honored;
    may your Kingdom come;
    may your will be done on earth as it is in
        heaven.
Give us today the food we need.
Forgive us the wrongs we have done,
    as we forgive the wrongs that others have
        done to us.
Do not bring us to hard testing,
    but keep us safe from the Evil One.'

"If you forgive others the wrongs they have done to you, your Father in heaven will also forgive you. But if you do not forgive others, then your Father will not forgive the wrongs you have done."

Mt 6:5-14

One day Jesus was praying in a certain place. When he had finished, one of his disciples said to him, "Lord, teach us to pray, just as John taught his disciples."

Jesus said to them, "When you pray, say this:

'Father:
    May your holy name be honored;
    may your Kingdom come.
    Give us day by day the food we need.
    Forgive us our sins,
        for we forgive everyone who does us
        wrong.
    And do not bring us to hard testing.' "

Lk 11:1-4

Do Not Be Worried

"You cannot serve both God and money. This is why I tell you: do not be worried about the food and drink you need in order to stay alive, or about clothes for your body. After all, isn't life worth more than food? And isn't the body worth more than clothes? Look at the birds: they do not plant seeds, gather a harvest and put it in barns; yet your Father in heaven takes care of them! Aren't you worth much more than birds? Can any of you live a bit longer by worrying about it?

"And why worry about clothes? Look how the wild flowers grow: they do not work or make clothes for themselves. But I tell you that not even King Solomon with all his wealth had clothes as beautiful as one of these flowers. It is God who clothes the wild grass—grass that is here today and gone tomorrow, burned up in the oven. Won't he be all the more sure to clothe you? What little faith you have!

"So do not start worrying: 'Where will my food come from? or my drink? or my clothes?' (These are the things the pagans are always concerned about.) Your Father in heaven knows that you need all these things. Instead, be concerned above everything else with the Kingdom of God and with what he requires of you, and he will provide you with all these other things. So do not worry about tomorrow; it will have enough worries of its own. There is no need to add to the troubles each day brings."

Mt 6:25-34
(Lk 12:22-31)

Ask, Seek, Knock

"Ask, and you will receive; seek and you will find; knock, and the door will be opened to you. For everyone who asks will receive, and anyone who seeks will find, and the door will be opened to him who knocks. Would any of you who are fathers give your son a stone when he asks for bread? Or would you give him a snake when he asks for a fish? As bad as you are, you know how to give good things to your children. How much more, then, will your Father in heaven give good things to those who ask him!"

Mt 7:7-11
(Lk 11:9-13)

Jesus Prays to the Father

"Father, Lord of heaven and earth!
I thank you because you have shown to the unlearned
what you have hidden from the wise and learned.

Yes, Father, this was how you were pleased to
    have it happen.

My Father has given me all things.
No one knows the Son except the Father,
    and no one knows the Father except the Son
    and those to whom the Son chooses to
      reveal him."

Mt 11:25-27
(Lk 10:21-22)

Come to Me and Rest

"Come to me,
all of you who are tired from carrying heavy
    loads,
and I will give you rest.
Take my yoke and put it on you,
and learn from me,
because I am gentle and humble of spirit;
and you will find rest.
For the yoke I will give you is easy,
and the load I will put on you is light."

Mt 11:28-30

Away to a Hill to Pray

Jesus made his disciples get into the boat and go
ahead of him to Bethsaida, on the other side of
the lake, while he sent the crowd away. After
saying good-bye to the people, he went away to a
hill to pray.

(Mt 14:22-33)
Mk 6:45-46

Anything You Pray For, It Will Be Done

"And I tell you more: whenever two of you on earth agree about anything you pray for, it will be done for you by my Father in heaven. For where two or three come together in my name, I am there with them."

Mt 18:19-20

Jesus Blesses the Little Children

Some people brought children to Jesus for him to place his hands on them and to pray for them, but the disciples scolded the people. Jesus said, "Let the children come to me and do not stop them, because the Kingdom of heaven belongs to such as these."

He placed his hands on them and then went away.

Mt 19:13
(Mk 10:14-15)
(Lk 15:16-17)

Blessed Is He Who Comes in the Name of the Lord

A large crowd of people spread their cloaks on the road while others cut branches from the trees and spread them on the road. The crowds walking in front of Jesus and those walking behind began to shout,

"Praise to David's Son!
God bless him who comes
    in the name of the Lord!
Praise be to God!"

Mt 21:8-9

"Praise God! God bless him who comes
   in the name of the Lord!
God bless the coming kingdom of
   King David, our Father!
Praise be to God!" *Mk 11:9-10*

"God bless the king who comes
   in the name of the Lord!
Peace in heaven and glory to God!" *Lk 19:38*

"Praise God!
God bless him who comes
   in the name of the Lord!
God bless the King of Israel!"

Jesus found a donkey and rode on it, just as the scripture says,

"Do not be afraid, city of Zion!
Here comes your king,
   riding on a young donkey." *Jn 12:13-15*

A House of Prayer

Jesus went into the Temple and drove out all those who were buying and selling there. He overturned the tables of the moneychangers and the stools of those who sold pigeons, and said to them:

"It is written in the Scriptures that God said, 'My Temple will be called a house of prayer.' But you are making it a hideout for thieves!"

Mt 21:12-13
(Mk 11:15-17)
(Lk 19:45-46)
(Jn 2:14-17)

412 ☧ Gospels and Acts

When You Pray . . . Believe

Lesson from the Fig Tree

On his way back to the city early next morning, Jesus was hungry. He saw a fig tree by the side of the road and went to it, but found nothing on it except leaves. So he said to the tree, "You will never again bear fruit!" At once the fig tree dried up.

The disciples saw this and were astounded. "How did the fig tree dry up so quickly?" they asked.

Jesus answered, "I assure you that if you believe and do not doubt, you will be able to do what I have done to this fig tree. And not only this, but you will even be able to say to this hill, 'Get up and throw yourself in the sea,' and it will. If you believe, you will receive whatever you ask for in prayer."

Mt 21:18-22
(Mk 11:20-25)

The Two Great Commandments

A teacher of the Law . . . came to him with a question: "Which commandment is the most important of all?"

Jesus replied, "The most important one is this: 'Listen, Israel! The Lord our God is the only Lord. Love the Lord your God with all your heart, with all your soul, with all your mind, and with all your strength.' The second most important commandment is this: 'Love your neighbor as you love yourself.' There is no other commandment more important than these two."

(Mt 22:34-40)
Mk 12:28-31
(Lk 10:15-28)

Jesus' Love for Jerusalem

"Jerusalem, Jerusalem!
You kill the prophets and stone the messengers
    God has sent you!
How many times I wanted to put my arms
    around all your people,
just as a hen gathers her chicks under her
    wings, but you would not let me!
And so your Temple will be abandoned and
    empty.
From now on, I tell you, you will never see me
    again until you say,
'God bless him who comes in the name of the
    Lord.' "

Mt 23:37-39
(Lk 13:34-35)

The Great Prayer of Thanksgiving

While they were eating, Jesus took a piece of bread, gave a prayer of thanks, broke it, and gave it to his disciples. "Take and eat it," he said; "this is my body."

Then he took a cup, gave thanks to God, and gave it to them. "Drink it, all of you," he said, "this is my blood, which seals God's covenant, my blood poured out for many for the forgiveness of sins. I tell you, I will never again drink this wine until the day I drink the new wine with you in my Father's Kingdom."

Then they sang a hymn and went out to the Mount of Olives.

Mt 26:26-30
(Mk 14:22-26)

When the hour came, Jesus took his place at the table with the apostles. He said to them, "I have wanted so much to eat this Passover meal with you before I suffer! For I tell you, I will never eat it until it is given its full meaning in the Kingdom of God."

Then Jesus took a cup, gave thanks to God, and said, "Take this and share it among yourselves. I tell you that from now on I will not drink this wine until the Kingdom of God comes."

Then he took a piece of bread, gave thanks to God, broke it, and gave it to them, saying, "This is my body, which is given for you. Do this in memory of me." In the same way, he gave them the cup after the supper, saying, "This cup is God's new covenant sealed with my blood, which is poured out for you."

Lk 22:14-20

For I received from the Lord the teaching that I passed on to you: that the Lord Jesus, on the night he was betrayed, took a piece of bread, gave thanks to God, broke it, and said, "This is my body, which is for you. Do this in memory of me." In the same way, after the supper he took the cup and said, "This cup is God's new covenant sealed with my blood. Whenever you drink it, do so in memory of me."

1 Cor 11:23-25

Jesus Prays in Gethsemane

Then Jesus went with his disciples to a place called Gethsemane, and he said to them, "Sit here while I go over there and pray." He took with him Peter and the two sons of Zebedee. Grief and anguish came over him, and he said to them, "The sorrow of my heart is so great that it almost crushes me. Stay here and keep watch with me."

He went a little farther on, threw himself face downward on the ground, and prayed,

"My Father, if it is possible,
take this cup of suffering from me!
Yet not what I want, but what you want."

Then he returned to the three disciples and found them asleep; and he said to Peter, "How is it that you three were not able to keep watch with me for even one hour? Keep watch and pray that you will not fall into temptation. The spirit is willing but the flesh is weak."

Once more Jesus went away and prayed,

"My Father, if this cup of suffering cannot be
taken away unless I drink it,
your will be done."

He returned once more and found the disciples asleep; they could not keep their eyes open.

Again Jesus left them, went away, and prayed a third time, saying the same words.

Mt 26:36-44
(Mk 14:32-39)
(Lk 22:39-45)

Last Words of Jesus

My God, My God!

At noon the whole country was covered with darkness, which lasted for three hours. At about three o'clock Jesus cried out with a loud shout:

"*Eli, Eli, lema sabachthani?*"
which means
"My God, my God, why did you abandon me?"

Mt 27:45-46
(Mk 15:33-34)

Father, Forgive Them

When they came to the place called "The Skull," they crucified Jesus there, and the two criminals, one on his right and the other on his left. Jesus said:

"Forgive them, Father!
They don't know what they are doing."

Lk 23:33-34

I Promise You

The other criminal said to Jesus, "Remember me
when you come as King!" Jesus said to him:

"I promise you that today you will
be in Paradise with me."

Lk 23:42-43

Father, in Your Hands

It was about twelve o'clock when the sun stopped
shining and darkness covered the whole country
until three o'clock; and the curtain hanging in
the Temple was torn in two. Jesus cried out in a
loud voice:

"Father! In your hands
I place my spirit."

Lk 23:44-46

She Is Your Mother

Standing close to Jesus' cross were his mother, his
mother's sister, Mary the wife of Clopas, and
Mary Magdalene. Jesus saw his mother and the
disciple he loved standing there; so he said to his
mother:

"He is your son."

Then he said to the disciple:

"She is your mother."

Jn 19:25-27

I Am Thirsty

Jesus knew that by now everything had been
completed; and in order to make the scripture
come true, he said,

"I am thirsty."   *Jn 19:28*

It Is Finished

A bowl was there, full of cheap wine; so a sponge was soaked in the wine, put on a stalk of hyssop, and lifted up to his lips. Jesus drank the wine and said,

"It is finished!"

Jn 19:29-30

* * *

God Sends His Angel to Mary

The angel Gabriel came to Mary and said, "Peace be with you! The Lord is with you and has greatly blessed you!"

Mary was deeply troubled by the angel's message, and she wondered what his words meant. The angel said to her, "Don't be afraid, Mary; God has been gracious to you. You will become pregnant and give birth to a son, and you will name him Jesus. He will be great and will be called the Son of the Most High God. The Lord God will make him a king, as his ancestor David was, and he will be the king of the descendants of Jacob forever; his kingdom will never end!"

Mary said to the angel, "I am a virgin. How, then, can this be?"

The angel answered, "The Holy Spirit will come on you, and God's power will rest upon you. For this reason the holy child will be called the Son of God. Remember your relative Elizabeth. It is said that she cannot have children, but she herself is now six months pregnant, even though she is very old. For there is nothing that God cannot do."

Mary's Prayer of Acceptance

"I am the Lord's servant," said Mary; "may it happen to me as you have said." And the angel left her.

Lk 1:28-38

The Hail Mary

The angel Gabriel came to her and said,

> "Hail, full of grace,
> the Lord is with you!"

When Elizabeth heard the greeting of Mary, the babe leaped in her womb; and Elizabeth was filled with the Holy Spirit and she exclaimed with a loud cry,

> "Blessed are you among women,
> and blessed is the fruit of your womb!"
> *Lk 1:28, 41-42 (RSV)*

Canticle of Mary

> My soul proclaims the greatness of the Lord,
> my spirit rejoices in God my savior;
> for he has looked with favor on his lowly
> servant.
>
> From this day all generations will call
> me blessed:

the Almighty has done great things for me,
    and holy is his Name.
He has mercy on those who fear him
    in every generation.

He has shown the strength of his arm,
    he has scattered the proud in their conceit.
He has cast down the mighty from their
        thrones,
    and lifted up the lowly.
He has filled the hungry with good things,
    and the rich he has sent away empty.

He has come to the help of his servant Israel
    for he remembered his promise of mercy,
the promise he made to our fathers,
    to Abraham and his children for ever.

Lk 1:46-55 (ICET)

Canticle of Zechariah

Blessed be the Lord, the God of Israel;
    he has come to his people and set them free.
He has raised up for us a mighty savior,
    born of the house of his servant David.

Through his holy prophets he promised of old
    that he would save us from our enemies,
    from the hands of all who hate us.
He promised to show mercy to our fathers
    and to remember his holy covenant.

This was the oath he swore to our father
        Abraham:
    to set us free from the hands of our enemies,

free to worship him without fear,
holy and righteous in his sight
   all the days of our life.

You, my child, shall be called the prophet of
   the Most High,
   for you will go before the Lord to prepare
    his way,
to give his people knowledge of salvation
   by the forgiveness of their sins.

In the tender compassion of our God
   the dawn from on high shall break upon us,
to shine on those who dwell in darkness and
   the shadow of death,
   and to guide our feet into the way of peace.

Lk 1:67-79 (ICET)

Glory to God in the Highest

Suddenly a great army of heaven's angels appeared with the angel, singing praises to God:

"Glory to God in the highest heaven,
   and peace on earth to those with whom he is
    pleased!"

Lk 2:13-14

Song of Simeon

Simeon took the child in his arms and gave thanks to God:

"Now, Lord, you have kept your promise,
   and you may let your servant go in peace.

With my own eyes I have seen your salvation,
　　which you have prepared in the presence of
　　all peoples:
A light to reveal your will to the Gentiles
　　and bring glory to your people Israel."

Lk 2:28-32

While Jesus Was Praying

After all the people had been baptized, Jesus also
was baptized. While he was praying, heaven was
opened, and the Holy Spirit came down upon
him in bodily form like a dove. And a voice came
from heaven,

"You are my own dear Son.
I am pleased with you."

Lk 3:21-22

At Daybreak

At daybreak Jesus left the town and went off to a
lonely place. The people started looking for him
and when they found him, they tried to keep him
from leaving.

Lk 4:42

Long Before Daylight

Very early the next morning, long before
daylight, Jesus got up and left the house. He
went out of town to a lonely place, where he
prayed. But Simon and his companions went out
searching for him, and when they found him,
they said, "Everyone is looking for you."

Mk 1:35-37

He Would Go Away to Lonely Places and Pray

But the news about Jesus spread all the more widely, and crowds of people came to hear him and be healed from their diseases. But he would go away to lonely places, where he prayed.

Lk 5:15-16

The Whole Night Praying

At that time Jesus went up a hill to pray and spent the whole night there praying to God. When day come, he called his disciples to him and chose twelve of them, whom he named apostles.

Lk 6:12-13

One Day When Jesus Was Praying Alone

One day when Jesus was praying alone, the disciples came to him. "Who do the crowds say I am?" he asked them.

"Some say that you are John the Baptist," they answered. "Others say that you are Elijah, while others say that one of the prophets of long ago has come back to life."

"What about you?" he asked them. "Who do you say I am?"

Peter answered, "You are God's Messiah."

Lk 9:18-20

While He Was Praying

About a week after he had said these things, Jesus took Peter, John, and James with him and went up a hill to pray. While he was praying, his face changed its appearance, and his clothes became dazzling white. . . . A voice said from the cloud, "This is my son, whom I have chosen—listen to him!"

Lk 9:28-29, 35

Just One Thing Is Needed

As Jesus and his disciples went on their way, he came to a village where a woman named Martha welcomed him in her home. She had a sister named Mary, who sat down at the feet of the Lord and listened to his teaching. Martha was upset over all the work she had to do, so she came and said, "Lord, don't you care that my sister has left me to do all the work by myself? Tell her to come and help me!"

The Lord answered her, "Martha, Martha! You are worried and troubled over so many things, but just one is needed. Mary has chosen the right thing, and it will not be taken away from her."

Lk 10:38-42

Keep On Asking

And Jesus said to his disciples, "Suppose one of you should go to a friend's house at midnight and say to him, 'Friend, let me borrow three loaves of bread. A friend of mine who is on a trip has just come to my house and I don't have any food for him!' And suppose your friend should answer from inside, 'Don't bother me! The door is already locked, and my children and I are in bed. I can't get up and give you anything.' Well, what then? I tell you that even if he will not get up and give you the bread because you are his friend, yet he will get up and give you everything you need because you are not ashamed to keep on asking

Lk 11:5-8

The Lost Son

Jesus went on to say, "There was once a man who had two sons. The younger one said to him, 'Father, give me my share of the property now.' So the man divided his property between his two sons. After a few days the younger son sold his part of the property and left home with the money. He went to a country far away, where he wasted his money in reckless living. He spent everything he had. Then a severe famine spread over that country, and he was left without a thing. So he went to work for one of the citizens of that country, who sent him out to his farm to take care of the pigs. He wished he could fill himself with the bean pods the pigs ate, but no one gave him anything to eat. At last he came to his senses and said, 'All my father's hired workers have more than they can eat and here I am about to starve! I will get up and go to my father and say, "Father, I have sinned against God and against you. I am no longer fit to be called your son; treat me as one of your hired workers." ' So he got up and started back to his father.

The Forgiving Father

"He was still a long way from home when his father saw him; his heart was filled with pity, and he ran, threw his arms around his son, and kissed him. 'Father,' the son said, 'I have sinned against God and against you. I am no longer fit to be called your son.' But the father called to his servants. 'Hurry!' he said. 'Bring the best robe and put it on him. Put a ring on his finger and shoes on his feet. Then go and get the prize calf and kill it, and let us celebrate with a feast! For this son of mine was dead, but now he is alive; he was lost, but now he has been found.' And so the feasting began.

The Older Son

"In the meantime the older son was out in the field. On his way back, when he came close to the house, he heard the music and dancing. So he called one of the servants and asked him, 'What's going on?' 'Your brother has come back home,' the servant answered, 'and your father has killed the prize calf, because he got him back safe and sound.' The older brother was so angry that he would not go into the house; so his father came out and begged him to come in. But he spoke back to his father, 'Look, all these years I have worked for you like a slave, and I have never disobeyed your orders. What have you given me? Not even a goat for me to have a feast with my friends! But this son of yours wasted all your property on prostitutes, and when he comes back home, you kill the prize calf for him!' 'My son,' the father answered, 'you are always here with me, and everything I have is yours. But we had to celebrate and be happy, because your brother was dead, but now he is alive; he was lost, but now he has been found.' "

Lk 15:11-32

Persistence In Prayer

Then Jesus told his disciples a parable to teach them that they should always pray and never become discouraged.

"In a certain town there was a judge who neither feared God nor respected man. And there was a widow in that same town who kept coming to him and pleading for her rights, saying, 'Help me against my opponent!' For a long time the judge refused to act, but at last he said to himself, 'Even though I don't fear God or respect man, yet because of all the trouble this widow is giving me, I will see to it that she gets her rights. If I don't, she will keep on coming and finally wear me out!' "

And the Lord continued, "Listen to what that corrupt judge said. Now, will God not judge in favor of his own people who cry to him day and night for help? Will he be slow to help them? I tell you, he will judge in their favor and do it quickly. But will the Son of Man find faith on earth when he comes?"

Lk 18:1-8

How to Pray and How Not to Pray

"Once there were two men who went up to the Temple to pray: one was a Pharisee, the other a tax collector. The Pharisee stood apart by himself and prayed,

'I thank you, God, that I am not greedy, dishonest, or an adulterer, like everybody else. I thank you that I am not like that tax collector over there. I fast two days a week, and I give you one tenth of all my income.'

"But the tax collector stood at a distance and would not even raise his face to heaven, but beat on his breast and said,

'God, have pity on me, a sinner!'

"I tell you," said Jesus, "the tax collector, and not the Pharisee, was in the right with God when he went home. For everyone who makes himself great will be humbled, and everyone who humbles himself will be made great."

Lk 18:10-14

Jesus Prays for Peter

"Simon, Simon! Listen! Satan has received permission to test all of you, to separate the good from the bad, as a farmer separates the wheat from the chaff. But I have prayed for you, Simon, that your faith will not fail. And when you turn back to me, you must strengthen your brothers."

Lk 22:31-32

Jesus Visits with Two Disciples

On that same day two of Jesus' followers were going to a village named Emmaus, about seven miles from Jerusalem, and they were talking to each other about all the things that had happened. As they talked and discussed, Jesus himself drew near and walked along with them; they saw him, but somehow did not recognize him. Jesus said to them, "What are you talking about to each other, as you walk along?"

They stood still, with sad faces. One of them, named Cleopas, asked him, "Are you the only visitor in Jerusalem who doesn't know the things that have been happening there these last few days?"

"What things?" he asked.

"The things that happened to Jesus of Nazareth," they answered. "This man was a prophet and was considered by God and by all the people to be powerful in everything he said and did. Our chief priests and rulers handed him over to be sentenced to death, and he was crucified. And we had hoped that he would be the one who was going to set Israel free! Besides all that, this is now the third day since it happened. Some of the women of our group surprised us; they went at dawn to the tomb, but could not find his body. They came back saying they had seen a vision of angels who told them that he is alive. Some of our group went to the tomb and found it exactly as the women said, but they did not see him."

Then Jesus said to them, "How foolish you are,

how slow you are to believe everything the prophets said! Was it not necessary for the Messiah to suffer these things and then to enter his glory?" And Jesus explained to them what was said about himself in all the Scriptures, beginning with the books of Moses and the writings of all the prophets.

As they came near the village to which they were going, Jesus acted as if he were going farther; but they held him back saying, "Stay with us; the day is almost over and it is getting dark." So he went in to stay with them. He sat down to eat with them, took the bread, and said the blessing; then he broke the bread and gave it to them. Then their eyes were opened and they recognized him, but he disappeared from their sight. They said to each other, "Wasn't it like a fire burning in us when he talked to us on the road and explained the Scriptures to us?"

Lk 24:13-32

*　　*　　*

Canticle of the Word

In the beginning was the Word:
the Word was with God
and the Word was God.
He was with God in the beginning.
Through him all things came to be,
not one thing had its being but through him.
All that came to be had life in him
and that life was the light of men,
a light that shines in the dark,
a light that darkness could not overpower.

A man came, sent by God.
His name was John.
He came as a witness,
as a witness to speak for the light,
so that everyone might believe through him.
He was not the light,
only a witness to speak for the light.

The Word was the true light
that enlightens all men;
and he was coming into the world.
He was in the world
that had its being through him,
and the world did not know him.
He came to his own domain
and his own people did not accept him.

But to all that did accept him
he gave power to become children of God,
to all who believe in the name of him
who was born not out of human stock
or urge of the flesh
or will of man
but of God himself.
The Word was made flesh,
he lived among us,
and we saw his glory,
the glory that is his as the only Son of the
    Father,
full of grace and truth.

Jn 1:1-15 (JB)

God So Loved the World

For God loved the world so much
that he gave his only Son,
so that everyone who believes in him
may not die but have eternal life.
For God did not send his Son into the world
to be its judge,
but to be its savior.

Jn 3:16-17

Song of the Good Shepherd

I have come
so that they may have life
and have it to the full.
I am the good shepherd:
the good shepherd is one who lays down his
      life for his sheep.
The hired man, since he is not the shepherd
and the sheep do not belong to him,
abandons the sheep and runs away
as soon as he sees a wolf coming,
and then the wolf attacks and scatters the
      sheep;
this is because he is only a hired man
and has no concern for the sheep.
I am the good shepherd;
I know my own
and my own know me,
just as the Father knows me
and I know the Father;
and I lay down my life for my sheep.
And there are other sheep I have

that are not of this fold,
and these I have to lead as well.
They too will listen to my voice,
and there will be only one flock
and one shepherd.
The Father loves me,
because I lay down my life
in order to take it up again.
No one takes it from me;
I lay it down of my own free will,
and as it is in my power to lay it down,
so it is in my power to take it up again;
and this is the command I have been given
by my Father.

Jn 10:10-18 (JB)

Jesus Prays at Lazarus' Tomb

"I am the resurrection and the life.
Whoever believes in me will live, even though
he dies;
and whoever lives and believes in me will
never die.
Do you believe this?"

Jesus said to Martha, "Didn't I tell you that you
would see God's glory if you believed?" They
took the stone away. Jesus looked up and said,

"I thank you, Father,
that you listen to me.
I know that you always listen to me,
but I say this for the sake of the people here,
so that they will believe that you sent me."

Jn 11:25-26, 40-42

The Hour Has Come

"The hour has now come for the Son of Man to receive great glory. I am telling you the truth: a grain of wheat remains no more than a single grain unless it is dropped into the ground and dies. If it does die, then it produces many grains. Whoever loves his own life will lose it; whoever hates his own life in this world will keep it for life eternal. Whoever wants to serve me must follow me, so that my servant will be with me where I am. And my Father will honor anyone who serves me.

"Now my heart is troubled—and what shall I say? Shall I say, 'Father, do not let this hour come upon me'? But that is why I came—so that I might go through this hour of suffering. Father, bring glory to your name!"

Jn 12:23-28

A New Commandment

"And now I give you a new commandment:
love one another.
As I have loved you,
so you must love one another.
If you have love for one another,
then everyone will know that you are my
    disciples."

Jn 13:34-35

Jesus Is the Way to the Father

"Do not be worried and upset.
Believe in God and believe also in me.
There are many rooms in my Father's house,
and I am going to prepare a place for you.
I would not tell you this if it were not so.
And after I go and prepare a place for you,
I will come back and take you to myself,
so that you will be where I am.
You know the way that leads to the place
    where I am going.

I am the way, the truth, and the life;
No one goes to the Father except by me.
Now that you have known me, you will know
    my Father also. . . .
Whoever has seen me has seen the Father.

I am telling you the truth:
whoever believes in me will do what I do—
yes, he will do even greater things,
because I am going to the Father.
And I will do whatever you ask for in my
    name,
so that the Father's glory will be shown
    through the Son.
If you ask me for anything in my name, I will
    do it."

Jn 14:1-4, 6-7, 9, 12-14

The Promise of the Holy Spirit

"If you love me, you will obey my
        commandments.
I will ask the Father,
and he will give you another Helper,
who will stay with you forever.
He is the Spirit,
who reveals the truth about God.
The world cannot receive him,
because it cannot see him or know him.
But you know him,
because he remains with you and is in you.

When I go, you will not be left alone;
I will come back to you.

Whoever loves me will obey my teaching.
My Father will love him,
and my Father and I will come to him
    and live with him.

I have told you these things while I am still
        with you.
The Helper, the Holy Spirit,
    whom the Father will send in my name,
will teach you everything
    and make you remember all that I have
        told you."

Jn 14:15-18, 23, 25-26

My Own Peace I Give You .

"Peace is what I leave with you;
it is my own peace that I give you.
I do not give it as the world does.

Do not be worried and upset; do not be afraid.
You heard me say to you,
'I am leaving, but I will come back to you.'
If you loved me, you would be glad that I am
    going to the Father;
for he is greater than I.
I have told you this now before it happens,
so that when it does happen, you will believe.
I cannot talk with you much longer,
because the ruler of this world is coming.
He has no power over me,
but the world must know that I love the
    Father;
that is why I do everything as he commands
    me."

Jn 14:27-31

Jesus Is the True Vine

"I am the real vine,
and my Father is the gardener.
He breaks off every branch in me that does not
    bear fruit,
and he prunes every branch that does
    bear fruit,
so that it will be clean and bear more fruit.
You have been made clean already
by the teaching I have given you.
Remain united to me,
and I will remain united to you.
A branch cannot bear fruit of itself;
it can do so only if it remains in the vine.
In the same way you cannot bear fruit
unless you remain in me.
I am the vine, and you are the branches.

Whoever remains in me, and I in him, will
      bear much fruit;
for you cannot do anything without me."

If You Remain in Me

"If you remain in me, and my words remain
      in you,
then you will ask for anything you wish,
and you shall have it.

If you obey my commands,
you will remain in my love,
just as I have obeyed my Father's commands
and remain in his love.

I have told you this so that my joy may be in
      you
and that your joy may be complete.
My commandment is this:
love one another, just as I love you.
The greatest love a person can have for his
      friends is to give his life for them."

You Are My Friends

"You are my friends
if you do what I command you.
I do not call you servants any longer,
because a servant does not know what his
      master is doing.
Instead, I call you friends,
because I have told you everything I heard
      from my Father.
You did not choose me;
I chose you and appointed you

to go and bear much fruit,
the kind of fruit that endures.
And so the Father will give you
whatever you ask of him in my name.
This, then, is what I command you:
love one another."   *Jn 15:1-5, 7, 10-17*

The Work of the Holy Spirit

"I did not tell you these things at the
        beginning,
for I was with you.
But now I am going to him who sent me.

If I do not go
the Helper will not come to you.
But if I do go away,
then I will send him to you.
And when he comes,
he will prove to the people of the world
that they are wrong about sin
and about what is right and about God's
        judgment.

When, however, the Spirit comes,
who reveals the truth about God,
he will lead you into all the truth.
He will not speak on his own authority,
but he will speak of what he hears
and will tell you of things to come.
He will give me glory,
because he will take what I say
and tell it to you.
All that my Father has is mine;
that is why I said that the Spirit will take
what I give him and tell it to you."
                            Jn 16:4-5, 7-8, 13-15

Whatever You Ask in My Name

"In a little while you will not see me any more,
and then a little while later you will see me.

I am telling you the truth:
you will cry and weep,
but the world will be glad;
you will be sad,
but your sadness will turn into gladness.
When a woman is about to give birth,
she is sad because her hour of suffering has
        come;
but when the baby is born, she forgets her
        suffering,
because she is happy that a baby has been born
        into the world.
That is how it is with you:
now you are sad, but I will see you again,
and your hearts will be filled with gladness,
the kind of gladness that no one can take away
        from you.

When that day comes,
you will not ask me for anything.
I am telling you the truth:
the Father will give you
whatever you ask of him in my name.
Until now you have not asked for anything in
        my name;
ask and you will receive,
so that your happiness may be complete."

                                            Jn 16:16, 20-24

The Priestly Prayer of Christ

"Father, the hour has come.
Give glory to your Son,
so that the Son may give glory to you.
For you gave him authority over all mankind,
so that he might give eternal life to all those
    you gave him.
And eternal life means to know you,
the only true God,
and to know Jesus Christ, whom you sent.
I have shown your glory on earth;
I have finished the work you gave me to do.
Father! Give me glory in your presence now,
the same glory I had with you before the world
    was made.

I have made you known to those you gave me
    out of the world.
They belonged to you, and you gave them to
    me.
They have obeyed your word,
and now they know everything you gave me
    comes from you.
I gave them the message that you gave me,
and they received it;
they know that it is true that I came from you,
and they believe that you sent me."

Jesus Prays for His Disciples

"I pray for them.
I do not pray for the world but for those you
    gave me,
for they belong to you.
All I have is yours, and all you have is mine;

and my glory is shown through them.
And now I am coming to you;
I am no longer in the world,
but they are in the world.
Holy Father! Keep them safe by the power of
    your name,
the name you gave me,
so that they may be one just as you and I are
    one.
While I was with them,
I kept them safe by the power of your name,
the name you gave me.
I protected them, and not one of them was
    lost,
except the man who was bound to be lost—
so that scripture might come true.
And now I am coming to you,
and I say these things in the world
so that they might have my joy in their hearts
    in all its fullness.
I gave them your message,
and the world hated them,
because they do not belong to the world,
just as I do not belong to the world.
I do not ask you to take them out of the world,
but I do ask you to keep them safe from the
    Evil One.
Just as I do not belong to the world,
they do not belong to the world.
Dedicate them to yourself by means of truth;
your word is truth.
I sent them into the world,
just as you sent me into the world.

And for their sake I dedicate myself to you,
in order that they, too, may be truly dedicated
     to you."

Jesus Prays for All Believers

"I pray not only for them,
but also for those who believe in me
because of their message.
I pray that they may all be one.
Father! May they be in us,
just as you are in me and I am in you.
May they be one, so that the world will believe
     that you sent me.
I gave them the same glory you gave me,
so that they may be one,
just as you and I are one:
I in them and you in me,
so that they may be completely one,
in order that the world may know that you
     sent me
and that you love them as you love me.

Father! You have given them to me,
and I want them to be with me where I am,
so that they may see my glory,
the glory you gave me;
for you loved me before the world was made.
Righteous Father!
The world does not know you,
but I know you,
and these know that you sent me.
I made you known to them,
and I will continue to do so,

in order that the love you have for me may
  be in them,
and so that I also may be in them."

Jn 17:1-26

Prayer and Praying
in the Acts of the Apostles

They Gathered Frequently to Pray

After Jesus was taken into heaven, the apostles
went back to Jerusalem from the Mount of
Olives, which is about half a mile away from the
city. They entered the city and went up to the
room where they were staying: Peter, John,
James and Andrew, Philip and Thomas, Bar-
tholomew and Matthew, James the son of
Alphaeus, Simon the Patriot, and Judas son of
James. They gathered frequently to pray as a
group, together with the women and with Mary
the mother of Jesus and with his brothers.

Acts 1:12-14

In Fellowship and Prayer

Many of them believed Peter's message and were
baptized, and about three thousand people were
added to the group that day. They spent their
time in learning from the apostles, taking part in
the fellowship, and sharing in the fellowship
meals and the prayers.

Acts 2:41-42

With Glad and Humble Hearts

Many miracles and wonders were being done through the apostles, and everyone was filled with awe. All the believers continued in close fellowship and shared their belongings with one another. They would sell their property and possessions, and distribute the money among all, according to what each one needed. Day after day they met as a group in the Temple, and they had their meals together in their homes, eating with glad and humble hearts, praising God, and enjoying the good will of all the people. And every day the Lord added to their group those who were being saved.

Acts 2:43-47

Walking and Jumping and Praising God

One day Peter and John went to the Temple at three o'clock in the afternoon, the hour for prayer. There at the Beautiful Gate, as it was called, was a man who had been lame all his life. Every day he was carried to the gate to beg for money from the people who were going into the Temple. When he saw Peter and John going in, he begged them to give him something. They looked straight at him, and Peter said, "Look at us!" So he looked at them, expecting to get something from them. But Peter said to him, "I have no money at all, but I give you what I have: in the name of Jesus Christ of Nazareth I order you to get up and walk!" Then he took him by his right hand and helped him up. At once the man's feet and ankles became strong; he jumped up, stood on his feet, and started walking around. Then he went into the Temple with them, walking and jumping and praising God. The people there saw him walking and praising God, and when they recognized him as the beggar who had sat at the Beautiful Gate, they were all surprised and amazed at what had happened to him.

Acts 3:1-10

The Believers Pray for Boldness

As soon as Peter and John were set free, they returned to their group and told them what the chief priests and the elders had said. When the believers heard it, they all joined together in prayer to God:

"Master and Creator of heaven, earth, and sea, and all that is in them! By means of the Holy Spirit you spoke through our ancestor David, your servant, when he said,
'Why were the Gentiles furious;
    why did people make their useless plots?
The kings of the earth prepared themselves,
    and the rulers met together
    against the Lord and his Messiah.'
For indeed Herod and Pontius Pilate met together in this city with the Gentiles and the people of Israel against Jesus, your holy Servant, whom you made Messiah. They gathered to do everything that you by your power and will had already decided would happen. And now, Lord, take notice of the threats they have made, and

allow us, your servants, to speak your message
with all boldness. Reach out your hand to heal,
and grant that wonders and miracles may be performed through the name of your holy Servant
Jesus."

Acts 4:23-30

The Seven Helpers

So the twelve apostles called the whole group of
believers together and said, "It is not right for us
to neglect the preaching of God's word in order
to handle finances. So then, brothers, choose
seven men among you who are known to be full
of the Holy Spirit and wisdom, and we will put
them in charge of this matter. We ourselves,
then, will give our full time to prayer and the
work of preaching."

The whole group was pleased with the
apostles' proposal, so they chose Stephen, a man
full of faith and the Holy Spirit (and six others).
The group presented them to the apostles, who
prayed and placed their hands on them.

Acts 6:2-6

*(Other instances of prayer and praying in the
Acts can be found in: 8:14-15, 8:20-24, 9:11-12,
9:40-41, 10:2-4, 10:9, 10:30-31, 11:4-5, 12:4-5,
12:12, 13:2-3, 14:23, 16:13-14, 16:16-18,
16:25-26, 20:36-37, 21:5, 22:17-18, 27:29,
28:8-9.)*

Epistles
of Paul

Prayer of Thanksgiving

First, I thank my God through Jesus Christ for all of you, because the whole world is hearing about your faith. God is my witness that what I say is true—the God whom I serve with all my heart by preaching the Good News about his Son. God knows that I remember you every time I pray. I ask that God in his good will may at last make it possible for me to visit you now. For I want very much to see you, in order to share a spiritual blessing with you to make you strong. What I mean is that both you and I will be helped at the same time, you by my faith and I by yours.

Rm 1:8-12

He Made Us His Friends

For when we were still helpless Christ died for the wicked at the time that God chose. It is a difficult thing for someone to die for a righteous person. It may even be that someone might dare to die for a good person. But God has shown us how much he loves us—it was while we were still sinners that Christ died for us! By his death we are now put right with God: how much more, then, will we be saved by him from God's anger! We were God's enemies, but he made us his friends through the death of his Son. Now that we are God's friends, how much more will we be saved by Christ's life! But that is not all; we rejoice because of what God has done through our Lord Jesus Christ, who has now made us God's friends.

Rm 5:6-11

A Hymn to God's Love

Who Can Separate Us from the Love of Christ?

In view of all this, what can we say? If God is for us, who can be against us? Certainly not God, who did not even keep back his own Son, but offered him for us all! He gave us his Son — will he not also freely give us all things? Who will accuse God's chosen people? God himself declares them not guilty! Who, then, will condemn them? Not Christ Jesus, who died, or rather, who was raised to life and is at the right side of God, pleading with him for us! Who, then, can separate us from the love of Christ? Can trouble do it, or hardship or persecution or hunger or poverty or danger or death?

Nothing Can Separate Us from Christ

No, in all these things we have complete victory through him who loved us! For I am certain that nothing can separate us from his love: neither death nor life, neither angels nor other heavenly rulers or powers, neither the present nor the future, neither the world above nor the world below — there is nothing in all creation that will ever be able to separate us from the love of God which is ours through Christ Jesus our Lord.

Rm 8:31-35, 37-39

Everyone Who Calls Out to the Lord Will Be Saved

If you confess that Jesus is Lord and believe that God raised him from death, you will be saved. For it is by our faith that we are put right with

God; it is by our confession that we are saved.
The scripture says, "Whoever believes in him will
not be disappointed." This includes everyone,
because there is no difference between Jews and
Gentiles; God is the same Lord of all and rightly
blesses all who call to him. As the scripture says,
"Everyone who calls out to the Lord for help will
be saved."

Rm 10:9-13

A Hymn to God's Wisdom

How great are God's riches!
How deep are his wisdom and knowledge!
Who can explain his decisions?
Who can understand his ways?
As the scripture says,

"Who knows the mind of the Lord?
    Who is able to give him advice?
Who has ever given him anything,
    so that he had to pay it back?"

For all things were created by him,
and all things exist through him and for him.
To God be the glory forever! Amen.

Rm 11:33-36

PRAY AT ALL TIMES

Let your hope keep you joyful,
be patient in your troubles,
and pray at all times.

Rm 12:12

Prayer of Praise

Let us give glory to God! He is able to make you stand firm in your faith, according to the Good News I preach about Jesus Christ and according to the revelation of the secret truth which was hidden for long ages in the past. Now, however, that truth has been brought out into the open through the writings of the prophets; and by the command of the eternal God it is made known to all nations, so that all may believe and obey.

To the only God, who alone is all-wise, be glory through Jesus Christ forever! Amen.

Rm 16:25-27

Blessings in Christ

May God our Father and the Lord Jesus Christ give you grace and peace.

I always give thanks to my God for you because of the grace he has given you through Christ Jesus. For in union with Christ you have become rich in all things, including all speech and knowledge. The message about Christ has become so firmly established in you that you have not failed to receive a single blessing, as you wait for our Lord Jesus Christ to be revealed. He will also keep you firm to the end, so that you will be faultless on the Day of our Lord Jesus Christ. God is to be trusted, the God who called you to have fellowship with his Son Jesus Christ, our Lord.

1 Cor 1:3-9

Paul's Canticle to Love

I may be able to speak the languages of men
      and even of angels,
but if I have no love,
my speech is no more than a noisy gong or
      a clanging bell.
I may have the gift of inspired preaching;
I may have all knowledge and understand all
      secrets;
I may have all the faith needed to move
      mountains—
but if I have no love, I am nothing.
I may give away everything I have,
and even give up my body to be burned—
but if I have no love, it does me no good.

Love is patient and kind;
it is not jealous or conceited or proud;
love is not ill-mannered or selfish or irritable;
love does not keep a record of wrongs;
love is not happy with evil,
but is happy with the truth.
Love never gives up;
and its faith, hope, and patience never fail.

Love Is Eternal

Love is eternal.
There are inspired messages, but they are
      temporary;
there are gifts of speaking in strange tongues,
      but they will cease;
there is knowledge, but it will pass.
For our gifts of knowledge and of inspired
      messages are only partial;

but when what is perfect comes,
then what is partial will disappear.

When I was a child, my speech, feelings, and
thinking were all those of a child;
now that I am a man, I have no more use for
childish ways.
What we see now is like a dim image in a
mirror;
then we shall see face to face.
What I know now is only partial;
then it will be complete —
as complete as God's knowledge of me.

Meanwhile these three remain:
faith, hope, and love;
and the greatest of these is love.

1 Cor 13:1-13

The Resurrection of Christ

I passed on to you what I received, which is of
the greatest importance: that Christ died for our
sins, as written in the Scriptures; that he was
buried and that he was raised to life three days
later, as written in the Scriptures; that he appeared to Peter and then to all twelve apostles.
Then he appeared to more than five hundred of
his followers at once, most of whom are still
alive, although some have died. Then he appeared to James, and afterward to all the
apostles.

Last of all he appeared also to me — even
though I am like someone whose birth was ab-
normal. For I am the least of all the apostles — I

do not even deserve to be called an apostle, because I persecuted God's church. But by God's grace I am what I am.

1 Cor 15:3-10

A Hymn to Christ's Victory

Then the end will come; Christ will overcome all spiritual rulers, authorities, and powers, and will hand over the Kingdom to God the Father. For Christ must rule until God defeats all enemies and puts them under his feet. The last enemy to be defeated will be death. For the scripture says, "God will put all things under his feet." It is clear, of course, that the words "all things" do not include God himself, who puts all things under Christ. But when all things have been placed under Christ's rule, then he himself, the Son, will place himself under God, who placed all things under him; and God will rule completely over all.

1 Cor 15:24-28

A Hymn of Triumph Over Death

Listen to this secret truth: we shall not all die, but when the last trumpet sounds, we shall all be changed in an instant, as quickly as the blinking of an eye. For when the trumpet sounds, the dead will be raised, never to die again, and we shall all be changed. For what is mortal must be changed into what is immortal; what will die must be changed into what cannot die. So when

this takes place, and the mortal has been changed
into the immortal, then the scripture will come
true:

"Death is destroyed;
victory is complete!
Where, Death, is your victory?
Where, Death, is your power to hurt?"

1 Cor 15:51-55

Thanks Be to God

May God our Father and the Lord Jesus Christ
give you grace and peace.

Let us give thanks to the God and Father of
our Lord Jesus Christ, the merciful Father, the
God from whom all help comes! He helps us in
all our troubles, so that we are able to help others
who have all kinds of troubles, using the same
help that we ourselves have received from God.
Just as we have a share in Christ's many sufferings, so also through Christ we share in God's
great help.

2 Cor 1:2-5

A Blessing

The grace of the Lord Jesus Christ, the love of
God, and the fellowship of the Holy Spirit be
with you all.

2 Cor 13:13

Abba, Abba

To show that you are his sons,
God sent the Spirit of his Son
    into our hearts,
the Spirit who cries out,
"Father, my Father."
So then, you are no longer a slave
    but a son.
And since you are his son,
God will give you all that he has
    for his sons.

Gal 4:6-7

<small>A PAULINE CANTICLE</small>

Spiritual Blessings in Christ

Let us give thanks to the God and Father of
    our Lord Jesus Christ!
    For in our union with Christ he has blessed
      us by giving us every spiritual blessing in
      the heavenly world.
Even before the world was made, God had
      already chosen us to be his through our
      union with Christ,
    so that we would be holy and without fault
      before him.
Because of his love God had already decided
      that through Jesus Christ he would
      make us his sons (daughters)
this was his pleasure and purpose.

How Great Is the Grace of God!

Let us praise God for his glorious grace,
   for the free gift he gave us in his dear Son!
For by the death of Christ we are set free, that
   is, our sins are forgiven.
How great is the grace of God, which he gave
   to us in such large measure!
In all his wisdom and insight God did what he
   had purposed,
   and made known to us the secret plan he
   had already decided to complete by
   means of Christ.
This plan which God will complete when the
   time is right, is to bring all creation
   together,
   everything in heaven and on earth, with
   Christ as head.

Let Us Praise God's Glory

All things are done according to God's plan
   and decision;
   and God chose us to be his own people in
   union with Christ because of his own
   purpose, based on what he had decided
   from the very beginning.
Let us, then, who were the first to hope in
   Christ, praise God's glory!
And you also became God's people when you
   heard the true message,
   the Good News that brought you salvation.
You believed in Christ, and God put his stamp
   of ownership on you by giving you the
   Holy Spirit he had promised.

The Spirit is the guarantee that we shall
     receive what God has promised his
     people,
   and this assures us that God will give
     complete freedom to those who are his.
   Let us praise his glory!

Eph 1:3-14

Paul's Prayer

For this reason, ever since I heard of your faith in
the Lord Jesus and your love for all of God's people, I have not stopped giving thanks to God for
you. I remember you in my prayers and ask the
God of our Lord Jesus Christ, the glorious
Father, to give you the Spirit, who will make you
wise and reveal God to you, so that you will
know him. I ask that your minds may be opened
to see his light, so that you will know what is the
hope to which he has called you, how rich are the
wonderful blessings he promises his people, and
how very great is his power at work in us who
believe. This power working in us is the same as
the mighty strength which he used when he
raised Christ from death and seated him at his
right side in the heavenly world. Christ rules
there above all heavenly rulers, authorities,
powers, and lords; he has a title superior to all
titles of authority in this world and in the next.
God put all things under Christ's feet and gave
him to the church as supreme Lord over all
things. The church is Christ's body, the comple-
tion of him who himself completes all things
everywhere.

Eph 1:15-23

I Fall on My Knees
Before the Father

For this reason I fall on my knees before the Father, from whom every family in heaven and on earth receives its true name. I ask God from the wealth of his glory to give you power through his Spirit to be strong in your inner selves, and I pray that Christ will make his home in your hearts through faith. I pray that you may have your roots and foundation in love, so that you, together with all God's people, may have the power to understand how broad and long, how high and deep, is Christ's love. Yes, may you come to know his love— although it can never be fully known—and so be completely filled with the very nature of God.

To him who by means of his power working in us is able to do so much more than we can ever ask for, or even think of: to God be the glory in the church and in Christ Jesus for all time, forever and ever! Amen.

Eph 3:14-21

There Is One Lord

There is one body and one Spirit,
just as there is one hope to which
   God has called you.
There is one Lord, one faith, one baptism;
there is one God and Father
   of all mankind,
who is Lord of all,
   works through all,
   and is in all.

Eph 4:4-6

With Psalms and Hymns

Be filled with the Spirit.
Speak to one another with the words of
    psalms, hymns, and sacred songs;
sing hymns and psalms to the Lord
    with praise in your hearts.
In the name of our Lord Jesus Christ,
always give thanks for everything
    to God the Father.

Eph 5:19-20

Put on the Armor of God
and Pray on Every Occasion

Finally, build up your strength in union with the Lord and by means of his mighty power. Put on all the armor that God gives you, so that you will be able to stand up against the Devil's evil tricks. For we are not fighting against human beings but against the wicked spiritual forces in the heavenly world, the rulers, authorities, and cosmic powers of this dark age. So put on God's armor now! Then when the evil day comes, you will be able to resist the enemy's attacks; and after fighting to the end, you will still hold your ground.

So stand ready, with truth as a belt tight around your waist, with righteousness as your breastplate, and as your shoes the readiness to announce the Good News of peace. At all times carry faith as a shield; for with it you will be able to put out all the burning arrows shot by the Evil One. And accept salvation as a helmet, and the word of God as the sword which the Spirit gives you. Do all this in prayer, asking for God's help. Pray on every occasion, as the Spirit leads. For this reason keep alert and never give up; pray always for all God's people. And pray also for me, that God will give me a message when I am ready to speak, so that I may speak boldly and make known the gospel's secret. For the sake of this gospel I am an ambassador, though now I am in prison. Pray that I may be bold in speaking about the gospel as I should.

Eph 6:10-20

A Blessing

May God the Father and the Lord Jesus Christ give to all Christian brothers and sisters peace and love with faith. May God's grace be with all those who love our Lord Jesus Christ with undying love.

Eph 6:23-24

Paul's Prayer for His Readers

May God our Father and the Lord Jesus Christ give you grace and peace.

I thank God for you every time I think of you; and every time I pray for you all, I pray with joy because of the way in which you have helped me in the work of the gospel from the very first day until now. And so I am sure that God, who began this good work in you, will carry it on until it is finished on the Day of Christ Jesus. You are always in my heart! . . . God is my witness that I tell the truth when I say that my deep feeling for you all comes from the heart of Christ Jesus himself.

I pray that your love will keep on growing more and more, together with true knowledge and perfect judgment, so that you will be able to choose what is best. Then you will be free from all impurity and blame on the Day of Christ. Your lives will be filled with the truly good qualities which only Jesus Christ can produce, for the glory and praise of God.

Phil 1:2-11

A PAULINE CANTICLE

Christ's Humility and Greatness

The attitude you should have is the one that Christ Jesus had:
>He always had the nature of God,
>>but he did not think that by force he should try to become equal to God.
>Instead of this, of his own free will he gave up all he had,
>>and took the nature of a servant.
>He became like man
>>and appeared in human likeness.
>He was humble and walked the path of obedience all the way to death —
>>his death on the cross.
>For this reason God raised him to the highest place above
>>and gave him the name that is greater than any other name.

And so, in honor of the name of Jesus
    all beings in heaven, on earth, and in the
      world below
    will fall on their knees,
and all will openly proclaim that Jesus Christ
    is Lord,
    to the glory of God the Father.

Phil 2:5-11

Ask for What You Need with a Thankful Heart

May you always be joyful in your union with the Lord. I say it again: rejoice!

Show a gentle attitude toward everyone. The Lord is coming soon. Don't worry about anything, but in all your prayers ask God for what you need, always asking him with a thankful heart. And God's peace, which is far beyond human understanding, will keep your hearts and minds safe in union with Christ Jesus.

My brothers, fill your minds with those things that are good and that deserve praise: things that are true, noble, right, pure, lovely, and honorable. . . . And God who gives us peace will be with you all.

Phil 4:4-9

A BLESSING

May the grace of the Lord Jesus Christ be with you all.

Phil 4:23

Prayer of Thanksgiving

We always give thanks to God, the Father of our Lord Jesus Christ, when we pray for you. For we have heard of your faith in Christ Jesus and of your love for all God's people. When the true message, the Good News, first came to you, you heard about the hope it offers. So your faith and love are based on what you hope for, which is kept safe for you in heaven. The gospel keeps bringing blessings and is spreading throughout the world, just as it has among you ever since the day you first heard about the grace of God and came to know it as it really is.

With Joy Give Thanks to the Father

For this reason we have always prayed for you, ever since we heard about you. We ask God to fill you with the knowledge of his will, with all the wisdom and understanding that his Spirit gives. Then you will be able to live as the Lord wants and will always do what pleases him. Your lives will produce all kinds of good deeds, and you will grow in your knowledge of God. May you be made strong with all the strength which comes from his glorious powers, so that you may be able to endure everything with patience. And with joy give thanks to the Father, who has made you fit to have your share of what God has reserved for his people in the kingdom of light. He rescued us from the power of darkness and brought us safe into the kingdom of his dear Son, by whom we are set free, that is, our sins are forgiven.

Col 1:3-6, 9-14

A Pauline Hymn to Christ

Christ is the visible likeness of the invisible God.

He is the first-born Son, superior to all created things.

For through him God created everything
in heaven and on earth,
the seen and the unseen things,

including spiritual powers, lords, rulers, and authorities.

God created the whole universe through him and for him.

Christ existed before all things,

and in union with him all things have their proper place.

He is the head of his body, the church;

he is the source of the body's life.

He is the first-born Son, who was raised from death,

in order that he alone might have the first place in all things.

For it was by God's own decision that the Son has in himself the full nature of God.

Through the Son, then, God decided to bring the whole universe back to himself.

God made peace through his Son's death on the cross

and so brought back to himself all things,
both on earth and in heaven.

Col 1:15-20

Set Your Hearts on Things That Are in Heaven

You have been raised to life with Christ, so set your hearts on the things that are in heaven, where Christ sits on his throne at the right side of God. Keep your minds fixed on things there, not on things here on earth. For you have died, and your life is hidden with Christ in God. Your real life is Christ and when he appears, then you too will appear with him and share his glory!

Col 3:1-4

Sing Psalms, Hymns, and Sacred Songs

You are the people of God;
he loved you and chose you for his own.
So then, you must clothe yourselves with
    compassion, kindness, humility,
    gentleness, and patience.
Be tolerant with one another and forgive one
    another . . . just as the Lord has forgiven
    you.
And to all these qualities add love,
which binds all things together in perfect
    unity.
The peace that Christ gives is to guide you in
    the decisions you make;
for it is to this peace that God has called you
    together in the one body.
And be thankful.
Christ's message in all its richness must live
    in your hearts.
Teach and instruct one another with all
    wisdom.

Sing psalms, hymns, and sacred songs;
sing to God with thanksgiving in your hearts.
Everything you do or say, then,
should be done in the name of the Lord Jesus,
as you give thanks through him to God the
    Father.

Col 3:12-17

Christ Is the Real Master You Serve

Whatever you do, work at it with all your heart,
as though you were working for the Lord and not
for men. Remember that the Lord will give you
as a reward what he has kept for his people. For
Christ is the real Master you serve.

Col 3:23-24

Be Persistent in Prayer

Be persistent in prayer, and keep alert as you
pray, giving thanks to God. At the same time
pray also for us, so that God will give us a good
opportunity to preach his message about the
secret of Christ. For that is why I am now in
prison. Pray, then, that I may speak, as I should,
in such a way as to make it clear.

Col 4:2-4

The Truth About Those Who Have Died

Our brothers, we want you to know the truth
about those who have died, so that you will not
be sad, as are those who have no hope. We

believe that Jesus died and rose again, and so we
believe that God will take back with Jesus those
who have died believing in him.

1 Thes 4:13-14

Pray at All Times

Be joyful always, pray at all times, be thankful in
all circumstances. This is what God wants from
you in your life in union with Christ Jesus.

Do not restrain the Holy Spirit; do not despise
inspired messages. Put all things to the test: keep
what is good and avoid every kind of evil.

May the God who gives us peace make you
holy in every way and keep your whole being—
spirit, soul, and body—free from every fault at
the coming of our Lord Jesus Christ. He who
calls you will do it, because he is faithful.

Pray also for us, brothers.

Greet all the believers with a brotherly kiss.

1 Thes 5:16-26

We Always Pray for You

That is why we always pray for you.
We ask our God to make you worthy
   of the life he has called you to live.
May he fulfill by his power all your desire
   for goodness and complete your work of
     faith.
In this way the name of our Lord Jesus will
   receive glory from you, and you from
     him,
by the grace of our God and of the Lord Jesus
   Christ.

2 Thes 1:11-12

You Are Chosen

We must thank God at all times for you, brothers, you whom the Lord loves. For God chose you as the first to be saved by the Spirit's power to make you his holy people and by your faith in the truth. God called you to this through the Good News we preached to you; he called you to possess your share of the glory of our Lord Jesus Christ.

May our Lord Jesus Christ himself and God our Father, who loved us and in his grace gave us unfailing courage and a firm hope, encourage you and strengthen you to always do and say what is good.

2 Thes 2:13-14, 16-17

The Lord Is Faithful

Finally, our brothers, pray for us that the Lord's message may continue to spread rapidly and be received with honor, just as it was among you. Pray also that God will rescue us from wicked and evil people; for not everyone believes the message.

But the Lord is faithful, and he will strengthen you and keep you safe from the Evil One. And the Lord gives us confidence in you, and we are sure that you are doing and will continue to do what we tell you.

May the Lord lead you into a greater understanding of God's love and the endurance that is given by Christ.

2 Thes 3:1-5

A BLESSING

May the Lord himself, who is our source of peace, give you peace at all times and in every way. The Lord be with you all.

May the grace of our Lord Jesus Christ be with you all.

2 Thes 3:16, 18

A Song of Gratitude for God's Mercy

I give thanks to Christ Jesus our Lord, who has given me strength for my work. I thank him for considering me worthy and appointing me to serve him, even though in the past I spoke evil of him. . . . But God was merciful to me because I did not yet have faith and so did not know what I was doing. And our Lord poured out his abundant grace on me and gave me the faith and love which are ours in union with Christ Jesus. This is a true saying, to be completely accepted and believed: Christ Jesus came into the world to save sinners. I am the worst of them, but God was merciful to me in order that Christ Jesus might show his full patience in dealing with me, the worst of sinners, as an example for all those who would later believe in him and receive eternal life.

To the eternal King,
immortal and invisible,
the only God—
to him be honor and glory
forever and ever! Amen.

1 Tm 1:12-17

The Great Secret

No one can deny how great is the secret of our religion:

> He appeared in human form,
>> was shown to be right by the Spirit,
>> and was seen by angels.
> He was preached among the nations,
>> was believed in throughout the world,
>> and was taken up to heaven.

1 Tm 3:16

King of Kings and Lord of Lords

Strive for righteousness, godliness, faith, love, endurance, and gentleness. Run your best in the race of faith, and win eternal life for yourself; for it was to this life that God called you when you firmly professed your faith before many witnesses. Before God, who gives life to all things, and before Christ Jesus, who firmly professed his faith before Pontius Pilate, I command you to obey your orders and keep them faithfully until the Day when our Lord Jesus Christ will appear.

> His appearing will be brought about
>> at the right time by God,
> the blessed and only Ruler,
> the King of kings and the Lord of lords.
> He alone is immortal;
> he lives in the light that no one can approach.
> No one has ever seen him;
> no one can ever see him.
> To him be honor and eternal power!
> Amen. *1 Tm 6:11-16*

Remember Jesus Christ

Remember Jesus Christ, who was raised from death, who was a descendant of David, as is taught in the Good News I preach. Because I preach the Good News, I suffer and I am even chained like a criminal. But the word of God is not in chains, and so I endure everything for the sake of God's chosen people, in order that they too may obtain the salvation that comes through Christ Jesus and brings eternal glory. This is a true saying:

"If we have died with him,
    we shall also live with him.
If we continue to endure,
    we shall also rule with him.
If we deny him,
    he also will deny us.
If we are not faithful,
    he remains faithful
    because he cannot be false to himself."

2 Tm 2:8-13

A Song of Anticipation

As for me, the hour has come for me to be
    sacrificed;
the time is here for me to leave this life.
I have done my best in the race,
I have run the full distance, and I have kept
    the faith.
And now there is waiting for me the prize of
    victory
awarded for a righteous life,

the prize which the Lord, the righteous
    Judge,
will give me on that Day — and not only to me,
but to all those who wait with love for him to
    appear.

2 Tm 4:6-8

A BLESSING

The Lord be with your spirit.
    God's grace be with you all.

2 Tm 4:22

Other
Epistles

A Hymn to God's Word

In the past God spoke to our ancestors many times in many ways through the prophets, but in these last days he has spoken to us through his Son.

He is the one through whom God created the universe,
the one whom God has chosen to possess all things at the end.
He reflects the brightness of God's glory
and is the exact likeness of God's own being,
sustaining the universe with his powerful word.
After achieving forgiveness for the sins of mankind,
He sat down in heaven at the right side of God,
the Supreme Power.

Heb 1:1-3

A Hymn to the Greatness of God's Son

The Son was made greater than the angels, just as the name that God gave him is greater than theirs.

For God never said to any of his angels,

"You are my Son;
today I have become your Father."

Nor did God say about any angel,

"I will be his Father,
and he will be my Son."

But when God was about to send his first-born Son into the world, he said,

"All of God's angels must worship him."

But about the angels God said,

"God makes his angels winds,
and his servants flames of fire."

About the Son, however, God said:

"Your kingdom, O God, will last forever and
ever!
You rule over your people with justice.
You love what is right and hate what is wrong.
That is why God, your God, has chosen you
and has given you the joy of an honor far
greater
than he gave to your companions."

He also said,

"You, Lord, in the beginning created the
earth,
and with your own hands you made the
heavens.
They will disappear, but you will remain;
they will all wear out like clothes.
You will fold them up like a coat,
and they will be changed like clothes.
But you are always the same,
and your life never ends."

God never said to any of his angels:

"Sit here at my right side
until I put your enemies as a footstool under
your feet."

What are the angels, then? They are spirits
who serve God and are sent by him to help those
who are to receive salvation.

Heb 1:4-14

Sharper Than a Two-edged Sword

The word of God is alive and active,
sharper than any double-edged sword.
It cuts all the way through,
to where soul and spirit meet,
to where joints and marrow come together.
It judges the desires and thoughts of man's
heart.
There is nothing that can be hid from God;
everything in all creation is exposed
and lies open before his eyes.
And it is to him that we must all give an
account of ourselves.

Heb 4:12-13

Because He Was Humble God Heard Him

In his life on earth Jesus made his prayers and requests with loud cries and tears to God, who
could save him from death. Because he was humble and devoted, God heard him. But even
though he was God's Son, he learned through his
sufferings to be obedient. When he was made

perfect, he became the source of eternal salvation for all those who obey him, and God declared him to be high priest, in the priestly order of Melchizedek.

Heb 5:7-10

Let Us Keep Our Eyes Fixed on Jesus

Let us keep our eyes fixed on Jesus
on whom our faith depends from beginning to
  end.
He did not give up because of the cross!
On the contrary, because of the joy that was
  waiting for him,
he thought nothing of the disgrace of dying on
  the cross,
and he is now seated at the right side of God's
  throne.

Heb 12:2-3

A BLESSING

God has raised from death our Lord Jesus, who is the Great Shepherd of the sheep as the result of his sacrificial death, by which the eternal covenant is sealed. May the God of peace provide you with every good thing you need in order to do his will, and may he, through Jesus Christ, do in us what pleases him. And to Christ be the glory forever and ever! Amen.

Heb 13:20-21

Every Good Gift Comes from God

Do not be deceived, my dear brothers!
Every good gift and every perfect present
 comes from heaven;
it comes down from God, the Creator of the
 heavenly lights,
who does not change or cause darkness by
 turning.
By his own will he brought us into being
 through the word of truth,
so that we should have first place among all his
 creatures.

Jas 1:16-18

An Exhortation to Prayer

Is anyone among you in trouble? He should pray.
Is anyone happy? He should sing praises. Is there
anyone who is sick? He should send for the
church elders, who will pray for him and rub
olive oil on him in the name of the Lord. This
prayer made in faith will heal the sick person;
the Lord will restore him to health, and the sins
he has committed will be forgiven. So then, confess your sins to one another and pray for one
another, so that you will be healed. The prayer
of a good person has a powerful effect. Elijah
was the same kind of person as we are. He prayed
earnestly that there would be no rain, and no
rain fell on the land for three and a half years.
Once again he prayed, and the sky poured out its
rain and the earth produced its crops.

Jas 5:13-18

GRACE AND PEACE IN FULL MEASURE

You were chosen according to the purpose of God the Father and were made a holy people by his Spirit, to obey Jesus Christ and be purified by his blood.

May grace and peace be yours in full measure.

1 Pt 1:2

Rich Blessings for God's People

Let us give thanks to the God and Father of our Lord Jesus Christ! Because of his great mercy he gave us new life by raising Jesus Christ from death. This fills us with a living hope, and so we look forward to possessing the rich blessings that God keeps for his people. He keeps them for you in heaven, where they cannot decay or spoil or fade away. They are for you, who through faith are kept safe by God's power for the salvation which is ready to be revealed at the end of time.

1 Pt 1:3-5

You Are Living Stones

Come to the Lord, the living stone rejected by man as worthless but chosen by God as valuable. Come as living stones, and let yourselves be used in building the spiritual temple, where you will serve as holy priests to offer spiritual and acceptable sacrifices to God through Jesus Christ.

You are the chosen race, the King's priests, the holy nation, God's own people, chosen to proclaim the wonderful acts of God, who called you out of darkness into his own marvelous light. At one time you were not God's people, but now you are his people; at one time you did not know God's mercy, but now you have received his mercy.

1 Pt 2:4-5, 9-10

Christ Carried Our Sins

If you endure suffering even when you have done right, God will bless you for it. It was to this that God called you, for Christ himself suffered for you and left you an example, so that you would follow in his steps.

He committed no sin,
and no one ever heard a lie come from his lips.
When he was insulted,
he did not answer back with an insult;
when he suffered, he did not threaten,
but placed his hopes in God,
the righteous Judge.
Christ himself carried our sins in his body to
the cross,
so that we might die to sin and live for
righteousness.
It is by his wounds that you have been healed.
You were like sheep that had lost their way,
but now you have been brought back
to follow the Shepherd and Keeper of your
souls.

1 Pt 2:20-25

The Apron of Humility

All of you must put on the apron of humility, to serve one another; for the scripture says, "God resists the proud, but shows favor to the humble." Humble yourselves, then, under God's mighty hand, so that he will lift you up in his own good time. Leave all your worries with him, because he cares for you.

1 Pt 5:5-7

A BLESSING

May peace be with all of you who belong to Christ. May grace and peace be yours in full measure through your knowledge of God and of Jesus our Lord. To him be the glory, now and forever! Amen.

1 Pt 5:16; 2 Pt 1:2; 3:18

The Word of Life

We write to you about the Word of life,
which has existed from the very beginning.
We have heard it,
and we have seen it with our eyes;
yes, we have seen it,
and our hands have touched it.
When this life became visible, we saw it;
so we speak of it and tell you about the eternal
      life which was with the Father and was
      made known to us.
What we have seen and heard
we announce to you also,

so that you will join with us in the fellowship
that we have with the Father and with his Son
    Jesus Christ.
We write this in order that our joy may be
    complete.

1 Jn 1:1-4

God Is Light

Now the message that we have heard from his
    Son
and announce is this:
God is light, and there is no darkness at all in
    him.
If, then, we say that we have fellowship with
    him,
yet at the same time live in darkness,
we are lying both in our words and in our
    actions.
But if we live in the light—
just as he is in the light—
then we have fellowship with one another,
and the blood of Jesus, his Son, purifies us
    from every sin.

1 Jn 1:5-7

THE NEW COMMAND

This command I am writing you is not new; it is
the old command, the one you have had from the
very beginning. The message you heard from the
very beginning is this: we must love one another.

1 Jn 2:7, 3:11

We Are God's Children

See how much the Father has loved us!
His love is so great that we are called God's
        children—
and so, in fact, we are.
This is why the world does not know us:
it has not known God.
My dear friends, we are now God's children,
but it is not yet clear what we shall become.
But we know that when Christ appears,
we shall be like him,
because we shall see him as he really is.
Everyone who has this hope in Christ
keeps himself pure,
just as Christ is pure.

1 Jn 3:1-3

WHAT LOVE IS

This is how we know what love is:
Christ gave his life for us.
We too, then, ought to give our lives
for our brothers!

1 Jn 3:16

God Is Love

Dear friends,
let us love one another,
because love comes from God.
Whoever loves is a child of God and knows
        God.

Whoever does not love does not know God,
for God is love.
And God showed his love for us
by sending his only Son into the world,
so that we might have life through him.
This is what love is:
it is not that we have loved God,
but that he loved us and sent his Son
to be the means by which our sins are forgiven.

We Should Love One Another

Dear friends,
if this is how God loved us,
then we should love one another.
No one has ever seen God,
but if we love one another,
God lives in union with us,
and his love is made perfect in us.

We are sure that we live in union with God
and that he lives in union with us,
because he has given us his Spirit.
And we have seen and tell others that the
    Father sent his Son to be the Savior of
    the world.
If anyone declares that Jesus is the Son
    of God,
he lives in union with God
and God lives in union with him.
And we ourselves know and believe the love
    which God has for us.

We Love Because God First Loved Us

God is love,
and whoever lives in love lives in union with
 God
and God lives in union with him.
Love is made perfect in us in order that we
 may have courage on the Judgment Day;
and we will have it because our life in this
 world is the same as Christ's.
There is no fear in love;
perfect love drives out all fear.
So then, love has not been made perfect
in anyone who is afraid,
because fear has to do with punishment.

We love because God first loved us.
If someone says he loves God,
but hates his brother, he is a liar.
For he cannot love God,
whom he has not seen,
if he does not love his brother,
whom he has seen.
The command that Christ has given us is this:
whoever loves God must love his brother also.

1 Jn 4:7-21

Pray for Sinners

We have courage in God's presence, because we are sure that he hears us if we ask him for anything that is according to his will. He hears us whenever we ask him; and since we know this is true, we know also that he gives us what we ask from him.

If you see your brother commit a sin that does not lead to death, you should pray to God, who will give him life. This applies to those whose sins do not lead to death. But there is sin which leads to death, and I do not say that you should pray to God about that. All wrongdoing is sin, but there is sin which does not lead to death.

1 Jn 5:14-17

Prayer of Praise

To those who have been called by God, who live in the love of God the Father and the protection of Jesus Christ:

May mercy, peace, and love be yours in full measure.

To him who is able to keep you from falling and to bring you faultless and joyful before his glorious presence — to the only God our Savior, through Jesus Christ our Lord, be glory, majesty, might, and authority, from all ages past, and now, and forever and ever! Amen.

Jude 1-2, 24-25

Revelation

Hymn of Thanksgiving to Christ

Grace and peace be yours from God
who is, who was, and who is to come,
and from the seven spirits in front of his
    throne,
and from Jesus Christ, the faithful witness,
the first-born Son, who was raised from death
    and who is also the ruler of the kings of the
    world.

He loves us, and by his death
he has freed us from our sins
and made us a kingdom of priests
to serve his God and Father.
To Jesus Christ be the glory and power forever
    and ever! Amen.

Look, he is coming on the clouds!
Everyone will see him, including those who
    pierced him.
All peoples on earth will mourn over him.
So shall it be!
"I am the first and the last,"
says the Lord God Almighty, who is, who was,
    and who is to come.

Rv 1:4-8

Blessings on Those Who Win the Victory

"If you have ears, then, listen to what the Spirit
says to the churches!

"To those who win the victory I will give the
right to eat the fruit of the tree of life that grows
in the garden of God. . . .

Rv 2:7

'Be faithful to me, even if it means death, and I will give you life as your prize of victory. Those who win the victory will not be hurt by the second death. . . .

Rv 2:10-11

"To those who win the victory I will give some of the hidden manna. I will also give each of them a white stone on which is written a new name that no one knows except the one who receives it. . . .

Rv 2:17

"To those who win the victory, who continue to the end to do what I want, I will give the same authority that I received from my Father: I will give them authority over the nations, to rule them with an iron rod and to break them to pieces like clay pots. I will also give them the morning star. . . .

Rv 2:26-28

"Those who win the victory will be clothed like this in white, and I will not remove their names from the book of the living. In the presence of my Father and of his angels I will declare openly that they belong to me. . . .

Rv 3:5-6

"I will make him who is victorious a pillar in the temple of my God, and he will never leave it. I will write on him the name of my God and the name of the city of my God, the new Jerusalem, which will come down out of heaven from my God. I will write on him my new name. . . .

Rv 3:12

"Listen! I stand at the door and knock; if anyone hears my voice and opens the door, I will come into his house and eat with him, and he will eat with me. To those who win the victory I will give the right to sit beside me on my throne, just as I have been victorious and now sit by my Father on his throne."

Rv 3:20-21

Song of Glory, Honor, and Thanks

Day and night they never stop singing:

"Holy, holy, holy, is the Lord God Almighty, who was, who is, and who is to come."

The four living creatures sing songs of glory and honor and thanks to the one who sits on the throne, who lives forever and ever. When they do so, the twenty-four elders fall down before the one who sits on the throne, and worship him who lives forever and ever. They throw their crowns down in front of the throne and say:

"Our Lord and God! You are worthy
   to receive glory, honor, and power.
For you created all things
   and by your will they were given existence
   and life."

Rv 4:8-11

A New Song

The Lamb went and took the scroll from the right hand of the one who sits on the throne. As he did so, the four living creatures and the

twenty-four elders fell down before the Lamb.
Each had a harp and gold bowls filled with in-
cense, which are the prayers of God's people.
They sang a new song:

"You are worthy to take the scroll
　　and to break open the seals.
For you were killed, and by your death you
　　　bought for God
　　people from every tribe, language, nation,
　　　and race.
You have made them a kingdom of priests
　　to serve our God,
　　and they shall rule on earth."

Again I looked, and I heard angels, thousands
and millions of them! They stood around the
throne, the four living creatures, and the elders,
and sang in a loud voice:

"The Lamb who was killed is worthy
　　to receive power, wealth, wisdom, and
　　　strength,
　　honor, glory, and praise!"

And I heard every creature in heaven, on earth,
in the world below, and in the sea — all living beings in the universe — and they were singing:

"To him who sits on the throne and to the
　　Lamb,
　　be praise and honor, glory and might,
　　forever and ever!"

The four living creatures answered, "Amen!"
And the elders fell down and worshiped.

Rv 5:7-14

The Saints Proclaim God's Glory

After this I looked, and there was an enormous crowd—no one could count all the people! They were from every race, tribe, nation, and language, and they stood in front of the throne and of the Lamb, dressed in white robes and holding palm branches in their hands. They called out in a loud voice:

> "Salvation comes from our God,
> who sits on the throne,
> and from the Lamb!"

All the angels stood around the throne, the elders, and the four living creatures. Then they threw themselves face downward in front of the throne and worshiped God, saying:

> "Amen! Praise, glory, wisdom,
> thanksgiving, honor, power, and might
> belong to our God forever and ever!
> Amen!"

One of the elders asked me, "Who are these people dressed in white robes, and where do they come from?"

"I don't know, sir. You do," I answered.

He said to me, "These are the people who have come safely through the terrible persecution. They have washed their robes and made them white with the blood of the Lamb. That is why they stand before God's throne and serve him day and night in his temple. He who sits on the throne will protect them with his presence. Never again will they hunger or thirst; neither

sun nor any scorching heat will burn them,
because the Lamb, who is in the center of the
throne, will be their shepherd, and he will guide
them to springs of life-giving water. And God
will wipe every tear from their eyes."

Rv 7:9-17

A Song of Worship

Then the seventh angel blew his trumpet, and
there were loud voices in heaven, saying:

> "The power to rule over the world
> belongs now to our Lord and his Messiah,
> and he will rule forever and ever!"

Then the twenty-four elders who sit on their
thrones in front of God threw themselves face
downward and worshiped God, saying:

> "Lord God Almighty, the one who is and who
> was!
> We thank you that you have taken your great
> power
> and have begun to rule!
> The heathen were filled with rage,
> because the time for your anger has come,
> the time for the dead to be judged.
> The time has come to reward your servants,
> the prophets,
> and all your people, all who have
> reverence for you,
> great and small alike.
> The time has come to destroy those who
> destroy the earth!"

Rv 11:15-18

Victory Song

Then I heard a loud voice in heaven saying:

"Now God's salvation has come!
Now God has shown his power as King!
Now his Messiah has shown his authority!

For the one who stood before our God and accused our brothers day and night has been thrown out of heaven. Our brothers won the victory over him by the blood of the Lamb and by the truth which they proclaimed; and they were willing to give up their lives and die. And so be glad, you heavens, and all you that live there! But how terrible for the earth and the sea! For the Devil has come down to you, and he is filled with rage, because he knows that he has only a little time left."

Rv 12:10-12

Eternal Message of Good News

Then I saw another angel flying high in the air, with an eternal message of Good News to announce to the peoples of the earth, to every race, tribe, language, and nation. He said in a loud voice:

"Honor God and praise his greatness!
For the time has come for him to judge
    mankind.
Worship him who made heaven, earth, sea,
    and the springs of water!"

Then I heard a voice from heaven saying, "Write

this: Happy are those who from now on die in the service of the Lord!"

"Yes indeed!" answers the Spirit. "They will enjoy rest from their hard work, because the results of their service go with them."

Rv 14:6-7, 13

The Song of the Lamb

"Lord God Almighty
   how great and wonderful are your deeds!
King of the nations,
   how right and true are your ways!
Who will not stand in awe of you, Lord?
   Who will refuse to declare your greatness?
   You alone are holy.
All the nations will come
   and worship you,
   because your just actions are seen by all."

Rv 15:3-4

Praise God!

After this I heard what sounded like the roar of a large crowd of people in heaven, saying:

"Praise God!
Salvation, glory, and power belong to our
    God!
True and just are his judgments!
He has condemned the prostitute who was
    corrupting the earth with her immorality.
God has punished her because she killed his
    servants."

Again they shouted,

> "Praise God!
> The smoke from the flames that consume the
>   great city go up forever and ever!"

The twenty-four elders and the four living creatures fell down and worshiped God, who was
seated on the throne. They said, "Amen! Praise
God!"

Rv 19:1-4

The Wedding Feast of the Lamb

Then there came from the throne the sound of a
voice, saying,

> "Praise our God,
> all his servants and all people,
> both great and small,
> who have reverence for him!"

Then I heard what sounded like a crowd, like the
sound of a roaring waterfall, like loud peals of
thunder. I heard them say,

> "Praise God! For the Lord,
> our Almighty God, is King!
> Let us rejoice and be glad;
> let us praise his greatness!
> For the time has come for the wedding of the
>   Lamb,
> and his bride has prepared herself for it.
> She has been given clean shining linen to
>   wear."
> (The linen is the good deeds of God's people.)

Then the angel said to me, "Write this: Happy are those who have been invited to the wedding feast of the Lamb." And the angel added, "These are the true words of God."

Rv 19:5-9

The New Heaven and the New Earth

Then I saw a new heaven and a new earth. The first heaven and the first earth disappeared, and the sea vanished. And I saw the Holy City, the new Jerusalem, coming down out of heaven from God, prepared and ready, like a bride dressed to meet her husband. I heard a loud voice speaking from the throne:

"Now God's home is with mankind!
He will live with them,
and they shall be his people.
God himself will be with them,
and he will be their God.
He will wipe away all tears from their eyes.
There will be no more death,
no more grief or crying or pain.
The old things have disappeared."

Then the one who sits on the throne said, "And now I make all things new!" He also said to me, "Write this because these words are true and can be trusted." And he said,

"It is done!
I am the first and the last,
the beginning and the end.
To anyone who is thirsty

I will give the right to drink from the spring
of the water of life without paying for it.
Whoever wins the victory will receive this
    from me:
  I will be his God,
  and he will be my son."

                                            Rv 21:1-7

The Temple Is the Lord
God Almighty and the Lamb

I did not see a temple in the city, because its temple is the Lord God Almighty and the Lamb. The
city has no need of the sun or the moon to shine
on it, because the glory of God shines on it, and
the Lamb is its lamp. The peoples of the world
will walk by its light, and the kings of the earth
will bring their wealth into it. The gates of the
city will stand open all day; they will never be
closed, because there will be no night there. The
greatness and the wealth of the nations will be
brought into the city. But nothing that is impure
will enter the city, nor anyone who does shame-
ful things or tells lies. Only those whose names
are written in the Lamb's book of the living will
enter the city.

                                         Rv 21:22-27

The Lord Will Be Their Light

The angel also showed me the river of the water
of life, sparkling like crystal, and coming from
the throne of God and of the Lamb and flowing
down the middle of the city's street. On each side

of the river was the tree of life, which bears fruit twelve times a year, once each month; and its leaves are for the healing of the nations. Nothing that is under God's curse will be found in the city.

The throne of God and of the Lamb will be in the city, and his servants will worship him. They will see his face, and his name will be written on their foreheads. There shall be no more night, and they will not need lamps or sunlight, because the Lord God will be their light, and they will rule as kings forever and ever.

Rv 22:1-5

The Spirit and the Bride Say "Come!"

"Listen!" says Jesus, "I am coming soon! I will bring my rewards with me, to give to each one according to what he has done. I am the first and the last, the beginning and the end."

Happy are those who wash their robes clean and so have the right to eat the fruit from the tree of life and to go through the gates into the city. But outside the city are the perverts and those who practice magic, the immoral and the murderers, those who worship idols and those who are liars both in words and deeds.

"I, Jesus, have sent my angel to announce these things to you in the churches. I am descended from the family of David; I am the bright morning star."

The Spirit and the Bride say, "Come!"

Everyone who hears this must also say, "Come!"

Come, whoever is thirsty; accept the water of life as a gift, whoever wants it.

So be it. Come Lord Jesus!
May the grace of the Lord Jesus be with
everyone.

Rv 22:12-17, 20-21

Contents-Index

Pentateuch

Historical Books

Wisdom Literature

Isaiah

Jeremiah, Ezekiel, Daniel

Minor Prophets

Psalms
Book One

Book Two

Book Three

Gospels and Acts

Other Epistles